NOTABLE LATINO WRITERS

MAGILL'S CHOICE

NOTABLE LATINO WRITERS

Volume 2

Griselda Gambaro — Sheila Ortiz Taylor

321 - 658

from

The Editors of Salem Press

SALEM PRESS, INC.

PASADENA, CALIFORNIA   HACKENSACK, NEW JERSEY

Essays originally appeared in *Cyclopedia of World Authors, Fourth Revised Edition* (2004), *Critical Survey of Drama* (2003), *Critical Survey of Poetry* (2002), *Critical Survey of Short Fiction* (2001), *Critical Survey of Long Fiction* (2000), and *Identities and Issues in Literature* (1997). New material has been added.

Library of Congress Cataloging-in-Publication Data

Notable Latino writers / from the editors of Salem Press.
     p. cm. – (Magill's choice)
     Includes bibliographical references and indexes.
     ISBN-13: 978-1-58765-243-1 (13-digit set : alk. paper)
     ISBN-13: 978-1-58765-245-5 (13-digit vol. 2 : alk. paper)
     ISBN-10: 1-58765-243-9 (set)
     ISBN-10: 1-58765-245-5 (vol. 2)
     1. American literature–Hispanic American authors–History and criticism.
2. Hispanic Americans–Intellectual life. 3. Hispanic Americans in literature.
I. Salem Press. II. Series.
     PS153.H56N68 2005
     810.9'868–dc22

                                                                    2005017567

First Printing

PRINTED IN THE UNITED STATES OF AMERICA

Table of Contents

Key to Pronunciation

Vowel Sounds

Symbol	Spelled (Pronounced)
a	answer (AN-suhr), laugh (laf), sample (SAM-puhl), that (that)
ah	father (FAH-thur), hospital (HAHS-pih-tuhl)
aw	awful (AW-fuhl), caught (kawt)
ay	blaze (blayz), fade (fayd), waiter (WAYT-ur), weigh (way)
eh	bed (behd), head (hehd), said (sehd)
ee	believe (bee-LEEV), cedar (SEE-dur), leader (LEED-ur), liter (LEE-tur)
ew	boot (bewt), lose (lewz)
i	buy (bi), height (hit), lie (li), surprise (sur-PRIZ)
ih	bitter (BIH-tur), pill (pihl)
o	cotton (KO-tuhn), hot (hot)
oh	below (bee-LOH), coat (koht), note (noht), wholesome (HOHL-suhm)
oo	good (good), look (look)
ow	couch (kowch), how (how)
oy	boy (boy), coin (koyn)
uh	about (uh-BOWT), butter (BUH-tuhr), enough (ee-NUHF), other (UH-thur)

Consonant Sounds

Symbol	Spelled (Pronounced)
ch	beach (beech), chimp (chihmp)
g	beg (behg), disguise (dihs-GIZ), get (geht)
j	digit (DIH-juht), edge (ehj), jet (jeht)
k	cat (kat), kitten (KIH-tuhn), hex (hehks)
s	cellar (SEHL-ur), save (sayv), scent (sehnt)
sh	champagne (sham-PAYN), issue (IH-shew), shop (shop)
ur	birth (burth), disturb (dihs-TURB), earth (urth), letter (LEH-tur)
y	useful (YEWS-fuhl), young (yuhng)
z	business (BIHZ-nehs), zest (zehst)
zh	vision (VIH-zhuhn)

Complete List of Articles

Volume 1

NOTABLE LATINO WRITERS

Griselda Gambaro

Argentine playwright

Born: Buenos Aires, Argentina; July 28, 1928

DRAMA: *Las paredes*, pr. 1964, pb. 1979 (English translation, 1992); *El desatino*, pr., pb. 1965; *Matrimonio*, pr. 1965; *Los siameses*, pr., pb. 1967 (*The Siamese Twins*, 1967); *El campo*, pb. 1967, pr. 1968 (*The Camp*, 1970); *Información para extranjeros*, wr. 1971, pb. 1987 (*Information for Foreigners*, 1992); *Nada que ver*, pr. 1972, pb. 1983; *Solo un aspecto*, pb. 1973, pr. 1974; *Sucede lo que pasa*, pr. 1976, pb. 1983; *Decir sí*, pb. 1978, pr. 1981; *El despojamiento*, pr., pb. 1981; *La malasangre*, pr. 1982, pb. 1984 (*Bad Blood*, 1994); *Real envido*, pr. 1983, pb. 1984; *Del sol naciente*, pr., pb. 1984; *Teatro*, pb. 1984-1996 (6 volumes).

LONG FICTION: *Una felicidad con menos pena*, 1967; *Nada que ver con otra historia*, 1972; *Ganarse la muerte*, 1976; *Dios no nos quiere contentos*, 1979; *Lo impenetrable*, 1984 (*The Impenetrable Madame X*, 1991); *Déspues del día de fiesta*, 1994; *El mar que nos trajo*, 2001.

SHORT FICTION: *Madrigal en ciudad*, 1963; *El desatino*, 1965; *Lo mejor que se tiene*, 1998.

NONFICTION: *Escritos inocentes*, 1999.

MISCELLANEOUS: *Conversaciónes con chicos*, 1966.

Griselda Gambaro (grih-ZEHL-dah gahm-BAH-roh) was born in Buenos Aires, Argentina, and has spent her life there, aside from a year in Rome in 1970 and almost three years in Barcelona (1977-1980). She is the daughter of a postal worker, and because she came from a family with limited economic means, after she finished high school in 1943 she went to work in the business office of a publishing company. Through her writing and its successes, she has enjoyed greater financial security. She is married to the sculptor Juan Carlos Distefano and is the mother of two children, Andrea, born in 1961, and Lucas, born in 1965. Many of the critics who meet Gambaro in Argentina or during one of her trips abroad are struck by her

> *Madam X, the last descendant of an aristocratic*
> *family, usually received mail early in the morning.*
> *If her mute intuition had found words to express*
> *itself, Madam X's life would have taken a different*
> *turn, perhaps less involved in overwhelming*
> *passions but filled with greater pleasure on a daily*
> *basis. A woman of neither profound reflections nor*
> *speculation, her slumbering intuition didn't prevent*
> *her from wondering who sent the huge envelope*
> *made of elegant paper.*
>
> —from *The Impenetrable Madam X*
> (trans. Evelyn Picon Garfield)

gentle manner and gracious demeanor, which belie the brutality, vigor, and cruelty expressed in her texts. Although she once called herself "a cowardly person," any reader or spectator of her work soon realizes that the texts also disprove this evaluation, for the writer of these plays must be brave indeed to face the types of bleak and cruel situations that are portrayed. The expectation is implied, however, that the works will bring forth the kind of participation needed to correct the real problems of today's sociopolitical environment.

According to her recollections, she was always writing; that is, from the moment she learned to read she also began to write. She threw away many pieces of work until she was sufficiently satisfied to offer as her first effort worthy of publishing *Madrigal en ciudad,* a collection of three short novellas that won the Prize of the Argentine Fondo Nacional de las Artes for narrative in 1963. Soon after, she received the Premio Emece in 1965 for the collection *El desatino,* also containing novellas and short stories. At the same time, two plays emerged from the prose pieces, *Las paredes* and *El desatino,* each winning theatrical prizes: for *Las paredes,* the Premio de la Asociacion de Teatros and the Fondo Nacional de las Artes in 1964, and for *El desatino,* the Prize of the Revista Teatro XX in 1965.

One of the characteristics of Gambaro's writing production that emerged from the beginning was her development of some of the prose pieces as dramatic works almost at the same time that she was writing the prose pieces. She continued this practice until 1972, the year in which she completed work on the novel *Nada que ver con otra historia* and the play *Nada que ver.* She no longer works in that almost parallel fashion in the two genres, finding that she now writes either a play or a piece of fiction independent of one or the other; the plays, however, have become more famous than her fiction and have been translated into several languages and staged around the world. In Argentina, she was closely associated with the experimental art group located at the Centro de Experimentación audiovisual del Instituto Torcuato Di Tella, a foundation formed in 1958 to patronize the fine arts and foster sociological investigations. The Institute, which closed in 1971, worked in part as a theatrical laboratory for young writers who were able to experiment with techniques and representation by adapting audiovisual phenomena to the stage. As part of its promotion of vanguardist and creative talents, the Institute published as well as produced a number of her plays. Jorge Petraglia, a noted Argentine director and actor, has also been associated with Gambaro's work in both of his talented capacities.

As a woman who writes in Latin America, Gambaro is often asked about her role as a woman writer, with questions ranging from the problematics of a feminine discourse to extraliterary problems concerning whether she has faced discrimination in her career because of gender. Her response is usually to present her own specific experiences rather than offer observations applicable to women in Latin America. Argentina, for example, has a long tradition of women writers, and there are many well-established women in literary circles. She sees any difficulties as related more to social class than to gender; all the successful women in Argentina have been from the upper class and appear to act with an inborn sense of security absent in a person from the lower classes. In regard to feminine discourse, she was asked to present a paper on the question, "¿Es posible y deseable una dramaturgia especificamente femenina?" (1980; is it possible or desirable to have a specifically feminine dramaturgy?), and her

W H A T   T O   R E A D

The Siamese Twins

The contrast between words and actions typical of Gambaro's dramatic images is graphically demonstrated in *The Siamese Twins* (1967). The play develops as a series of encounters in which Lorenzo, the dominant member of the pair alluded to in the title, is driven by envy to cause the destruction of Ignacio. This relationship re-creates the Cain and Abel motif, yet the play never makes explicit that the two are blood brothers; their fraternal relationship seems to be a myth exploited by Lorenzo or, if true, a fact not willingly accepted by Ignacio.

Lorenzo's attempt at domination is dramatically expressed in the scene in which he forces Ignacio to walk with him as if the two were real Siamese twins, attached physically. This theatrical gesture contradicts the verbal messages that indicate that the two are physically separate and psychologically different. Lorenzo is cunning, envious, and treacherous while Ignacio is ingenuous, compassionate, and good-natured. Lorenzo's need to rid himself of Ignacio is predicated on the erroneous belief that without Ignacio he will somehow be more whole, more independent. By the end of the play, Lorenzo has finally succeeded in implicating Ignacio in some deed for which the police torture and kill him. In the final scene, Lorenzo realizes too late that his destruction of Ignacio has left him not whole but deficient.

The impact of the final scene is strengthened by its power to recall the final moments of Samuel Beckett's *Waiting for Godot* (1954). Lorenzo is alone on an empty stage, ironically assuming the identity of Ignacio by re-creating the latter's fetal position as a dead man. Like Estragon's famous *Allons* ("Let's go"), which brings no action, Lorenzo, too, announces his imminent departure but goes nowhere. His inability to act contradicts his words and his very existence; the completion of his goal has brought his own destruction.

— *Sandra Messinger Cypess*

answer is that one writes naturally, without thinking of gender, and the result is the particular view of the writer, showing his or her particular characteristics. The women characters in her own work fit no particular pattern and seem to reflect the greater division Gambaro has perceived in human behavior: Some people are victims of the oppressive acts of others, but at any one moment, anyone can become a victim.

Of the many successful Argentine dramatists, Gambaro is consistently named among the top playwrights of her country and of Latin America in general. Despite working within a confined sociopolitical context, she has been successful in creating a theatrical experience that relates to the particular problems of her country yet is couched in a universal theatrical idiom. She won the Argentores Prize from the Society of Argentinian Authors first in 1968 for *The Camp* and in 1976 for *Sucede lo que pasa*. *The Camp* also earned her awards from the Municipality of Buenos Aires, *Talia* magazine, and "Theatrical Broadcast News" of Municipal Radio of Buenos Aires. In 1982 she was granted a Guggenheim Fellowship.

Because her view of the human condition transcends national boundaries and her plays are richly textured in terms of theme and technique, Gambaro's work has been the focus of an increasing number of articles and dissertations in the United States, Canada, and Europe. In general, her work may be characterized as having a contemporary sociopolitical message that is conveyed with intense visual images of compelling dramatic interest that work well onstage.

— Sandra Messinger Cypess

Learn More

Boling, Becky. "Reenacting Politics: The Theater of Griselda Gambaro." In *Latin American Women Dramatists: Theater, Texts, and Theories*, edited by Catherine Larson and Margarita Vargas. Bloomington: Indiana University Press, 1998. Analyzes the treatment of political power, justice, and morality in Gambaro's plays.

Gladhart, Amalia. *Leper in Blue: Coercive Performance and the Contemporary Latin American Theater.* Chapel Hill: University of

North Carolina Press, 2000. Gambaro's work is among the plays that are analyzed in this examination of works by Latin American playwrights.

Jehenson, Myriam Yvonne. "Staging Cultural Violence: Griselda Gambaro and Argentina's 'Dirty War.'" *Mosaic: A Journal for the Interdisciplinary Study of Literature* 32, no. 1 (March, 1999): 85-104. Examines Gambaro's play *Information for Foreigners* and its link between politics and art, drawing parallels to the mechanisms of Argentina's repressive regime in the 1970's.

López-Calvo, Ignacio. "Lesbianism and Caricature in Griselda Gambaro's *Lo impenetrable.*" In *Latina Lesbian Writers and Artists*, edited by Maria Dolores Costa. New York: Harrington Park Press, 2003. One of eight essays examining works by Latina lesbians.

Magnarelli, Sharon. "Acting/Seeing Women: Griselda Gambaro's *El despojamiento.*" In *Latin American Women's Writing: Feminist Readings in Theory and Crisis*, edited by Anny Brooksbank Jones and Catherine Davies. New York: Oxford University Press, 1996. Focuses on Gambaro's use of the theatrical element as a thematic thread in *El despojamiento*, itself an allegory for Argentina's military regime.

Reinelt, Janice, ed. *Crucibles of Crisis: Performing Social Change.* Ann Arbor: University of Michigan Press, 1996. Essay by Diane Taylor uses *Information for Foreigners* to explore the intersection of theater and terror, examining especially the theater's ability to prevent or conceal violence.

Taylor, Claire. *Bodies and Texts: Configurations of Identity in the Works of Griselda Gambaro, Albalucía Angel, and Laura Esquivel.* Leeds, England: Maney, 2003. Analyzes the formation of feminine identity in *Nada que ver con otra historia* and *Dios no nos quiere contentos.*

Witte, Ann. *Guiding the Plot: Politics and Feminism in the Work of Women Playwrights from Spain and Argentina.* New York: Peter Lang, 1996. Focuses on the theater in Argentina and Spain between 1960 to 1990, a period of important sociopolitical change in both countries. Examines the way in which playwrights can provide an oppositional stance to those in power and work within the confines of an oppressive environment.

Cristina García

Cuban American novelist

Born: Havana, Cuba; July 4, 1958

LONG FICTION: *Dreaming in Cuban*, 1992; *The Agüero Sisters*, 1997;
Monkey Hunting, 2003.
NONFICTION: *Cars of Cuba*, 1995.
EDITED TEXT: *Cubanisimo! The Vintage Book of Contemporary Cuban
Literature*, 2003.

Cristina García (krihs-TEE-nah gahr-SEE-ah) is a highly regarded Cuban American writer. Born in Havana, Cuba,
she was brought to the United States at the age of two, when her
family emigrated after Fidel Castro came to power. She grew
up in New York City, studied in Catholic schools, and attended
Barnard College and the School of Advanced International
Studies at The Johns Hopkins University. In 1993, after working
for *Time* magazine as a journalist in Miami, San Francisco, and
Los Angeles, García was a Hodder Fellow at Princeton University. She then moved to Los Angeles.

As a young adult García read American, Russian, and French
novelists. Later she discovered her Latin American literary heritage. She cites Wallace Stevens, Gabriel García Márquez, and
Toni Morrison as particular literary inspirations for her when
writing her novels. Perhaps her greatest inspiration, however,
was a trip back to Cuba in 1984, where she learned about her
family and, as for so many bicultural writers, regained a sense of
her own culture of origin and her part in it from the experience
of "going home."

As a bicultural Cuban American writer, García is part of a vi-
brant group of individuals of various ethnicities who draw on
the contradictions of being simultaneously both and neither.
Other American writers sharing this multiethnic common
ground are Julia Alvarez, Gloria Anzaldúa, Sandra Cisneros,

Amy Tan, Maxine Hong Kingston, Diana Abu-Jaber, Oscar Hijuelos, Pablo Medina, and Omar Torres. They too write of the delicate balance, double consciousness, and multiple resonances of living "on the borderlands," as Anzaldúa phrased it. They share an ability to "pass," as well as the knowledge, sometimes painful yet often a source of great pride, of their difference from mainstream American culture. They chronicle intergenerational immigrant experience and displacement, exile and double exile, for even the culture of origin feels like a strange place to the hybrid child who, unlike its parents, has become at least partially

Norma I. Quintana

> *In Cuba, aging was not such a disgraceful affair.*
> *Most elderly women were venerated and sought after*
> *for counsel. They were surrounded by their families*
> *and often lived to see their great-grandchildren grow*
> *up. The* abuelitas *were the eyes and ears of a clan,*
> *the peacemakers, the storytellers and historians. They*
> *held each young destiny in their hands.*
>
> —from *The Agüero Sisters*

identified with the adopted American culture. The formation of identity, in all its complex manifestations, is the overarching theme in this kind of work.

The relativity of perception is another powerful theme in the works of these writers, and García is particularly skillful in the way her narrative structure and chronology reflect this relativity. Given the element of the autobiographical in novels that explore identity formation, it is no surprise that García has experienced this relativity personally, not only culturally but also politically. When interviewed by Allan Vorda in 1993 García mentioned that her parents were extremely anti-Communist, but that her other relatives, whom she had met on her 1984 trip, were pro-Communist if not Party members.

Dreaming in Cuban is set alternately in Brooklyn and Havana, with multiple narrators tracing their memories, their family lines, and their complex interconnections. Granddaughter Pilar and grandmother Celia communicate wordlessly over the years, and only when the grandchild comes to visit do both feel complete again. In her novel García plays with Magical Realism, politics, the diary and epistolary forms, and the accretion of layers of culture. The locations shift, just as do the barriers of time and space, life and death, and García draws on the puzzle that is memory to show how identity is formed. The novel was nominated for the National Book Award in 1992, and in 1994 García received a Guggenheim Fellowship.

WHAT TO READ

Dreaming in Cuban

Dreaming in Cuban (1992), Cristina García's first novel, chronicles the lives of three generations of women as they strive for self-fulfillment. This bittersweet novel also illustrates the Cuban American immigrant experience in the United States, focusing on the search for cultural identity in exile. In Cuba, for twenty-five years, the matriarch Celia del Pino writes letters to Gustavo, a long lost lover. She never sends the self-revealing correspondence, and stops writing in 1959, at the time of the Cuban Revolution, when the family becomes divided by politics and her granddaughter Pilar is born.

Celia, who believes that "to survive is an act of hope," sublimates her unfulfilled romantic desires by imagining herself as a heroine of the revolution. In need of recognition, she supports Fidel Castro devotedly. As her husband Jorge del Pino leaves her to join their daughter Lourdes in the United States, she spends her days scanning the sea for American invaders and daydreaming about a more exciting life.

Felicia, Celia's youngest daughter, abused and abandoned by her first husband, Hugo Villaverde, suffers

The Agüero Sisters draws upon the pro- and anti-Communist allegiances found in García's own family. The novel contrasts two sisters, Constancia, who fled Cuba when Castro came to power, and Reina, who remained. Each has achieved a different kind of success in her chosen environment. Like *Dreaming in Cuban, The Agüero Sisters* is strongly marked by Magical Realism. *Monkey Hunting* is also about Cuban Americans, but this time Chinese Cuban Americans, tracing the Chen family from 1857 to the present as they emigrate from country to country.

— *Tanya Gardiner-Scott*

from fits of madness and violence. A stranger to herself and her children, she seeks refuge in music and the Afro-Cuban cult of Santeria; after becoming a priestess, she finds peace in death. Lourdes, Celia's eldest daughter, is raped and tortured by the revolutionaries and loses her unborn son. She escapes from Castro's Cuba with her husband Rufino del Puente and their daughter Pilar. Emotionally unfulfilled, she develops eating disorders; while her family dreams of returning to Cuba, she supports the anti-Castro movement, establishes a chain of Yankee Doodle bakeries, and focuses on achieving the American Dream.

Raised in Brooklyn, in conflict with her Americanized mother, Pilar identifies with her grandmother Celia in Cuba. She visits the homeland in search of her true identity and, as she receives Celia's legacy of letters and family stories, she becomes aware of the magic inner voice that inspires artistic creativity. Pilar returns to America with a positive self-image, accepting her double identity as a bilingual and bicultural Latina.

Dreaming in Cuban represents the coming-of-age memoir narrative. Through recollections and nostalgic remembrances, the novel illustrates issues of identity and separation, women's survival strategies, and cultural dualism.

— *Ludmila Kapschutschenko-Schmitt*

Learn More

Alvarez-Borland, Isabel. "Displacements and Autobiography in Cuban-American Fiction." In *Twayne Companion to Contemporary World Literature: From the Editors of Literature Today*, edited by Pamela A. Genova. New York: Twayne/Thomson Gale, 2003. Compares García with two other Cuban American writers, Omar Torres and Pablo Medina, and looks at the semi-autobiographical nature of their novels.

Brogan, Kathleen. *Cultural Haunting: Ghosts and Ethnicity in Recent American Literature*. Charlottesville: University of Virginia Press, 1998. Brogan analyzes García's *Dreaming in Cuban* and work by Toni Morrison and Louise Erdich to examine how minority writers use modern ghost stories as a means of exploring and recreating their ethnic identity.

Davis, Rocio G. "Back to the Future: Mothers, Languages, and Homes in Cristina García's *Dreaming in Cuban.*" In *Twayne Companion to Contemporary World Literature: From the Editors of Literature Today*, edited by Pamela A. Genova. New York: Twayne/Thomson Gale, 2003. Explores the complicated negotiations of mother-daughter bonds in García's novel.

McCracken, Ellen. *New Latina Narrative: The Feminine Space of Postmodern Ethnicity.* Tucson: University of Arizona Press, 1999. García's work is included in this analysis of writing by Cuban American, Puerto Rican American, Mexican American, and Dominican American writers. McCracken explains how these writers have redefined concepts of multiculturalism and diversity in American society.

Pérez Firmat, Gustavo. *Life on the Hyphen: The Cuban-American Way.* Austin: University of Texas Press, 1994. Sets García's work in the context of the popular culture created by Cuban Americans who moved to the United States when they were children.

Viera, Joseph M., and Deborah Kay Ferrell. "Cristina García, 1958-   " In *American Writers: A Collection of Literary Biographies*, edited by Jay Parini. Supplement XI: Toni Cade Bambara to Richard Yates. New York: Scribner's, 2002. Includes an essay discussing García's life and work, and a bibliography.

Yagoda, Ben. *The Sound on the Page: Style and Voice in Writing.* New York: HarperResource, 2004. Yagoda seeks to define literary style and to learn how a writer develops his or her own unique voice. He interviews García and other writers who explain how they approach style and how their style has been influenced by other writers.

Lionel G. García

Mexican American
novelist and short-story writer

Born: San Diego, Texas; August 20, 1935

LONG FICTION: *Leaving Home*, 1985; *A Shroud in the Family*, 1987;
Hardscrub, 1990; *To a Widow with Children*, 1994.
SHORT FICTION: *I Can Hear the Cowbells Ring*, 1994; *The Day They
Took My Uncle, and Other Stories*, 2001.
DRAMA: *An Acorn on the Moon*, pr. 1995.
CHILDREN'S/YOUNG ADULT LITERATURE: *The Elephant and the
Ant*, 2000.

B orn in 1935 in the remote brush country of Texas near the
Mexican border to Gonzalo Guzman and Maria Saenz
García, Lionel G. García (LIOH-nehl gahr-SEE-ah) was later to
write fiction for nearly three decades before seeing significant
publication of and attention to his works. A regional writer,
García has lived most of his life in this desolate, drought-ridden
part of the United States.

Interested in science and biology, García entered Texas A&M
University. He earned a B.S. in 1956; he also took classes in and
otherwise pursued creative writing as an undergraduate. García

---

*He was an alcoholic. Which brings me to the
supposed cause of his bedevilment. He had been
possessed, my grandmother told us, when he
accidentally drank the dregs of a bottle of beer that
had been laced with a special potion, a potion so
powerful it would cause insanity. It was, she said, a
potion meant for someone else.*

—from "The Day They Took My Uncle"

twice served two-year terms in the U.S. Army, the first of which was in 1957-1958. A year after leaving the military, he married Noemi Barrera. He returned to active duty in 1959.

Resolved not to pursue a military career, he returned to Texas A&M in the early 1960's, where he eventually earned the D.V.M. degree, which would provide most of his life's work outside the literary world. He became a practicing veterinarian in the late 1960's, after spending three years as an assistant professor of anatomy, again at Texas A&M. Perhaps surprisingly, though, he makes little use of his biology and primary profession in his fiction.

Arte Público Press

While serving in the military and teaching college classes, García's side interest—perhaps at heart it was always his main one—was writing short stories. He had published his first story in the undergraduate literary magazine during his senior year of college, continuing to write thereafter. It was not until 1983, however, that he would receive recognition for his work; he was awarded the PEN Southwest Discovery Prize for his first novel, *Leaving Home*, which at the time was unpublished.

Like the terrain in South Texas, García's characters—while colorful—are often bleak and desolate in their attitudes and behavior. Both *Leaving Home* and *A Shroud in the Family* are about family life among first- and second-generation immigrants coming from Mexico to Texas. About this time, he also began to give public readings of his fiction, a mode of performance that well serves his storytelling abilities.

His next novel, *Hardscrub*, is set in the 1950's and also tells of a family confronting the problems of everyday life in South Texas. It won several honors, all regional in nature, including the Texas Literary Award. In the mid-1990's García changed his focus to other subgenres of fiction: He published the highly autobiographical collection of personal writings titled *I Can Hear the Cowbells Ring*, and he tried his luck with a play called *An Acorn on the Moon*, which was locally produced but never published. He also wrote a children's book, *The Elephant and the Ant*. In the late 1990's he collected his stories, most of which had been previously published, in *The Day They Took My Uncle, and Other Stories*. García's works have generally been well received as popular fiction, regional in scope but more than expansive in their appreciation of the experience of Mexican immigrants coming to make lives in the southwestern United States.

— *Carl Singleton*

Learn More

Anhalt, Diana. "South Texas Buckshot Stories." *The Texas Observer*, November 9, 2001. A detailed, favorable review of *The Day They Took My Uncle, and Other Stories*. Anhalt focuses on local-color characters appearing in the collection of short fiction.

W H A T   T O   R E A D

Leaving Home

Lionel G. García's *Leaving Home* (1985) offers an intimate view of one Latino family in the early 1940's. The novel traces the wanderings of the aging Adolfo, a former baseball pitcher who ruined his career with alcohol, as he moves from the home of his sister Maria to San Diego, hoping to live with his former lover, Isabel. Carmen, Maria's daughter, goes with Adolfo, hoping to move in with an aunt and find a better job.

Turned away by her aunt, Carmen is allowed to stay with Isabel. Adolfo, however, is forced to return to Maria's house. Maria promises to help him find a job, but his pride prevents him from working in the fields or holding down a gardener's job. He travels to Los Angeles, meeting a con artist, Antonia, who persuades him to move in with her so she can get his pension checks. She eventually throws him out, and he moves in with the Professor, another of Antonia's victims.

When the United States enters World War II, the Professor returns to Tijuana to avoid the draft. Adolfo accompanies him and marries a prostitute. He soon leaves her, however, and returns to Maria's house.

In the meantime, Carmen applies for a job at the Navy hospital in San Diego and shortly thereafter is recommended for nurses' training in the U.S. Navy. She graduates at the top of her class and becomes an officer. Although Carmen is capable, her promotion is partly based on the fact that she is Latina. When Carmen becomes engaged to a white naval officer in the Philippines, Maria believes that she has lost Carmen.

Maria, too, experiences significant changes. She begins to question God's judgment when Carmen gets sick. When one of her sons is killed in battle, she loses her faith in God. She is alone and lonely. When Adolfo returns, Maria feels happy again. The two agree that Adolfo has wasted his life, but they are happy to have each other.

— *Wilma Shires*

Golden, Dorothy. Review of *To a Widow with Children,* by Lionel G. García. *Library Journal* 119, no. 6 (April 1, 1994): 131. A brief, favorable review which praises the novel for its success in the absence of sex and violence as it studies the problems of the family.

Mutter, John. Review of *A Shroud in the Family,* by Lionel G. García. *Publishers Weekly* 232, no. 4 (July 24, 1987): 181. A review of the novel. The critic calls the work a satire which ridicules the use of Hispanic stereotypes while endorsing stereotypes of white, mainstream Americans.

Ray, Karen. Review of *Hardscrub,* by Lionel G. García. *The New York Times Book Review* 125, no. 1705 (February 25, 1990): 7, 24. A detailed review of the novel, in which the critic finds much humor and irony, with special attention given to characters.

Gabriel García Márquez

Colombian
novelist and short-story writer

Born: Aracataca, Colombia; March 6, 1928
Also known as: Gabriel José García Márquez

LONG FICTION: *La hojarasca*, 1955 (novella; as *Leaf Storm* in *Leaf Storm, and Other Stories*, 1972); *El coronel no tiene quien le escriba*, 1961 (novella; *No One Writes to the Colonel*, 1968); *La mala hora*, 1962, revised 1966 (*In Evil Hour*, 1979); *Cien años de soledad*, 1967 (*One Hundred Years of Solitude*, 1970); *El otoño del patriarca*, 1975 (*The Autumn of the Patriarch*, 1975); *Crónica de una muerte anunciada*, 1981 (*Chronicle of a Death Foretold*, 1982); *El amor en los tiempos del cólera*, 1985 (*Love in the Time of Cholera*, 1988); *El general en su laberinto*, 1989 (*The General in His Labyrinth*, 1990); *Collected Novellas*, 1990; *Del amor y otros demonios*, 1994 (*Of Love and Other Demons*, 1995); *Memoria de mis putas tristes*, 2004.

SHORT FICTION: *Los funerales de la Mamá Grande*, 1962 (*Big Mama's Funeral*, stories included in *No One Writes to the Colonel, and Other Stories*, 1968); *Isabel viendo llover en Macondo*, 1967 (*Monologue of Isabel Watching It Rain in Macondo*, 1972); *No One Writes to the Colonel, and Other Stories*, 1968; *Relato de un náufrago: Que estuvo diez días a la deriva en una balsa sin comer ni beber, que fue proclamado héroe de la patria, besado por las reinas de la belleza y hecho rico por la publicidad, y luego aborrecido por el gobierno y olvidado para siempre*, 1970 (*The Story of a Shipwrecked Sailor: Who Drifted on a Liferaft for Ten Days Without Food or Water, Was Proclaimed a National Hero, Kissed by Beauty Queens, Made Rich Through Publicity, and Then Spurned by the Government and Forgotten for All Time*, 1986); *La increíble y triste historia de la Cándida Eréndira y de su abuela desalmada*, 1972 (*Innocent Eréndira, and Other Stories*, 1978); *Leaf Storm, and Other Stories*, 1972; *El negro que hizo esperar a los ángeles*, 1972; *Ojos de perro azul,* 1972; *Todos los cuentos de Gabriel García Márquez,* 1975 (*Collected Stories,* 1984); *Doce cuentos peregrinos,* 1992 (*Strange Pilgrims: Twelve Stories,* 1993).

NONFICTION: *La novela en América Latina: Diálogo,* 1968 (with Mario Vargas Llosa); *Cuando era feliz e indocumentado,* 1973; *Chile, el golpe y los gringos,* 1974; *Crónicas y reportajes,* 1976; *Operación Carlota,* 1977; *Periodismo militante,* 1978; *De viaje por los países socialistas,* 1978; *Obra periodística,* 1981-1999 (5 volumes; includes *Textos costeños,* 1981; *Entre cachacos,* 1982; *De Europa y América, 1955-1960,* 1983; *Por la libre, 1974-1995,* 1999; *Notas de prensa, 1961-1984,* 1999); *El olor de la guayaba: Conversaciones con Plinio Apuleyo Mendoza,* 1982 (*The Fragrance of the Guava: Plinio Apuleyo Mendoza in Conversation with Gabriel García Márquez,* 1983; also known as *The Smell of Guava,* 1984); *La aventura de Miguel Littín, clandestino en Chile,* 1986 (*Clandestine in Chile: The Adventures of Miguel Littín,* 1987); *Por un país al alcance de los niños,* 1996 (*For the Sake of a Country Within Reach of the Children,* 1998); *Noticia de un secuestro,* 1996 (*News of a Kidnapping,* 1997); *Vivir para contarla,* 2002 (*Living to Tell the Tale,* 2003).

Gabriel García Márquez (GAH-bryehl gahr-SEE-ah MAHR-kays) is among the major figures in the great surge of creativity, from the late 1940's to the early 1970's, that placed Latin America in the forefront of the global literary scene. García Márquez was born in a Colombian village on the Caribbean coast. He was the first of twelve children. Owing to his parents' indigence, he was reared by his maternal grandparents, who provided him with the stories, legends, and superstitions of Aracataca that were in time to inform a number of his short stories as well as his monumental novel *One Hundred Years of Solitude.* He was sent to school at the age of eight, after the death of his grandfather. Completing his early and secondary education at Barranquilla and Zipaquirá, he matriculated in 1947 at the National University of Colombia in Bogotá.

During the 1940's he read the modern writers, especially Franz Kafka and William Faulkner. In his freshman year in Bogotá his law studies were punctuated by his reading of fiction and by the publication of his first story, "The Third Resignation," a chilling Kafkaesque narrative about a comatose male who lives from the age of seven to the age of twenty-five in a coffin.

The volatile political situation in Colombia, marked by the conflict between the Liberal and Conservative parties, culminated in 1949 with the assassination of Jorge Eliécer Gaitán, the Liberal candidate for president, and initiated a decade of civil bloodshed known as *la violencia* (the violence). The university in Bogotá had closed during the preceding year, and García Márquez continued his studies at Cartagena, where he abandoned law studies in favor of journalism.

In 1950 he moved to Barranquilla and became a columnist for the newspaper *El Heraldo*. Four years later he returned to Bogotá and became a writer for *El Espectador*, the newspaper that had published his first story. His determination to become a writer had been fostered by his reading of Faulkner, and his first long fictional work, *Leaf Storm* (a Faulknerian rendition of the thoughts during a funeral that occupy the minds of the deceased's son, mother, and grandfather), was published in 1955. In the same year he was sent by *El Espectador* to Geneva, where he was left without resources after the military government shut

> *Many years later, as he faced the firing squad, Colonel Aureliano Buendía was to remember that distant afternoon when his father took him to discover ice. At that time Macondo was a village of twenty adobe houses, built on the bank of a river of clear water that ran along a bed of polished stones. . . . The world was so recent that many things lacked names, and in order to indicate them it was necessary to point.*
>
> —from *One Hundred Years of Solitude*
> (trans. Gregory Rabassa)

© The Nobel Foundation

down the newspaper. He then spent some three years in Paris, living in poverty and continuing his writing. He traveled extensively to Europe, the Soviet Union, and Venezuela, where he edited *Momento* and, in 1958, married Mercedes Barcha. From 1959, the year of Cuba's revolution, until 1961 he worked as a journalist for Fidel Castro's *Prensa Latina*. In 1961 he, with his wife and son, journeyed from New York through Faulkner's South to Mexico, where in the following year he saw the publication of eight of his stories in one volume.

After the publication of more stories and novellas, García Márquez went into seclusion. He emerged in 1967, having written *One Hundred Years of Solitude*, a novel that resists and revises conventional notions of temporality, morality, and the demarcations between life and death. The immediate international success of this novel established its author as a major figure of twentieth century literature. In *One Hundred Years of Solitude* the history of the New World and of the human spirit is encapsulated in the generations of the Buendía family, the founders and chief residents of the fictional town of Macondo. In the novel the most ordinary events are related as though they were miracles, while ostensibly extraordinary events are presented as mere matters of fact.

García Márquez's distaste for extremist politics, especially dictatorships, is evident in his writing. *The Autumn of the Patriarch* is based upon the Venezuelan dictator of the 1950's, Marcos Pérez Jiménez. The novel's fictional counterpart, Zacarías Alvarado, is a grotesque whose atrocious tyranny is recorded in an unrelenting style that retains the humor of *One Hundred Years of Solitude* but darkens it with grisly and diabolic details. The regime of Augusto Pinochet in Chile is depicted as oppressive in *Clandestine in Chile: The Adventures of Miguel Littín.* Pro-Marxism is much in evidence in this historically based first-person narrative of filmmaker Littín, who returned in disguise to Chile to compile a cinematic documentary of life under Pinochet twelve years after the violent overthrow of the Marxist president Salvador Allende in 1973.

While his views on world events are well known and have been published under fictional guise and in journalistic form since 1968, it is for his Magical Realism that García Márquez has won international acclaim. He was awarded the Nobel Prize in Literature for 1982, and his *Love in the Time of Cholera* —with its assumption of the immortality of the lover's vow, in which physical resurrection is implicit—was well received upon its translation into English in 1988. Critics and reviewers continued their praise of his talent and creative imagination upon the appearance of his short novel *Of Love and Other Demons*, recounting a twelve-year-old girl's "possession" (the effects of an attack by a rabid dog) and a priest's being possessed by rabid love in his attendance on her.

In his prologue to *Strange Pilgrims*, a collection of twelve short stories written between 1976 and 1982, García Márquez is explicit about his concept of nonlinear narrative: A "story has no

W H A T   T O   R E A D

One Hundred Years of Solitude

One Hundred Years of Solitude (1967) is the story of five generations of the Buendía family. It begins with the foundation of Macondo by José Arcadio Buendía and his wife Ursula. Despite their fear that the consummation of their marriage will result in the birth of a child with a pig's tail (there is a family precedent for such an event), José decides to challenge fate.

Macondo begins as a kind of primitive paradise. Modern civilization finally reaches Macondo, however, and with the arrival of the national political parties come civil wars caused by their conflicts. The Americans bring economic prosperity but exploit the workers. These intrusions of foreigners and modernity are eliminated by a flood that washes them away and returns Macondo to a state similar to its original paradise. In the end, Macondo is not a paradise, however, but a fiction: A member of the Buendía family deciphers a parchment written in Sanskrit which foretold the entire story of the family and Macondo from beginning to the end—that is, the story of *One Hundred Years of Solitude*. History is the completion of a fiction.

Perhaps the most important achievement of this novel is its expression of a mythic reality. Entrance into the magical world of Macondo is an acceptance of the negation of rationality; in fact, the novel is recognized as one of the earliest to use Magical Realism. One aspect of this is mythic time that negates linear time. The repetition of numerous cycles, such as the names of the members of the Buendía family, create this sense of an eternal present. There is also a biblical level of reading that develops myth from Creation and Original Sin to the apocalyptic ending. García Márquez's creation of a traditional yet fascinating story, his mastery of narrative technique, and his creation of myth make *One Hundred Years of Solitude* one of the most important novels of the twentieth century.

— *Raymond L. Williams*

beginning, no ending: it either works or it does not." Scholars consistently make profound inquiries into the revolutionary art of García Márquez, with its inventive voice and its inexhaustible thematic constitutions, and readers delight in the strangely realistic humor of this creative artist, whom Thomas Pynchon once called a "straight-faced teller of tall tales."

— Roy Arthur Swanson

Learn More

Bell, Michael. *Gabriel García Márquez: Solitude and Solidarity.* New York: St. Martin's Press, 1993. This book explores García Márquez's works from a number of different perspectives, ranging from comparative literary criticism to political and social critiques. Also included are commentaries on García Márquez's styles, including journalism and Magical Realism.

Bell-Villada, Gene H. *García Márquez: The Man and His Work.* Chapel Hill: University of North Carolina Press, 1990. Includes biographical information on García Márquez, analyses of his major works, an index, and a bibliography.

_____, ed. *Gabriel García Márquez's "One Hundred Years of Solitude": A Casebook.* New York: Oxford University Press, 2002. A dozen essays on García Márquez's masterpiece, comprising a wide range of critical approaches.

Bloom, Harold, ed. *Gabriel García Márquez.* New York: Chelsea House, 1989. Includes eighteen critical essays on García Márquez, arranged in order of their original publication. Also features an index and a bibliography.

Gárcia Márquez, Gabriel. *Living to Tell the Tale.* Translated by Edith Grossman. New York: A. A. Knopf, 2003. The first in a projected three-volume autobiography. This volume covers Gárcia Márquez's life from his youth until the mid-1950's.

González, Nelly Sfeir de, comp. *Bibliographic Guide to Gabriel García Márquez, 1986-1992.* Westport, Conn.: Greenwood Press, 1994. An annotated bibliography that includes works by García Márquez, criticism and sources for him, and an index of audio and visual materials related to the author and his works.

McMurray, George R., ed. *Critical Essays on Gabriel García Márquez.* Boston: G. K. Hall, 1987. A collection of book reviews, articles, and essays covering the full range of García Márquez's fictional work. Very useful for an introduction to specific novels and collections of short stories. Also includes an introductory overview by the editor and an index.

Mellen, Joan. *Gabriel Gárcia Márquez.* Literary Masters 5. Detroit: Gale Group, 2000. An overview of Gárcia Márquez's life and work designed to support the research of high school and college students. Includes a glossary, annotated bibliography, and study list of questions.

Pelayo, Rubén. *Gabriel Gárcia Márquez: A Critical Companion.* Westport, Conn.: Greenwood Press, 2001. An account of Gárcia Márquez's life, work, and literary style, helping students place him within the canon of Western literature.

Solanet, Mariana. *García Márquez for Beginners.* New York: Writers and Readers, 2001. Part of the "Beginners" series of brief introductions to major writers and their works. Very basic, but a good starting point.

Enrique González Martínez

Mexican poet

Born: Guadalajara, Mexico; April 13, 1871
Died: Mexico City, Mexico; February 19, 1952

POETRY: *Preludios,* 1903; *Lirismos,* 1907; *Silénter,* 1909; *Los senderos ocultos,* 1911; *La muerte del cisne,* 1915; *El libro de la fuerza, de la bondad y del ensueño,* 1917; *Parábolas, y otras poemas,* 1918; *Jardins de Francia,* 1919 (translation); *La palabra del viento,* 1921; *El romero alucinado,* 1923; *Las señales furtivas,* 1925; *Poemas truncas,* 1935; *Ausencia y canto,* 1937; *El diluvio del fuego,* 1938; *Tres rosas en el ánfora,* 1939; *Bajo el signo mortal,* 1942; *Segundo despertar, y otras poemas,* 1945; *Vilano al viento,* 1948; *Babel, poema al margen del tiempo,* 1949; *El nuevo narciso, y otras poemas,* 1952.

SHORT FICTION: "Una hembra," 1895; "La chiquilla," 1907; "A vuelo," 1908.

NONFICTION: "Algunos aspectos de la lírica mexicana," 1932; *El hombre del búho,* 1944; *La apacible locura,* 1951.

Enrique González Martínez (ehn-REE-kay gahn-ZAH-lehs mahr-TEE-nehs) achieved his first literary success at an early age. When he was fourteen years old, he won first prize in a contest organized by the English-Spanish newspaper of Guadalajara, *The Sun,* for his translation of an English poem about John Milton. Later in his life, he was Effective Member of the prestigious Mexican Academy of Language, president of the Athenaeum of the Youth of Mexico, member of the Seminary of Mexican Culture, Founding Member of the renowned National College of Mexico, and a professor of language and literature at various institutions of higher education. He received the 1944 Manuel Ávila Camacho Literary Award, was president of the organizing committee of the American Continental Congress of Peace, and, in 1949, was a candidate for the Nobel Prize in Literature.

González Martínez was born in Guadalajara, the capital of

the state of Jalisco, Mexico, on April 13, 1871. He was the son of a schoolteacher, José María González, and his wife, Feliciana Martínez. González Martínez attended the grade school directed by his father, and in 1881, he entered the preparatory school run by the Church in the Conciliar Seminary of his native city. Five years later, when he was only fifteen, he entered the School of Medicine of Guadalajara.

González Martínez's fondness for poetry began at a very early age. As a child, he often amazed his parents and other adults with his achievements as a student as well as with his ability to write verse. Although he devoted himself with enthusiasm to the study of medicine during his student years, his interest in poetry grew. When he was graduated as a medical doctor in 1893, he had already published a number of poems in newspapers and magazines, earning for himself a reputation as a provincial poet.

Despite his appointment upon graduation as an adjunct professor of physiology in the School of Medicine in Guadalajara, González Martínez did not have much success practicing medicine in his native city. At this time, González Martínez's father was offered the post of headmaster in a school that was going to be opened in Culiacán, the capital of the state of Sinaloa. It was an excellent opportunity to improve the family's economic situ-

Wring the swan's neck who with deceiving plumage
inscribes his whiteness on the azure stream;
he merely vaunts his grace and nothing feels
of nature's voice or of the soul of things.
Every form eschew and every language
whose processes with deep life's inner rhythm
are out of harmony . . . and greatly worship
life, and let life understand your homage.

—from "Wring the Swan's Neck"
(trans. Samuel Beckett)

ation, and since González Martínez had yet to establish himself as a physician, he decided to move to Culiacán with his parents and his younger sister, Josefina. They arrived there at the end of 1895, and for the next six months González Martínez tried without success to establish his professional practice. After this time, he decided to move to the small town of Sinaloa, where he finally established himself and resided for the next fifteen years. In 1898, González Martínez married Luisa Rojo y Fonseca, a girl who had strongly impressed him when he had first seen her on his initial visit to Sinaloa. Their marriage produced four children—Enrique, María Luisa, Héctor, and Jorge—the youngest child, however, only lived sixteen months.

The fifteen years that González Martínez lived in Sinaloa were a period of intense professional activity as a doctor as well as of incessant literary production. For some time, the poet seemed to be content with publishing his poems in newspapers and magazines of the provinces as well as the capital, where he

Instituto Nacional de Bellas Artes, Mexico

was beginning to be known. Nevertheless, in 1900, an event took place that prompted González Martínez to publish his first book of poetry. For reasons not yet fully understood, a newspaper in Guadalajara published a false report of his death. Several publications in different cities expressed their sorrow for the early death of such a promising poet and reprinted poems of his that had previously appeared in their pages. One of González Martínez's friends published a long article lamenting the death of the poet, recalling his life, listing his successes, and praising his virtues as a physician, a man of letters, and a citizen. When all of this came to the attention of González Martínez in the small town where he lived, the poet rushed to deny the false information, and in a letter written in a joking tone he thanked his friend from Guadalajara for the informative and sorrowful article. After the uproar occasioned by this event had passed, the poet concluded that his poems must be good enough to be published in book form, and thus his first collection, titled *Preludios* (preludes), appeared in 1903.

Although González Martínez continued practicing medicine, his other activities seemed to multiply after the publication of his first book. In 1907, he published *Lirismos* (lyricisms), his second book of poetry, and between 1907 and 1909 he edited, along with his friend Sixto Osuna, the magazine *Arte*, which was published in Mocorito. Between 1907 and 1911, he occupied the position of Political Prefect in the districts of Mocorito, El Fuerte, and Mazatlán in the state of Sinaloa, and at the beginning of the Revolution of 1910, he was the Secretary General of the government in Culiacán, the capital of the state of Sinaloa. In 1909, he published another book of poetry, *Silénter* (silently), and was appointed Correspondent Member of the Mexican Academy of Language.

The year 1911 was of special importance in the life of González Martínez. It was during this year that he published his book *Los senderos ocultos* (the concealed paths). It was also the year in which he decided to abandon his medical career completely in order to devote the rest of his life to poetry, changing his residence and that of his family to Mexico City. There, he began to work as an editorial writer for the newspaper *El Imparcial.*

In 1912, he founded the magazine *Argos*, which appeared for only one year, and in 1913, he was appointed Under Secretary of Public Instruction and Fine Arts. After occupying this position for a year, he spent a year as Secretary General of the government in Puebla. In 1915, he returned to Mexico City to devote himself to teaching and was appointed a professor of Spanish language and literature and of general literature in the National Preparatory School, as well as in the Normal School for Women. He was also appointed a professor of French literature in the School of Higher Studies, later called the Faculty of Philosophy and Letters. He soon lost his professorial positions, however, for political reasons.

After 1915, the poetic production of González Martínez increased, and his books of poetry followed one another with a frequency uncommon even among the most prolific poets. Nevertheless, despite his constant dedication to poetry, in 1917 he went back to work for a newspaper, this time as an editorial writer for *El Heraldo de México*, while at the same time acting as coeditor of the magazine *Pegaso*.

In 1920, González Martínez began his diplomatic career with an appointment as Minister Plenipotentiary to Chile, whence he was transferred to a similar position in Argentina two years later. After another two years, he was appointed Minister Plenipotentiary for Mexico in Spain and Portugal, and he held this position for six years, until 1931.

The relatively peaceful life of González Martínez suffered two serious disruptions. The first was the death of his wife, Luisa, in 1935, and the second was the death of his son Enrique in 1939. The poet expressed in his poems the sorrow and the solitude that these two deaths caused him.

In 1942, González Martínez was admitted into the Seminary of Mexican Culture. A year later, he was appointed Founding Member of the important cultural organization the National College of Mexico, and in 1944, he received the Manuel Ávila Camacho Literary Award. In 1949, he presided over the organizing committee of the American Continental Congress of Peace, and he was nominated for the Nobel Prize for Literature. He died as he was approaching his eighty-first birthday, on February 19, 1952.

W H A T   T O   R E A D

"Wring the Swan's Neck"

Although he was only four years younger than the Nicaraguan poet Rubén Darío and several years older than other major *Modernistas* Leopoldo Lugones (from Argentina) and Julio Herrera y Reissig (from Uruguay), Enrique González Martínez fits better among the postmodernists. It must be considered that this Mexican poet published his first book of poetry in 1903, when he was already thirty-two years old, and that he reached his peak when *Modernismo* was fading and postmodernism was at its apex. In this connection, the sonnet "Tuércele el cuello al cisne" ("Wring the Swan's Neck") should be mentioned.

This is the famous poem in which González Martínez recommended the death of the swan, the symbol of *Modernismo,* and its replacement by the owl as less ornamental but wiser and more thoughtful:

> His grace is not the swan's, but his unquiet
> pupil, boring into the gloom, interprets
> the secret book of the nocturnal still.

The poet himself said that his sonnet was not intended as an attack on Darío and the other first-class *Modernistas*; rather, it was directed against Darío's epigones. Nevertheless, González Martínez's poem was widely regarded as the death blow to *Modernismo* and the beginning of postmodernism. González Martínez's aesthetic was fundamentally different from that of the *Modernistas*: He was inclined toward meditation and the patient study of the mysteries of life, rather than toward verbal brilliance for its own sake.

González Martínez began to write when the poetic environment in the Hispanic world was dominated by *Modernismo*. The great Nicaraguan poet Rubén Darío had succeeded in imposing his peculiar modality on this movement not only in Latin America but also in Spain. *Modernista* poetry was greatly influenced by the Parnassian and Symbolist schools of French origin, often featuring landscapes of ancient Greece or of eighteenth century France and including all kinds of exotic plants and flowers. The preferred fauna were animals known for their beauty, such as the peacock and the swan—especially the latter, which became a symbol of the movement. Metals and precious stones were used constantly as poetic motifs. The language of the *Modernistas* was musical and richly textured; adjectives were used profusely, and the imagery evoked strange impressions and sensations, synesthesia appearing with extraordinary frequency.

It was only natural that a movement so generalized and powerful as *Modernismo* had an influence on a young poet such as González Martínez, who had an expansive concept of poetry and who was well equipped for artistic creation to the most refined degree. In his poetry can be found Parnassian and Symbolist notes, Satyrs and beautiful animals, musically elegant adjectives and synesthesia—everything with the clear desire to produce a refined artistic creation. For these reasons, many would consider González Martínez a member of the *Modernismo* movement.

Nevertheless, González Martínez was never a *Modernista* in the style of Darío. His Satyrs and nymphs suffer from a lack of realism, and his fowls and stones—they are not always precious—do not function as mere ornaments in his poetry but contribute to the development of its ideas as well as communicate emotion. Closer connections could be found between González Martínez and *Modernistas* with the tendencies of the Cuban José Martí and the Colombian José Asunción Silva or with Darío in his later years, when his poetry was richer in insight and profundity. In González Martínez, interior concentration, simplicity of expression, and directness of communication are dominant characteristics.

— *Rogelio A. de la Torre*

Learn More

Brushwood, John S. *Enrique González Martínez*. New York: Twayne, 1969. An introductory biographical study and critical analysis of selected works by González Martínez. Includes bibliographic references.

Geist, Anthony L., and José B. Monleón, eds. *Modernism and Its Margins: Reinscribing Cultural Modernity from Spain and Latin America*. New York: Garland, 1999. A rereading of Modernism and the Modernist canon from a double distance: geographical and temporal. It is a revision not only from the periphery (Spain and Latin America), but from this new *fin de siècle* as well, a revisiting of modernity and its cultural artifacts from that same postmodernity.

Goldberg, I. *Studies in Spanish American Literature*. Port Washington, N.Y.: Kennikat Press, 1968. A critical study of Modernism in Latin American literature.

Nicolás Guillén

Cuban poet

Born: Camagüey, Cuba; July 10, 1902
Died: Havana, Cuba; July 16, 1989

POETRY: *Motivos de son,* 1930; *Sóngoro cosongo,* 1931; *West Indies, Ltd.,*1934; *Cantos para soldados y sones para turistas,* 1937; *España: Poema en cuatro angustias y una esperanza,* 1937; *Elegía a Jacques Roumain en el cielo de Haiti,* 1948; *Cuba Libre; Poems by Nicolás Guillén,* 1948; *Elegía a Jesús Menéndez,* 1951; *Elegía cubana,* 1952; *La paloma de vuelo popular: Elegías,* 1958; *Buenos días, Fidel,* 1959; *Poemas de amor,* 1964; *Tengo,* 1964 (English translation, 1974); *Antología mayor: El son entero y otros poemas,* 1964; *Che comandante,* 1967; *El gran zoo,* 1967 (*The Great Zoo,* 2004); *Cuatro canciones para el Che,* 1969; *El diario que a diario,* 1972 (*The Daily Daily,* 1989); *La rueda dentada,* 1972; *Man-Making Words: Selected Poems of Nicolás Guillén,* 1972; *¡Patria o muerte! The Great Zoo and Other Poems,* 1972; *El corazón con que vivo,* 1975; *Poemas manuables,* 1975; *Por el mar de las Antillas anda un barco de papel,* 1977; *Música de cámara,* 1979; *Sol de domingo,* 1982; *New Love Poetry: In Some Springtime Place,* 1994.

NONFICTION: *Prosa de prisa: Crónicas,* 1962; *Prosa de prisa, 1929-1972,* 1975-1976 (3 volumes); *Páginas vueltas: Memorias,* 1982.

Though he is widely considered one of Latin America's most notable poets, Nicolás Guillén (nih-koh-LAHS gwee-YEN) has been a particularly influential leader in the fields of African American and Afro-Caribbean literature. Raised in the central Cuban town of Camagüey, Guillén started writing poems in 1916, and his work was first published in 1919 in the journal *Camagüey Gráfico.* Unsatisfied after a year in law school in Havana, he returned to Camagüey in 1922 and began working as a printer (a trade he had learned from his father, who had been the editor of the local newspaper *Las Dos Repúblicas* before his death in a 1917 military uprising).

Though he became deeply involved in journalistic pursuits, Guillén never abandoned poetry. He wrote a substantial amount in the early stages of his career (though most of it was not published for many years) and also coedited the literary section of *Las Dos Repúblicas* before founding a literary journal, *Lis*, with his brother Francisco. Some of his earliest poems were published in the journal; most of these were included again in an appendix to Ángel I. Augier's *Nicolás Guillén: Estudio biográfico-crítico* (1965). Guillén published no poetry between 1923 and 1927, returning to Havana in 1927 after a family friend helped him find a position at the Ministry of the Interior. He resumed work on his poems in 1927 but continued to have mixed feelings about Havana; for this reason many of the pieces written between 1927 and 1931 were published in journals in Mazanillo and other Cuban cities. These were eventually compiled in *Obra poetica* (1972). In 1930, the first versions of Guillén's groundbreaking collection *Motivos de son* (motifs of son) appeared in the newspaper column "Ideales de una raza" in *Diario de la Marina*. Guillén's insights into the Afro-Caribbean community—of which he was becoming an increasingly vocal part—continued to be solicited by his friend Gustavo E. Urritia until 1931, when the column was discontinued. It was not long, though, before

Your English,
only a bit more shaky than your feeble Spanish,
is good enough inside the ring
for you to understand that filthy slang
spit from the jaws of those you waste
jab by jab.

—from "Small Ode to a Black Cuban Boxer"
(trans. Robert Márquez and
David Arthur McMurray)

W H A T   T O   R E A D

Motivos de son

Although Guillén's earliest poetry followed the Modernist tradition begun by Rubén Darío and others, his astute political sensibilities soon led him to focus his literary energies on the unique heritage of the Afro-Cuban and mestizo populations. The results of these efforts were first published in *Motivos de son* (1930; motifs of son), whose eight poems have since been anthologized in several English-language editions. The *son* (sweet song) is a traditional Afro-Cuban form of rhythm and song, and its inclusion in the title is the first of many clear nods to African (primarily West African) influences on Cuban culture. These references are apparent throughout the collection—and through all of Guillén's work—whether in the inclusion of traditional African call-and-response patterns of speech and song or in pointed indictments of slavery in the Americas:

Do you know my other last name, the one that comes
to me from that enormous land, the captured,
bloody last name, that came across the sea
in chains, which came in chains across the sea.

Guillén began to collaborate with the Afro-Cuban leader Lino Dou on a new column, "La marcha de una raza," which appeared in the newspaper *El Mundo*.

These years also marked the official debut of two of Guillén's major poetry collections. The first, *Motivos de son*, would exert significant influence on the African-based negritude and Latin American literary movements. The book abandoned the Modernist poetry of Guillén's earlier work and rejected the *negrista* approach adopted by many of his contemporaries. Traditionally, these movements viewed Afro-Caribbean and African American culture through European eyes, sometimes with the aim of projecting a sense of Old World legitimacy onto New World cre-

Motivos de son encountered a vehement but short-lived backlash among Afro-Cubans and an equally short-lived welcome among whites. Superficially, the collection seems to adhere to a legacy of portraying the *negro bembón*, a stereotype of African Americans that portrays them as ignorant and poor but satisfied and happy-go-lucky. Gradually, however, both populations realized that Guillén had created literature from centuries-old African oral tradition. His deceptively simple use of alliteration, allegory, and metaphor might have appeared to justify long-held prejudices about black people's ignorance, but a close read revealed the poems to be condemnations of the circumstances that created these prejudices.

However, *Motivos de son* is not merely a lamentation of Cuba's social ills. Instead, Guillén suggests that the rich heritage of African-influenced speech, rhythms, and music are tools that Afro-Caribbeans should embrace with pride. Though he rejects the tendency to "exoticize" black people in the Americas, Guillén views their cultural contributions—such as the *son*, the rumba, the bongo, and the songs of plantation workers—as the basis on which any African American identity must be built.

— *Anna A. Moore*

ations. Guillén saw these notions as backward-looking and instead adopted a decidedly more political approach, one that acknowledged the legacies of slavery and socioeconomic oppression and incorporated elements of the African diaspora's rich heritage.

Sóngoro cosongo, Guillén's highly politicized second volume, solidified the poet's already strong ties to Cuba's political left wing. This alliance, whose early roots can be traced back to the sudden death of Guillén's politically progressive father and to his own racially mixed roots, was energized by popular discontent under Gerardo Machado's dictatorship, which fell in 1933. The following year, Guillén's *West Indies, Ltd.* appeared. Like its predecessor, this book takes a harsh view of the United States' increasing dominance, as well as colonial hierarchies and their influences on modern Caribbean (particularly Cuban) cultures. This collection, however, is particularly remarkable for the diversity of forms it employs, including both formal Alexandrine sonnets and rhythmic African-inspired *jitanjáforas* (made-up words).

Meanwhile, Guillén's political activity continued to intensify, and in 1935, it cost him his job at Havana's Department of Culture. He started working at the journal *Resumen*, which was formally affiliated with the Cuban Communist Party, before moving on to *Mediodía* in 1936. As this latter periodical became increasingly influential and controversial, so did Guillén's place in Cuba's literary circles, and he was ultimately named the publication's director. He moved to Spain in 1937, partly because of growing political persecution in his homeland, and joined the International Congress for the Defense of Culture as well as the Cuban Communist Party. After observing and writing about the Spanish Civil War (1936-1939), he returned to Cuba to write for the Communist newspaper *Hoy*. An unsuccessful run for mayor of Camagüey eventually led to his departure in 1942 for a lecture and poetry-reading tour through Haiti and several South American countries. The tour continued until the 1948 murder of Guillén's friend Jesús Menendez, an official in the National Federation of Sugar Workers, an event that inspired one of Guillén's *elegías* (elegies). In 1951, *Hoy* was shut down by the government of Carlos Prio Socarras, and Guillén left for a tour of Eastern Europe, returning to Cuba shortly after the May, 1952, installation of dictator Fulgencio Batista. The new regime responded to Guillén's satires in the newspaper *La Última Hora* by forcing him into exile in 1953. He remained without a country for six years, traveling during the first two and finding a safe if uneasy harbor in France until 1958, when Argentina offered him asylum. *La paloma de vuelo popular* (the dove of popular flight) deals primarily with Guillén's political and personal frustrations, feelings that portended the impending Cuban Revolution. When Batista fled Fidel Castro's rebel forces on January 1, 1959, Guillén returned as quickly as possible. His homecoming on January 23 was large and joyous, and Castro's new government welcomed him warmly. In 1961, the Union of Writers and Artists of Cuba was established under Guillén's direction, and he remained the organization's leader until his death. Meanwhile, he also resumed his work as a journalist, and was appointed ambassador-at-large and plenipotentiary minister in 1962.

Guillén's post-Revolution poetry was published in *Tengo* (*I Have*, 1974) and *El gran zoo* (*The Great Zoo*, 2004), which continued his extraordinary tradition of combining powerful social commentary with creative use of poetic forms. His attention to the subtleties of daily life and his unwavering support of Castro's socialist government are apparent in *La rueda dentada* (the gear wheel) and in the two nonfiction collections published in 1972: *Prosa de prisa 1929-1972* and *El diario que a diario* (*The Daily Daily*). By the early 1980's, Guillén's work had been translated into more than thirty languages. He was nominated by many contemporaries for the Nobel Prize and awarded Cuba's highest honor, the José Martí National Order, but in 1986 he began to succumb to Parkinson's disease, and died shortly after receiving the Maurice Bishop Prize (the only major regional award he had not won) in 1989.

— Anna A. Moore

Learn More

Ellis, Keith. *Nicolás Guillén: A Bilingual Anthology.* Havana: Editorial José Martí, 2004. This anthology is preceded by an excellent introduction that gives in-depth analysis of Guillén's life and works. Pieces are carefully organized to support Ellis's thesis that love is the driving force behind each of Guillén's poems.

Kaup, Monica. "'Our America' That Is Not One: Transnational Black Atlantic Disclosures in Nicolás Guillén and Langston Hughes." *Discourse* 22, no. 3 (Fall, 2000): 87-105. Focuses on the concept of blackness and the black experience as they are celebrated in the poetry of Guillén and Hughes. Studies the poets' language as a tool used to denounce colonialism.

Miller, Marilyn. "(Gypsy) Rhythm and (Cuban) Blues: The Neo-American Dream in Guillén and Hughes." *Comparative Literature* 51, no. 4 (Fall, 1999): 324-345. A comparative study that addresses the distinct ways in which Langston Hughes and Nicolás Guillén problematized the notion of the American Dream in the United States and across the Americas.

Yovanovich, Gordana. "Play as a Mode of Empowerment for Women and as a Model for Poetics in the Early Poetry of Nicolás Guillén." *Hispanic Review* 69, no. 1 (Winter, 2001): 15-31. Explains the ways in which Guillén's poetry uses playfulness as a method of empowering women.

João Guimarães Rosa
Brazilian short-story writer and novelist

Born: Cordisburgo, Minas Gerais, Brazil;
June 27, 1908
Died: Rio de Janeiro, Brazil; November 19, 1967

SHORT FICTION: *Sagarana*, 1946, 1966; *Corpo de Baile*, 1956 (subsequent editions in 3 volumes: *Manuelzão e Miguilim, No Urubúquaquá, no Pinhém,* and *Noites do Sertão*); *Primeiras estórias*, 1962, 1968 (*The Third Bank of the River, and Other Stories,* 1968); *Tutaméia,* 1967; *Estas estórias,* 1969; *Ave, Palavra,* 1970; *The Jaguar, and Other Stories,* 2001.
LONG FICTION: *Grande Sertão: Veredas,* 1956 (*The Devil to Pay in the Backlands,* 1963).

João Guimarães Rosa (zhwown gee-ma-RAYNS ROH-sa) is generally regarded as the most important writer of fiction in twentieth century Brazil. The eldest of six children of a well-to-do businessman, he was born in the small town of Cordisburgo in central Brazil. He attended school in the state capital of Belo Horizonte and later completed medical school in the same city. He practiced medicine in the interior for some years, first as a private physician and later with the Brazilian National Guard. In 1934 he passed the Foreign Service examination, entered the Ministry of Foreign Affairs, and enjoyed a distinguished career in the Brazilian diplomatic service, attaining the rank of ambassador in 1958. Twice married, he had two daughters by his first wife.

Although the bulk of his work was short fiction, Guimarães Rosa is probably best known for his single novel, *The Devil to Pay in the Backlands*, the monologue of a former bandit about the meaning of life, particularly the significance of evil and love. The chapterless text runs to more than five hundred pages in length and is characterized not only by the thematic breadth and suggestive resonance of the narrative but also by the daunting complexity and novelty of the language in which it is told. In fact, all Guimarães Rosa's fiction is marked by linguistic experimentation, a feature that accounts for the unevenness of the quality of the translations and also helps to explain why so few of such an important author's works are available in any of the major European languages.

Even though the density and intricacy of language is a constant, many of Guimarães Rosa's works have a fairly conventional narrative structure. *Sagarana*, his first work, for example, contains nine tales that resemble very traditional forms such as the trickster tale, the fable, and the saint's tale. Guimarães Rosa wrote the first draft of this book in the late 1930's. When it garnered only second place in a national contest, he left it in a drawer and was not persuaded to edit and publish it until almost a decade later.

Yet another decade passed before his second book appeared, and many had begun to think Guimarães Rosa had exhausted his imagination on the first book. In 1956, however, he published not one but two books. The first, *Corpo de Baile* (corps de

> *Father was a reliable, law-abiding, practical man,*
> *and had been ever since he was a boy, as various*
> *people of good sense testified when I asked them*
> *about him. I don't remember that he seemed any*
> *crazier or even any moodier than anyone else we*
> *knew. He just didn't talk much. It was our mother*
> *who gave the orders and scolded us every day—my*
> *sister, my brother, and me. Then one day my father*
> *ordered a canoe for himself.*
>
> —from *The Third Bank of the River*
> (trans. Barbara Shelby)

ballet), contained tales of such length that the book first appeared in two volumes, and later editions appeared in three. There are only seven stories in the book, which naturally piqued interest in the question of genre, since the tales were impossibly long to be considered short stories yet not quite long enough to qualify as novels. The second book to appear in 1956 was *The Devil to Pay in the Backlands*, a massive narrative; again critics called this work a novel only for lack of an alternative term. In both works, the stories proceed with an almost unnerving leisureliness; in both, a philosophical inquiry lurks behind every rustic; and in both the diction is aggressively experimental.

One year after publishing these two books, Guimarães Rosa stood as a candidate for membership in the Brazilian Academy of Letters. He was not elected. Four years later, in 1961, the academy unexpectedly presented Guimarães Rosa with an award for the excellence of his collected works.

The author's diplomatic career was somewhat smoother. In 1958, he was promoted to Minister First Class with the rank of ambassador, and in 1962 he was named Chief of the Borders Division of the Brazilian State Department. In the same year, he published *The Third Bank of the River, and Other Stories*. This book offered some surprises, being the shortest yet to appear. It contains twenty-one narratives, which seemed to be a clear denial of the

---

W H A T   T O   R E A D

"The Thin Edge of Happiness"

Guimarães Rosa's "The Thin Edge of Happiness" seems simple: a five-page story broken into five vignettes that describe a young child's sadness. Taken by an aunt and uncle to visit a new city being carved out of the wilderness (probably modeled on Brazil's futuristic capital, Brasília), the boy, who remains nameless, is thrilled by the hustle and bustle of the frontier city, which is being built almost overnight by powerful machines, and the lush and seductive wilderness at his doorstep.

The story is a parody of children's once-upon-a-time tales: "This is the story: A little boy went with his aunt and uncle to spend a few days in a place where the great city was being built." The narrator describes matter-of-factly, using short sentences, how the boy leaves behind his parents to fly with his aunt and uncle to the unknown frontier, how the plane trip is a child's delight of new sensations, and how the place where he arrives is like a fairyland.

One of these new things is a spectacular turkey, an animal unknown in the city; but no sooner is the boy's

---

trend toward ever longer and more inclusive fictions. Although there are rural characters and scenes, it is also the first of his books in which locale is, even on a superficial level, of not much import. Critical reaction to the volume was mixed, because although the prose is unmistakably Guimarães Rosa's—some considered it almost self-parodic—the tales are, in comparison with his other works, terse almost to the point of abruptness. Yet many gave the work high praise, and the Academy of Letters unanimously elected Guimarães Rosa to its ranks the following year.

In 1967, Guimarães Rosa published *Tutaméia* (trifle), which contained not only forty stories but no less than four prefaces as well. That same year, the author finally scheduled his long-delayed formal seating in the Academy of Letters. Three days af-

delight with the animal described than it "disappears," slaughtered for a birthday meal. The boy's awe turns to terror: The turkey's absence foregrounds the threatening wilderness from which the animal's strutting had distracted him. The boy is then treated to what the adults intend as a marvelous display of the power of the machines used to carve the metropolis out of the jungle: A sort of juggernaut machete slashes down a tree so efficiently that the boy does not even see it fall. The boy feels sick as he contemplates the "astonished and blue" sky, exposed so brutally by the slash of the machine.

In rapid succession the narrative juxtaposes implied opposites: known experiences versus unknown delights, childlike joy versus unfocused anxiety, wild nature versus "wild" machines, the wilderness versus civilization and progress, childlike wonderment versus adult matter-of-factness, and the comforting versus the terrifying. More than a tale of the brutal shattering of youthful innocence, "The Thin Edge of Happiness" reveals typical Latin American conflicts: the natural versus the mechanical, spontaneous sentiment versus artificial power, the human versus the artificial and destructive.

— *David W. Foster*

ter the ceremony, he died of a brain hemorrhage. In 1969, *Estas estórias* (these stories), which the author had been organizing shortly before his death, appeared, and in 1970 the miscellanea of four decades of writing appeared as *Ave, Palavra* (hail, word).

Guimarães Rosa had no rival as the most important and original prose writer in Brazil in the twentieth century. He is widely regarded as a watershed figure, much as Joaquim Maria Machado de Assis is regarded for the nineteenth century. He is also considered by many to be Brazil's principal figure in the Latin American fiction "boom" of the second half of the twentieth century. His name is known to virtually all literate Brazilians, although it may be that his name is better known than his works because of the difficulties they present to readers. Because he is so demanding of his readers, his most enthusiastic following abroad is composed mainly of writers, critics, and translators. In Brazil, his works attained best-seller status at least briefly.

Guimarães Rosa's works are demanding above all because the variety of linguistic novelties affects everything, starting with the title page. Many of the titles contain invented or deformed words, and the prose is hyperexpressive; in his variety of Portuguese, nothing is impossible. Guimarães Rosa spoke six languages and read fourteen others, and many of these languages crept into his prose in subtle and at times confounding ways. Diction in his works is further complicated by his willingness to use Latinate or Tupi forms, ungrammatical constructions, and neologisms.

The style is also complicated by the fact that Guimarães Rosa was a medical doctor, an amateur naturalist, a student of Eastern mysticism, and a prodigious and omnivorous reader. The sources of names, motifs, and entire tales may be found in anything from Danish myth to the Brothers Grimm to Zen Buddhism, possibly all in the same story. It is not always necessary or even particularly enlightening to discover such sources, but the fact that such eclectic roots have been proven to exist in his fiction is a measure of their perverse originality.

Yet, although these stories are not always accessible on first reading, all of them are sufficiently enchanting to make a second reading worthwhile, and further study often provides unexpected discoveries and delights. Guimarães Rosa's literary career was an astonishment not only because he produced his fiction in his spare time but also because of the inventiveness of language, the range of theme, and the attention he paid to every detail.

—*Jon S. Vincent*

Learn More

Armstrong, Piers. *Third World Literary Fortunes: Brazilian Culture and Its International Reception.* Lewisberg, Pa.: Bucknell University Press, 1999. Examines the domestic and international receptions of Brazilian writers. Contrasts Guimarães Rosa, the "Brazilian James Joyce," with Jorge Amado, who celebrates negritude and has been successful in turning Brazilian popular culture into literature.

Coutinho, Eduardo de Faria. "João Guimarães Rosa." In *Latin*

American Writers, edited by Carlos A. Solé and Maria Isabel Abreu. 3 vols. New York: Charles Scribner's Sons, 1989. An excellent introduction to the complete works, including remarks on language, causality, regionalism and universality, the use of myth, the importance of emotion, and the unusual position in Guimarães Rosa's works of madmen, poets, and children.

_____. *The Synthesis Novel in Latin America: A Study on João Guimarães Rosa's "Grande Sertão: Veredas."* Chapel Hill: North Carolina University Press, 1991. A critical study.

Harss, Luis, and Barbara Dohmann. *Into the Mainstream: Conversations with Latin-American Writers.* New York: Harper and Row, 1967. Contains a fascinating and sometimes illuminating interview with Guimarães Rosa.

Martins, Wilson. "Structural Perspectivism in Guimarães Rosa." In *The Brazilian Novel,* edited by Heitor Martins. Bloomington: Indiana University Press, 1976. Though focusing largely on *The Devil to Pay in the Backlands*, this study is relevant to the short fiction for its discussion of Guimarães Rosa as both a radical innovator of style and a "classic" writer in the traditions of Brazilian regionalism.

Perrone, Charles A. "Guimarães Rosa Through the Prism of Magic Realism." In *Tropical Paths: Essays on Modern Brazilian Literature.* New York: Garland, 1993. Discusses some of Guimarães Rosa's short stories from the perspective of their Magical Realism; analyzes their relationship to modernity.

Vessels, Gary M. "The Search for Motives: Carnivalized Heroes and Paternal Abandonment in Some Recent Brazilian Fiction." *Luso-Brazilian Review* 31 (Summer, 1994): 57-65. Discusses the carnivalisque element in the heroes of such Brazilian writers as Jorge Amado and Guimarães Rosa; also discusses the mystery of motivation in Guimarães Rosa's theme of the abandonment by the father.

Vincent, Jon S. *João Guimarães Rosa.* Boston: Twayne, 1978. The first study of the complete works in any language. This critical study contains a brief summary of Guimarães Rosa's life and is divided into seven chapters, one on each of the short fiction books and one on the novel. The bibliography is, however, dated.

Ricardo Güiraldes

Argentine novelist

Born: Buenos Aires, Argentina; February 13, 1886
Died: Paris, France; October 8, 1927

LONG FICTION: *Raucho*, 1917; *Rosaura*, 1922; *Don Segundo Sombra*,
1926 (*Don Segundo Sombra: Shadows on the Pampas*, 1935).
SHORT FICTION: *Cuentos de muerte y de sangre*, 1915.
NONFICTION: *Xaimaca*, 1923 (travel sketches).

Ricardo Güiraldes (rih-KAHR-doh gee-RAHL-days), the son
of a wealthy Argentine rancher, was born on his father's estate near Buenos Aires. France attracted him at an early age, and
he was reading French by the time he entered high school. This

> *I went to school. I learned to swallow my tears and to mistrust sweet words. My aunts soon got tired of their new toy, and spent the day grumbling. The only thing they agreed on was that I was a lazy, dirty good-for-nothing, and to blame for everything that went wrong in the house.*
>
> —from *Don Segundo Sombra*
> (trans. Harriet de Onís)

influence is revealed in the volume of poetry he published at the age of twenty-nine. He spent much of his life in Paris and died there in 1927.

His boyhood on the ranch threw him into the company of the gauchos, or Argentine cowboys, one of whom, Segundo, was his teacher in the lore of the pampas, the Argentine plains. Segundo became the inspiration for at least one of his short stories of violence, published in 1915, and for the novel about his childhood, written while he lived in Paris, which established his fame.

Initially, Güiraldes was influenced by the Vanguardist movement, which is reflected in the two novels *Raucho* and *Rosaura* and the travel book *Xaimaca*. While living in Paris, however, he developed a nostalgia for Argentina that led him to turn back to the influences of his youth. His poetic sensitivity transmuted the crude material of early gaucho literature into the novel *Don Segundo Sombra*, a story that became as popular with children as with adults. The book transforms the Argentine cultural heritage of the gaucho into a national myth. The gaucho tradition combined with the telluric strength of the pampas create a healing environment for the young orphan protagonist, who becomes a man in the course of the narrative. The novel became a classic and one of Argentina's founding fictions.

Güiraldes was involved in activities other than writing. He was a congressman and at one time the mayor of Buenos Aires.

W H A T   T O   R E A D

Don Segundo Sombra

Don Segundo Sombra (1926) is based on the author's recollections of his early life on the *pampas*. Influenced by works such as Mark Twain's *Adventures of Huckleberry Finn* (1884), the narrative illustrates the experience of growing up in the countryside, having the ideal gaucho as a mentor and role model. *Don Segundo Sombra* symbolizes the *pampas* and its inhabitants and represents the gaucho culture as it once existed, before the invasion of economic and industrial progress. Often compared to Don Quixote in Miguel de Cervantes' *Don Quixote de la Mancha* (1605, 1615), Don Segundo is the last representative of a special kind of life that was disappearing.

The coming-of-age story is told by the protagonist, a misdirected orphan named Fabio. In the first part of the novel, he meets and becomes the apprentice of Don Segundo Sombra. Fabio sees his destiny in a nomadic free life, hoping to become a real gaucho. In the second part, Fabio reviews the five years spent learning gaucho skills and overcoming physical and spiritual tests. In the third part, the reader sees him returning to his town of origin, ready to take over his new position as a ranch owner upon the news of his legitimate right to the possessions of his father, who recognized him as his heir before dying. In the last three chapters, Fabio recalls the departure of Don Segundo.

The image of Don Segundo is seen through Fabio's eyes. He admires gauchos and transfers his image of them to his mentor, who becomes a hero and father figure for him. Fabio is the protagonist, but Don Segundo is the main character of his recollections. He embodies the virtues of the gaucho Fabio wants to become: laconic, serene, proud, stoic, and respectful of others, prizing freedom above all else. In his journey with Don Segundo through the *pampas*, this delinquent, lazy orphan grows up to be an honest, hardworking member of society.

— *Ludmila Kapschutschenko-Schmitt*

His poetry is frivolous and mystic, and his stories are romantic and realistic, but his love for his native country and his ability as a writer found their ideal expression in one novel, *Don Segundo Sombra.*

— *Emil Volek*

Learn More

Alonso, Carlos J. *The Spanish American Regional Novel: Modernity and Autochthony.* New York: Cambridge University Press, 1990. A study of regional novels and their role in the development of twentieth century Latin American fiction. Alonso illustrates his general observations about the genre with an analysis of three regional novels, including Güiraldes's *Don Segundo Sombra.*

Beardsell, Peter R. "Güiraldes' Role in the Avant-Garde of Buenos Aires." *Hispanic Review* 42 (Summer, 1974). Places Güiraldes within the context of Argentinian culture.

Flores, Angel. "Latin American Writers: Ricardo Güiraldes." *Panorama,* December, 1940. A review of Güiraldes's life and work.

Previtali, Giovanni. *Ricardo Güiraldes and "Don Segundo Sombra."* New York: Hispanic Institute in the United States, 1963. An examination of Güiraldes's best-known novel.

Scott, Nina M. *Language, Humor, and Myth in the Frontier Novels of the Americas: Wister, Güiraldes, and Amado.* Amherst: University of Massachusetts, 1983. Compares how the three novelists tell stories of the frontier and the "wild west," focusing on Güiraldes's *Don Segundo Sombra,* Jorge Amado's *Terras do sem fin,* and Owen Wister's *The Virginian.*

Spell, Jefferson R. *Contemporary Spanish American Fiction.* 1944. Reprint. New York: Biblo and Tannen, 1968. Includes information about Güiraldes's work.

Martín Luis Guzmán
Mexican novelist and biographer

Born: Chihuahua, Mexico; October 6, 1887
Died: Mexico City, Mexico; December 22, 1976

LONG FICTION: *El águila y la serpiente*, 1928 (*The Eagle and the Serpent*, 1930); *La sombra del caudillo*, 1929; *Memorias de Pancho Villa*, 1938-1940, 1951 (4 volumes; *Memoirs of Pancho Villa*, 1965).

SCREENPLAY: *Islas Marias, novela y drama*, 1959.

NONFICTION: *La querella de Mexico*, 1915; *A orillas del Hudson*, 1920; *Javier Mina, héroe de Espana y de Mexico*, 1932 (biography; originally published as *Mina el Mozo, héroe de Navarra*); *Filadelfia paraíso de conspiradores*, 1933 (history); *Apunte sobre una personalidad*, 1954 (biography); *Muertes históricas*, 1958 (biography); *Crónicas de mi Destierro*, 1963 (biography); *Necesidad de cumplir las Leyes de Reforma*, 1963.

MISCELLANEOUS: *Obras completas*, 1961-1963 (2 volumes).

Martín Luis Guzmán (mahr-TEEN lwees gews-MAHN), one of the most vigorous writers on the Mexican Revolution,

---

Ciudad Juárez is a sad sight; sad in itself, and still sadder when compared with the bright orderliness of that opposite river-bank, close but foreign. Yet if our faces burned with shame to look at it, nevertheless, or perhaps for that very reason, it made our hearts dance as we felt the roots of our being sink into something we had known, possessed, and loved for centuries. . . . Not for nothing were we Mexicans.

—from "My First Glimpse of Pancho Villa"
(trans. Harriet de Onís)

was born in 1887 in the capital of Chihuahua, which later became the main field of operations of the famous revolutionary warrior Pancho Villa. Guzmán's father, a colonel of the federal army, and his mother, who was related to wealthy families of Chihuahua, moved later the same year to Tacubaya, at that time on the outskirts of Mexico City, close to the famous Chapultepec Castle. The daily contemplation of this building, so important in the political history of Mexico, gave the boy a deep sense of history that eventually oriented his literary work. In the city of Veracruz, at the age of fourteen, he continued his studies and published his first newspaper, *La Juventud*, a work of ephemeral importance.

The Eagle and the Serpent

According to legend, the Aztecs' capital city (present-day Mexico City) was founded in the spot where they found an eagle, devouring a serpent, perched upon a nopal. These images form the basis for this book, but to understand it, the reader must also take into account the history of the Mexican Revolution (1910-1920) and the centuries of oppression that preceded it.

The Eagle and the Serpent (1928) is divided into two parts: "Revolutionary Hopes" and "At the Hour of the Triumph." In the first part, Guzmán, the author-narrator, tells of his adventures before the fighting peaked. In the second section, he tells of deeds that occurred during the most turbulent years of the conflict.

The story opens when Guzmán embarks for northern Mexico so that he can help the revolutionary Venustiano Carranza in his fight against provisional president and usurper Victoriano Huerta. Unable to carry out his plan to contact Carranza, Guzmán returns to Mexico City, but his enthusiasm for the Revolution causes him to leave

Afterward, Guzmán entered the National Preparatory School and the National School of Law in Mexico City. After his marriage, he traveled to Phoenix, Arizona, to fill a diplomatic post. He returned to Mexico in 1910, a crucial year for the country, for it marked the beginning of the revolution against the dictatorship of Porfirio Díaz. Guzmán joined Francisco Madero, the leader of the opposition, and participated enthusiastically in several nonmilitary tasks. In 1911, he associated with the group called El Ateneo de la Juventud, a young intellectual movement of great importance in the revival of Mexican culture. To denounce the opponents of the revolution, he founded the newspaper *El Honor Nacional*. After Victoriano Huerta murdered President Madero and usurped the presidency, Guzmán trav-

again. In Ciudad Juárez the author meets Pancho Villa, who is for him the chief hero of the Revolution. Finally, he is introduced to Carranza and gradually begins to realize that personal ambitions will inevitably cause deep disagreements among the fighters.

Several episodes are intermingled in this part of the work, and they may be the most interesting and representative material in the novel. Among them, "A Night in Culiacan," and "The Murdering Spider," emerge as masterpieces of suspense and narrative vigor.

The second part of the novel deals with the triumph of the Revolution, in which Guzmán abandons Carranza, who he sees as too ambitious and corrupt, and joins Villa (despite his impression that the legendary warrior and his pistol were a single thing; from Villa's gun, all of his friendships and enmities were born). Late in the book, Guzmán exultantly writes the most lyric pages he has ever composed. The sight of Mexico City and the volcanoes, the inhalation of the thin air of the plateau, the bath of clarity, and the perfect balance of person and environment deeply impress the "rebel who returned," as Guzmán calls himself. Ultimately, though, Guzmán is caught between divided loyalties and finally expatriates himself to the United States.

eled to the northern boundary of Mexico to join the "Division of the North" that was commanded by Villa, and he eventually became Villa's private secretary. When a schism developed between Villa and Venustiano Carranza, the new leader of the revolution, Guzmán supported Villa and was imprisoned in Mexico City. He was liberated by the Convention of Aguascalientes, when a new government appeared under the leadership of General Eulalio Gutiérrez.

A new discord between this regime and Villa ensued, and Guzmán, caught between the obedience to the Convention of Aguascalientes and loyalty to Villa, chose to expatriate himself voluntarily in 1915. He traveled in the United States, France, and Spain and finally settled in New York, where he collaborated in the publication of Spanish magazines. In 1920, he returned to Mexico. Again intervening in politics, he was appointed federal deputy and served in that post from 1922 through 1924 before political turmoil again necessitated exile, this time in Spain, where he remained almost twelve years. In 1936, he returned to Mexico and again devoted himself to journalism, publishing a weekly magazine of Mexican liberalism, *Tiempo*. He was elected a member of the Mexican Academy of the Language.

Guzmán's best works center on the Mexican Revolution. As an eyewitness of many revolutionary deeds and an actor in others, Guzmán was very well qualified to write about this drama of Mexican history. *The Eagle and the Serpent, La sombra del caudillo*, and *Memoirs of Pancho Villa* constitute a trilogy of great historical density. Although the term "novel" cannot be fully applied to his works, which appear more like a series of episodes or a mosaic of short stories linked together by the common denominator of the Revolution, Guzmán's mastery of narrative and descriptive techniques, his keenness of observation of the revolutionary leaders, especially Villa, and the dynamism and elegance of his prose make him one of the outstanding writers of Mexican literature. Whereas Mariano Azuela preferred to write about *Los de abajo* (1916; *The Underdogs*, 1929) of the Revolution, Guzmán chose to present with great psychological acumen an intimate portrait of its leaders, with their ambition, nobility, instinctiveness, and desperation. Many historical episodes he relates are as full of suspense as fiction. His contribution was recognized when, in 1951, he was appointed the Mexican ambassador to the United Nations. In 1958, he received the Mexican National Award for Literature.

— *Emil Volek*

Learn More

Bruce-Novoa, J. "Martín Luis Guzmán's Necessary Overtures." *Discurso literario* 4, no. 1 (Autumn, 1986). Studies the narrative structure and the characterization in two of Guzmán's novels: *El águila y la serpiente*, and *La sombra del caudillo*.

Brushwood, John S. *Mexico in Its Novel: A Nation's Search for Iden-*

tity. Austin: University of Texas Press, 1966. Brushwood includes a brief discussion of Guzmán in his study of the Mexican novel's development.

Duffey, J. Patrick. "Pancho Villa at the Movies: Cinematic Techniques in the Works of Guzmán and Muñoz." In *Latin American Literature and Mass Media,* edited by Edmundo Paz-Soldán and Debra A. Castillo. New York: Garland, 2001. Describes how *The Eagle and the Serpent* uses literary techniques similar to close-up shots in films, and compares the book's treatment of the Mexican Revolution and Pancho Villa to the film adaption of Rafael Felipe Muñoz's book, *¡Vámanos con Poncho Villa!*

Grimes, Larry M. *The Revolutionary Cycle in the Literary Production of Martín Luis Guzmán.* Cuernavaca, Mexico: Centro Intercultural de Documentacion, 1969. An examination of Guzmán's work by an author specializing in the study of Mexican literature.

Langford, Walter M. *The Mexican Novel Comes of Age.* Notre Dame, Ind.: University of Notre Dame Press, 1971. Includes several pages of information about Guzmán's contributions to the Mexican novel.

McLynn, Frank. *Villa and Zapata: A History of the Mexican Revolution.* New York: Carroll & Graf, 2001. McLynn makes reference to Guzmán in his chronicle of the revolution.

Sommers, Joseph. *After the Storm: Landmarks of the Modern Mexican Novel.* Albuquerque: University of New Mexico Press, 1968. Guzmán's work is included in this examination of Mexican literature.

José María Heredia

Cuban poet

Born: Santiago, Cuba; December 31, 1803
Died: Toluca, Mexico; May 2, 1839

POETRY: *En el teocalli de Cholula*, 1820; *En una tempestad*, 1822; *Niagara*, 1824; *Al sol*, 1825; *Selections*, 1844; *Obras poeticas*, 1875.
DRAMA: *Eduardo IV*, pr. 1818; *Los últimos romanos*, pr. 1829.
NONFICTION: *Lecciones de historia universal*, 1830-1831 (4 volumes).

José María Heredia (hoh-SAY mah-REE-ah ay-RAYTH-yah), Cuba's national poet, is considered one of the New World's first Romantic poets, despite the classical form of most of his verse, because of the intensity of his melancholy and introspective emotion and his deep feeling for nature. He was also one of the first to write about the American landscape. His *En el teocalli de Cholula* (on the temple pyramid of Cholula), written during a visit to Mexico when he was only seventeen, preceded the first Romantic poetry in Spain by thirteen years. His reaction to nature is shown in *En una tempestad* (in a hurricane), and especially in his ode about visiting Niagara Falls after having been turned down by his Cuban sweetheart.

> *Cuba, Cuba, what life you gave me,*
> *sweet land of light and beauty,*
> *how many dreams of fate and glory*
> *have I tied to your happy soil!*
> *I look at you again! . . . How heavily*
> *the harshness of my luck weighs upon me!*
> *Oppression threatens me with death*
> *in the fields where to the world I was born.*
>
> —from "Hymn of the Exile"
> (trans. Pablo Peschiera)

As a young boy, José María Heredia y Campuzano, related to the famous Cuban-born French poet of the same name (the author of the 1895 *The Trophies*), traveled with his parents to Florida, Santo Domingo, Venezuela, and Mexico, then returned to Havana to study law. Poetry and the theater also attracted him. At the age of fifteen, he wrote *Eduardo IV*, in which he and his contemporary, poet-dramatist Gertrudis Gómez de Avella-

---

WHAT TO READ

"On the Temple Pyramid of Cholula"

In 1830 the youthful Argentine poet Esteban Echeverría returned to his native Buenos Aires after spending five years among the Romantic poets of France; his advice to his fellow writers was to break away from literary dependence on Spain and to hymn the natural beauties of the New World. José María Heredia was already using poetry to paint the American scene and express Romantic ideas in classic verse forms. In "On the Temple Pyramid of Cholula" he used ten-syllable unrhymed lines resembling English blank verse.

Seated in the ancient Aztec temple, the youthful poet watches the sun setting behind the volcano Iztaccíhual, whose snowcap is tinged with gold. The stars come out, and as the moon descends, the shadow of Popocatépetl, like a colossal ghost, extend until it covers the earth. This eclipse of nature causes the poet to ponder the passing of the cruel Aztec rulers and all their glory. In this passing he sees how temporary is human fury and madness.

In the poem, the reader finds such classical touches as a mention—in an American landscape—of the olive tree "sacred to Minerva" and of Titan and his struggle against the gods of Olympus. With the subjectivity of later Romantic poets, Heredia, though describing a scene in Mexico through the eyes of a seventeen-year-old, was actually poetizing his soul and its agony at what it saw.

---

neda, both performed. That was her only recorded stage appearance, but she continued to write plays, as did Heredia, in Cuba and in France.

In 1823, Heredia received his law degree and was admitted to the bar, but that same year, because of his liberal ideas and revolutionary activities, he was permanently banished from Cuba. In New York, in 1825, he published a volume of poetry that attracted wide attention, *Al sol.* William Cullen Bryant's version of his "Ode to Niagara" was the first Latin American poetry translation published in the United States. Heredia reissued the book in an enlarged form in two volumes in 1832. He made several trips to France. Finally, he was invited by the president of Mexico to make his home there, and he became a Mexican citizen.

Some criticism has suggested that Heredia might qualify as the author of one of the earliest Spanish American novels, *Jicoténcal,* which appeared anonymously in Philadelphia in 1826. *Jicoténcal* is a historical novel dealing with the conquest of Mexico, following the spirit of the Enlightenment pretty much attuned to Heredia's own vision of Mexican history as expressed in his earlier poem *En el teocalli de Cholula.* Other critics, however, insist on the authorship of another Cuban, Father Félix Varela (1788-1853).

— Emil Volek

Learn More

Fontanella, Lee. "J. M. Heredia: A Case for Critical Inclusivism." *Revista hispánica moderna* 37 (1972-1973). A reassessment of Heredia's poetry.

Kahiluoto-Rudat, Eva M. "From Enlightenment to Romanticism in Spanish America: An Aesthetic Approach." *Hispanic Journal* 2 (Fall, 1980). Kahiluoto-Rudat focuses on Heredia's poetry as an example of changing styles and philosophies in nineteenth-century Spanish American literature.

McVay, Ted E., Jr. "The Sublime Aesthetic in the Poetry of José María Heredia." *Dieciocho* 17 (Spring, 1994). Examines the treatment of the sublime in *En una tempestad,* describing how Heredia drew upon philosophical theories of the sublime to create this work.

José Hernández

Argentine poet

Born: Chacra de Pueyrredón, Buenos Aires,
Argentina; November 10, 1834
Died: Belgrano, near Buenos Aires, Argentina;
October 21, 1886

POETRY: *El Gaucho Martín Fierro*, 1872 (*The Gaucho Martin Fierro*,
1935); *La vuelta de Martín Fierro*, 1879 (*The Return of Martin
Fierro*, 1935, included in *The Gaucho Martin Fierro*).

J osé Hernández (hoh-SAY ehr-NAHN-thays), Argentine poet,
soldier, political office holder, and champion of minorities,
was born at the Estancia Pueyrredón, province of Buenos Aires,
on November 10, 1834; he died in Belgrano on October 21,
1886. He lacked the education of other Argentine writers such
as Bartolomé Hidalgo, Estanislao del Campo, and Hilario Asca-
subi, who are important figures in Gauchesque literature, because illness halted his formal education. Yet he was the poet
read by the gauchos about whom he wrote. The unprecedented
success of his narrative poem was such that in less than two years
there were eight printings of it. However, sixty thousand copies

> *If they catch him enjoying himself*
> *they call him a drunk,*
> *and he's a "bad character"*
> *if they find him at a dance—*
> *if he puts up a fight, he's doing wrong,*
> *and if he doesn't, he's . . . done for.*
>
> —from "Martín Fierro" (trans. C. E. Ward)

W H A T   T O   R E A D

The Gaucho Martin Fierro

Martin Fierro, the hero of this poem (published in 1872), is a gaucho, born and raised on the rolling plains of Argentina. A gaucho was a mixture of the Spaniard and the Moor (or Spanish Muslim), transplanted to South America and mixed again with aboriginal Indians. The poem tells us that he was God-fearing, brutal, superstitious, ignorant, lazy, and kind, and while he roamed the plains he became a legend. Martin Fierro played his guitar and sang, telling of the sorrows of gauchos all over the land.

The poem tells of the gaucho's passing, which occurred after the 1850's, when the last native tribes were being pushed northward. At the same time, the gaucho was being supplanted by progress in the form of barbed wire, railroads, immigrants, wheat, and the herds of pure-bred cattle and sheep and thoroughbred horses that have made Argentina famous. In telling the tragic story of Martin Fierro and his lost family and home, the poem includes many epic themes: the fight against injustice, governmental power, and nature, as well as the yearning for

---

of the first part of his epic poem, *The Gaucho Martin Fierro*, were sold before he could persuade himself to go on with its sequel. Country pulperías stocked copies, along with other essentials such as tobacco and food, for the cattle herders to purchase and read around their campfires. Hernández was an active participant in the delicate political situation of Argentina prior to the period of national organization and, later, he was an active opponent of the oligarchical interests of the ruling class. He was so closely identified with his work that as the robust, bearded man strode along Buenos Aires streets, people addressed him as "Don Martín."

The first part of *The Gaucho Martin Fierro* introduces the image of an individual whose family life is destroyed by the politi-

lost freedom and lost loved ones during bitter years of exile. It also incorporates such motifs as the temporary flight to the land of a hated enemy and the rescue of a maiden in distress. Drenched with the pampas' earthiness, the redoubtable but bigoted Fierro symbolizes the pampas and the gaucho himself.

The poem presents the life cycle of both a place and of a group of people clearly representative of Argentina. The poetic style is brisk and clear, even though the language is replete with gaucho vocabulary and speech patterns. Martin Fierro's character projects itself over the poem: The reader can empathize with him for the loss of his home and family; all the lonely bitterness of his cruel military years fighting the raiding Indians on the far frontier; and his sadness when he finally returns home to find his little cabin abandoned, his wife and children gone, and only one familiar figure, his old cat prowling unhappily around the well. The poem holds the reader's interest throughout its stanzas and stands at the summit of Argentine gaucho literature. It has attracted attention in Spanish America, Brazil, and Spain, where famed author Miguel de Unamuno often read it aloud to his classes at Salamanca University.

— *William Freitas*

cal decisions of the authorities. The poem does not limit itself to presenting a conflict between individuals and society; it also makes room for the display of the perspective of the marginalized, along with descriptions of rural customs and beliefs. The second part, in which the author pleads for fair treatment for the gaucho by the government, continues the narrative line and incorporates a character, old Vizcacha, who supposedly espouses the essence of the gaucho philosophy.

The poet married Carolina González del Solar in 1863. In one of the many places where they settled, he founded the newspaper *Río de la Plata* and ran it for a year before his enemy, President Domingo Faustino Sarmiento, closed it. In his newspaper articles, Hernández stated his opposition to the official policy of frontiers and his strong defense of the gauchos. He also wrote a handbook on farming and animal husbandry in 1881, but nothing else from his pen will have the permanence of his rhymed yarn of the gaucho, told in the literary language that Hernández helped to establish as a naturalized vehicle for expressing folk culture. Since it was first published, the poem and the main character have become key ideological aspects of Argentine intellectual history.

— *Daniel Altamiranda*

Learn More

Benson, Nettie Lee, ed. *Catalogue of "Martín Fierro" Materials in the University of Texas Library.* Austin: University of Texas Press, 1972. In commemoration of the one hundredth anniversary of the publication of *The Gaucho Martín Fierro.*

Borges, Jorge Luis. *The Spanish Language in South America: A Literary Problem.* London: Hispanic & Luso-Brazilian Councils, 1964. Includes a lecture on *The Gaucho Martín Fierro.*

Foster, David William. *Argentine Literature: A Research Guide.* 2d rev. and expanded ed. New York: Garland, 1982. A long chapter is dedicated to Hernández.

Papanikolas, Zeese. "The Cowboy and the Gaucho." In *Reading the Virginian in the New West,* edited by Melody Graulich and Stephen Tatum. Lincoln: University of Nebraska Press, 2003. Compares the cowboy myth in the westerns of Owen Wister to the gaucho depicted in Hernandez's works about Martín Fierro.

Scroggins, Daniel. *A Concordance of José Hernández' "Martín Fierro."* Columbia: University of Missouri Press, 1971. A useful research tool.

Oscar Hijuelos

Cuban American novelist

Born: New York, New York; August 24, 1951

LONG FICTION: *Our House in the Last World*, 1983; *The Mambo Kings Play Songs of Love*, 1989; *The Fourteen Sisters of Emilio Montez O'Brien*, 1993; *Mr. Ives' Christmas*, 1995; *Empress of the Splendid Season*, 1999; *A Simple Habana Melody: From When the World Was Good*, 2002.

Oscar Hijuelos (AHS-kahr ee-WAYL-ohs) is widely regarded as a successful writer who has moved Latino cultural expression from the margins to the center of mainstream recognition. He was born to immigrant Cuban parents in the Spanish Harlem section of New York City. In his childhood, he witnessed the ordeals of his family in exile, and he suffered the turmoils of growing up Latino in the United States.

Hijuelos's father, Pascual, who worked as a dishwasher and a cook, died when Hijuelos was a teenager; his mother, Magdalena, was a homemaker who yearned to write poetry. His first novel, *Our House in the Last World*, published in 1983, is dedicated to them. This autobiographical work illustrates immigrant experiences similar to those lived by his family. The protagonists attach themselves to memories of a privileged life in Cuba while struggling to achieve success in the United States as members of an underprivileged ethnic minority. The isolation imposed by a different culture and language leads to feelings of alienation and powerlessness and often to violence and death.

The visit of Hijuelos to Cuba when he was three years old is portrayed in the novel. After returning from the sunny and warm island, the young protagonists, Héctor and his brother, encounter the cold reality of the urban world in New York. They are ridiculed by other children for being Hispanic; at the same time they are called "Whitey" or "Pinky" because of their light

ONI

Roberto Koch

> *It was a Saturday afternoon on La Salle Street,*
> *years and years ago when I was a little kid, and*
> *around three o'clock Mrs. Shannon, the heavy Irish*
> *woman in her perpetually soup-stained dress, opened*
> *her back window and shouted out into the*
> *courtyard, "Hey, Cesar, yoo-hoo, I think you're on*
> *television, I swear it's you!"*
>
> —from *The Mambo Kings Play Songs of Love*

skin. The concept of being "Cuban" is questioned when other Hispanics consider them "American." Like his characters, Hijuelos grew up with a sense of marginality and with a need to establish an identity within the two cultures. The use of Spanish words in the novel reflects bilingual and bicultural influences. His work becomes an expression of self-affirmation and the articulation of identity. Nostalgia for Cuba is a source of inspiration for poetic creation.

Ghosts appear in the novel, in an imagined house which represents memory. The writing of recollections and remembrances constitutes a form of survival. Like his protagonist Héctor, the author finished college; his efforts were rewarded when he received bachelor of arts and master's degrees from City College of New York. The novel won Hijuelos the Rome Prize for literature from the American Academy and Institute of Arts and Letters.

Hijuelos's interest in Hispanic and Afro-Caribbean music and its strong influence on American popular culture is reflected in his second novel, *The Mambo Kings Play Songs of Love* (1989). The research-based novel is a well-documented chronicle of the 1930's and 1940's music scene in Cuba and the times and spirit of the 1940's and 1950's in New York. In this family saga, where glories of the past and complex relationships are relived through memory and imagination, musical creation allows the expression of emotions and spiritual survival.

The search for the American Dream leads two Cuban immigrants—Cesar and Néstor Castillo, the Mambo Kings—to musical stardom and romantic adventures. The flamboyant Latin lovers, who fear a lifelong loneliness without love, have a macho, sexist attitude toward women. The younger generation, represented by Eugenio, born in America, recreates in the 1980's the memories of his ancestors and the influence of their culture in America.

The novel's narrative movement is provided by the shifts from one character's story to the next, going back and forth in time, with narrations in the first and third person. There are fluid transitions between English and Spanish. Extensive footnotes add to the monologues and dialogues in the text. During the writing of the novel, the author received fellowships from the National Endowment for the Arts, the New York Foundation for the Arts, and the Ingram Merrill Foundation. The bestselling book was awarded the 1990 Pulitzer Prize in fiction and was made into a motion picture.

The epic novel *The Fourteen Sisters of Emilio Montez O'Brien* appeared in 1993, offering the view of a woman's world, in contrast to the male perspective of the previous work. In this saga of an immigrant Pennsylvania family with a Cuban mother and an Irish father, the large number of sisters portrayed seems to reflect the reality of Hijuelos's family: The author's father had nine sisters, and his mother had three (Hijuelos himself had only one brother). The patriarch of the O'Brien family, Nelson, marries the aristocratic Mariela Montez when he goes to Cuba as a photographer during the Spanish-American War in 1898.

The Montez O'Briens' first daughter, Margarita, is born at sea in 1902, en route to the United States. They settle in a rural Pennsylvania town, where the other daughters and finally a son, Emilio, are born. Readers follow their lives and loves in a chronicle spanning the twentieth century, moving from one character to another, from dreams and hopes to disappointments and tragedies. In this novel Hijuelos provides, once again, a colorful and heartfelt portrait of immigrant life in the United States.

W H A T   T O   R E A D

The Mambo Kings Play Songs of Love

Oscar Hijuelos's life in an advertising agency had little to do with his passion for writing. When he first began thinking of the story that would become *The Mambo Kings Play Songs of Love* (1989), he knew that an uncle and an elevator operator would be his models. The uncle, a musician with Xavier Cugat in the 1930's, and a building superintendent patterned after an elevator-operator-musician merged to become Cesar Castillo, the Mambo King. Cesar's brother, Nestor—laconic, retrospective, and lamenting the loss of a lover he left behind in Cuba—writes the song in her memory that draws the attention of Ricky Ricardo. He hears "Beautiful María of My Soul" as he catches the Mambo Kings in a seedy nightclub where gigs are cheap but long. Ricky's interest changes their lives. The book altered Hijuelos's literary career by winning the Pulitzer Prize for fiction in 1990.

As the story opens, Cesar rots with his half-empty whiskey glass tipped at a TV beaming reruns. He seeks the *I Love Lucy* spot featuring Nestor and him as the Mambo Kings. Nestor has died. Cesar pathetically broods on the aging process, cirrhosis, and the loss of flamboyant times. Cesar's old, scratchy records—brittle and warped—resurrect his music stardom. He laments his brother's death by leafing through fading pictures.

In *The Mambo Kings Play Songs of Love*, Hijuelos presents pre-Castro Cubans, who, after World War II, streamed to New York. All communities may strive for the American Dream, but in Latino quarters, music, the mainstream of a culture, sought to free the oppressed. Hijuelos pursues thematic progression: The Castillo brothers become, for a moment, cultural icons by their appearance on *I Love Lucy*. Their fame does not last, however; Nestor dies suddenly, and Cesar comforts his ego with debauchery before committing suicide at the ironically named Hotel Splendour.

— *Craig Gilbert*

Mr. Ives' Christmas is a story of a man who must, over his life, cope with both a mystical vision and his son's murder on Christmas Eve. The murder causes him to question his faith, but ultimately he finds spiritual peace. In *Empress of the Splendid Season*, Hijuelos follows the fortunes of Lydia España over half a century, from being exiled by her Cuban family for a sexual indiscretion to making a life for herself in New York. *A Simple Habana Melody: From When the World Was Good* is also epic in scope, tracing the fortunes of a Cuban musician, Israel Levis, from the 1920's to the 1950's. Levis gains fame as the composer of a popular rumba, enjoys café society in the 1930's, and then is mistakenly interned at Buchenwald when his last name is taken to be Jewish. The novel contrasts the expansive, luxury-loving Levis with the increasingly niggardly, mean-spirited world he lives in.

— *Ludmila Kapschutschenko-Schmitt*

Learn More

Kevane, Bridget. *Latino Literature in America.* Westport, Conn.: Greenwood Press, 2003. This study of eight authors includes an analysis of *The Mambo Kings Play Songs of Love.*

Luis, William. *Dance Between Two Cultures: Latino Caribbean Literature Written in the United States.* Nashville, Tenn.: Vanderbilt University, 1997. Examines the work of Cuban American, Dominican American, and Puerto Rican American authors, focusing on Hijuelos and other prominent writers. Places these writers in a broader social, historical, political, and racial perspective.

Muller, Gilbert H. *New Strangers in Paradise: The Immigrant Experience and Contemporary American Fiction.* Lexington: University Press of Kentucky, 1999. Examines literature by Hijuelos and other writers whose work portrays immigrants seeking a new identity and the American dream.

Pérez Firmat, Gustavo. *Life on the Hyphen: The Cuban-American Way.* Austin: University of Texas Press, 1994. A scholarly study of Hijuelos and other Cuban American writers and performers who have become cultural figures.

Seyhan, Azade. *Writing Outside the Nation.* Princeton, N.J.: Princeton University Press, 2001. A study of writers who have emigrated to other countries, including the work of Hijuelos and other bilingual and bicultural writers living in the United States.

Shorris, Earl. *Latinos: A Biography of the People.* 1992. Reprint. New York: W. W. Norton, 2001. Focuses on the commercial and critical success of Hijuelos and his literary themes.

Smorkaloff, Pamela Maria. *Cuban Writers On and Off the Island: Contemporary Narrative Fiction.* New York: Twayne, 1999. Includes a discussion of Hijuelos and Cuban-born writers who began their literary careers outside their native country.

Rolando Hinojosa

Mexican American novelist

Born: Mercedes, Texas; January 21, 1929
Also known as: Roland Hinojosa-Smith (given name)

LONG FICTION: *Estampas del valle, y otras obras/Sketches of the Valley, and Other Works*, 1973 (English revision, *The Valley*, 1983); *Klail City y sus alrededores*, 1976 (*Klail City: A Novel*, 1987); *Mi querido Rafa*, 1981 (*Dear Rafe*, 1985); *Rites and Witnesses*, 1982; *Partners in Crime: A Rafe Buenrostro Mystery*, 1985; *Claros varones de Belken*, 1986 (*Fair Gentlemen of Belken County*, 1986); *Becky and Her Friends*, 1990; *The Useless Servants*, 1993; *Ask a Policeman*, 1998.

POETRY: *Korean Love Songs from Klail City Death Trip*, 1978 (printed 1980, includes some prose).

EDITED TEXT: *Tomás Rivera, 1935-1984: The Man and His Work*, 1988 (with Gary D. Keller and Vernon E. Lattin).

MISCELLANEOUS: *Generaciones, Notas, y Brechas/Generations, Notes, and Trails*, 1978; *Agricultural Workers of the Rio Grande and Rio Bravo Valleys*, 1984.

Rolando Hinojosa (roh-LAN-doh ee-noh-HOH-sah) views his various works as a single, ongoing novel. Entitled *The Klail City Death Trip*, this collective novel is still incomplete, although it constitutes a substantial body of writing: more than half a dozen works of prose fiction as well as *Korean Love Songs from Klail City Death Trip*, a work that intermixes prose and poetry. Each component of the collective work, excepting the mixed-genre work, is set in the area just north of the Mexican border in south Texas that is called "The Valley." *Korean Love Songs from Klail City Death Trip*, although much of it is set in Korea during the 1950's, focuses on military personnel conscripted from "The Valley," as does *The Useless Servants*.

Rolando was the youngest of the five children of Carrie Smith and Manuel Guzmán Hinojosa. The family became U.S.

citizens in the 1840's when a new boundary line between Mexico and the United States fell three miles south of where Manuel's family had lived for more than a century. Carrie Smith had arrived in the Valley when she was six months old and her father, a Union soldier during the Civil War, moved to the area around Mercedes.

Rolando was born in that area. Hinojosa's mother, a schoolteacher who had been raised in a completely bilingual and bicultural environment, had a deep respect for Mexican culture. Both she and her husband, Manuel, insisted that their son attend private, Spanish-language schools so that he would develop an interest and pride in his Hispanic culture. Rolando thus absorbed the folklore and lifestyles of the Mexican Americans in the area, accumulating the store of detail that would later color his prose fiction.

As a young man, Hinojosa was too close to his materials to realize their literary potential. During two years in the army, from 1946 to 1948, he distanced himself somewhat from the Valley, but it was not until 1951, when he was called back to serve in Korea, that he began to have a real sense of what he must write.

After his Korean service he resumed his interrupted studies at the University of Texas at Austin and graduated with a bachelor's degree in 1953. For a time Hinojosa returned to the Valley as a teacher. He then went on to earn a master's degree and fi-

> *Before the year was out, Viola hooked up with don Javier Leguizamón; he owns those lands over to Edgerton there; those were old mexicano lands taken over by Anglo Texans first and by the Leguizamóns after that. Viola was with don Javier up to her twentieth, maybe her twenty-first birthday; it happened that she was replaced by Gela Maldonado, but that's another story.*
>
> —from "When It Comes to Class: Viola Barragán"

Arte Público Press

nally a doctorate in Spanish from the University of Illinois. In 1970 he began teaching in San Antonio's Trinity University. There he met Tomás Rivera, who encouraged his writing. Upon Rivera's urging, Hinojosa submitted his *Estampas del valle, y otras obras/ Sketches of the Valley, and Other Works* to Quinto Sol Publications, who published it and named it recipient of their prize for fiction in 1972.

As in most of Hinojosa's writing, this initial publication contains disparate sketches of life in and around Mercedes. Some of the tales contradict others in the collection, but Hinojosa is undisturbed by this, contending that it is because he is offering different points of view that some of his characters contradict others. Such, he contends, is the nature of life.

WHAT TO READ

Klail City

Klail City (1976), part of the *Klail City Death Trip*, a chronicle of the Texas Rio Grande Valley, moves between past and present so that the two often appear to be the same. Like most of Rolando Hinojosa's novels, *Klail City* lacks linear plot development. A series of vignettes create a sense of place and ultimately present a picture of a changing world. Several narrators, including the main characters of the series, Rafe Buenrostro ("good face") and Jehú Malacara ("bad face") tell the stories.

P. Galindo, Esteban Echevarría (a kind of wise man throughout the series), Rafe, and Jehú recount a variety of tales ranging from tales of the Texas Rangers' abuse of Mexican Americans to the story of how Alejandro Leguizamón planned the murder of Rafe's father, Jesús, and the revenge exacted by Jesús' brother, don Julián. There is also a kind of interior monologue by Jehú as he and Rafe attend their twenty-second high school class reunion.

In "The Searchers," P. Galindo tells the stories of migrant workers as they leave their homes in the valley to travel north to pick produce. Rafe gives a personal account of what it was like in the 1940's for Mexican American students in the American high school, and Jehú recounts some of his experiences as an orphan, an acolyte, and a traveling evangelist with Brother Imás. There is also an account of how the whites used "bought" Mexicans to get their hand-picked candidates elected. In this and other stories, Hinojosa interweaves the past and present, particularly in the scenes that occur in the bars, where the old men, the *viejitos*, sit drinking and talking until don Manuel Guzmán, Klail City's only Mexican American police officer, comes to take them home.

In 1976, this eclectic collection of vignettes won Latin America's most prestigious literary award, the Casa de las Américas prize.

— *Joyce J. Glover*

Hinojosa chooses to write sometimes in Spanish, sometimes in English, and sometimes in both languages. *Estampas del valley, y otras obras* and *Klail City y sus alrededores* were both written in Spanish and translated into English by others. Hinojosa wrote *Korean Love Songs* in English, because it was about Americans in Asia, but he wrote *Mi querido Rafa*, set in south Texas, first in Spanish and only then translated it into English.

Perhaps the most typical of Hinojosa's books is *Becky and Her Friends*. Many characters from earlier books reappear in this novel, which is essentially a collection of sketches and fragmented reminiscences about Becky, the wife of Jehú Malacara, from twenty-seven people who have known her in various contexts. By presenting Becky in this way, Hinojosa also reveals a great deal about the people discussing her. What emerges from this brief novel, as from much of his other fiction, is a composite picture of the social structure of the Valley.

— *R. Baird Shuman*

Learn More

Hernandez, Guillermo E. *Chicano Satire: A Study in Literary Culture.* Austin: University of Texas Press, 1991. This work explores how satire figures into the works of three Chicanos: Luis Miguel Valdez, José Montoya, and Rolando Hinojosa. It provides insights into some of the books in The Klail City Death Trip series.

Karem, Jeff. *The Romance of Authencity: The Cultural Politics of Regional and Ethnic Literatures.* Charlottesville: University of Virginia Press, 2004. Describes how stereotypical ideas about authenticity place constraints on the content and interpretation of works by regional and ethnic writers, including Hinojosa.

Kaup, Monika. *Rewriting North American Borders in Chicano and Chicana Narrative.* New York: P. Lang, 2001. Examines Chicano literature since the 1960's to analyze how Hinojosa and other writers approach the theme of the border between the United States and Mexico.

Lee, Joyce Glover. *Rolando Hinojosa and the American Dream.* Denton: University of North Texas Press, 1997. A good book-length work in English on Hinojosa's works. Attempts to bring a biographical and psychological analysis to The Klail City Death Trip series.

Pilkington, Tom. *State of Mind: Texas Literature and Culture.* College Station: Texas A&M University Press, 1998. In this analysis of Hinojosa and other Texas writers, Pilkington seeks to determine the characteristics unique to Texas literature.

Saldivar, José David, ed. *The Rolando Hinojosa Reader: Essays Historical and Critical.* Houston: Arte Público Press, 1985. This work contains essays by Hinojosa and by a small number of scholars treating Hinojosa's works. Shows how early scholars analyzed The Klail City Death Trip series.

Saldívar, Ramón. *Chicano Narrative: The Dialectics of Difference.* Madison: University of Wisconsin Press, 1990. One of the most important works of Chicano literary criticism, this book contains a chapter treating *Korean Love Songs from Klail City Death Trip* and The Klail City Death Trip series. Saldívar's analysis covers many of the most significant Chicano literary texts.

Zilles, Klaus. *Rolando Hinojosa: A Reader's Guide.* Albuquerque: University of New Mexico Press, 2001. A guide to the Valley and its inhabitants, focusing on the theme of oral history represented in the series.

W. H. Hudson

Argentine-born English novelist and naturalist

Born: Quilmes, Argentina; August 4, 1841
Died: London, England; August 18, 1922
Also known as: William Henry Hudson, Henry Harford

LONG FICTION: *The Purple Land*, 1885 (originally pb. as *The Purple Land That England Lost*); *A Crystal Age*, 1887; *Fan: The Story of a Young Girl's Life*, 1892 (as Henry Harford); *El Ombú*, 1902 (reissued as *South American Sketches*, 1909; pb. in U.S. as *Tales of the Pampas*, 1916); *Green Mansions*, 1904; *A Little Boy Lost*, 1905.

SHORT FICTION: *Dead Man's Plack and An Old Thorn*, 1920.

NONFICTION: *Argentine Ornithology*, 1888-1889 (with Philip Lutley Sclater); *The Naturalist in La Plata*, 1892; *Birds in a Village*, 1893; *Idle Days in Patagonia*, 1893; *British Birds*, 1895; *Nature in Downland*, 1900; *Birds and Man*, 1901; *Hampshire Days*, 1903; *The Land's End*, 1908; *Afoot in England*, 1909; *A Shepherd's Life*, 1910; *Adventures Among Birds*, 1913; *Far Away and Long Ago*, 1918; *The Book of a Naturalist*, 1919; *Birds of La Plata*, 1920; *A Traveller in Little Things*, 1921; *A Hind in Richmond Park*, 1922; *One Hundred Fifty-three Letters from W. H. Hudson*, 1923 (with Edward Garnett, editor); *Men, Books, and Birds*, 1925.

The naturalist and writer William Henry Hudson was born at Quilmes, a short distance west of Buenos Aires, on August 4, 1841. His father, Daniel Hudson, who was of English descent and born in Massachusetts, had left New England under threat of tuberculosis to seek a gentler climate in Argentina. There, he and his wife, Katherine Kimball, who came from Maine, raised a family of six children. William Henry, the fourth of their five sons, was a strong, alert child who rode his pony about the pampas and developed an absorbing interest in the bird life of the great plains. From these contacts with nature he learned much that was of later benefit to him, quite possibly more than he learned from the ill-equipped tutors with whom he had his formal training.

At the age of twenty-eight, Hudson left South America to take up permanent residence in England. During his teens, an attack

W H A T   T O   R E A D

The Purple Land

The Purple Land (1885) is a documentary novel containing no plot. Rather, it is an imaginary travelogue set in the Banda Oriental (now Uruguay). Its protagonist, Richard Lamb, has been forced to flee to Montevideo after eloping with the daughter of a powerful Argentinean family, and the story concerns Lamb's wanderings in connection with an abortive attempt to find a job managing an inland plantation. At one point, he becomes entangled in the affairs of the rebel general Santa Coloma and fights with him in an ill-fated revolution.

He also attracts the attention of several women, including two very beautiful girls who mistake him for a single man and are bitterly disappointed when he informs them belatedly of his unavailability. One of these women, however, he rescues from an awkward predicament and smuggles her back to Argentina in spite of the risk to himself (the reader has already been told in the first chapter that these wanderings preceded a long spell in jail, an event that was instigated by his vengeful father-in-law and broke his wife's heart).

The attractive features of this novel are the local color and the attention to anthropological detail. It offers a convincing picture of the life of the country, and one can easily believe that some of the episodes are based on experience, and that Hudson actually heard some of the tall stories that are told to Lamb by Santa Coloma's rebel gauchos.

— *Brian Stableford*

of rheumatic fever had left him with a weakened heart, and he decided that Argentina was no place for someone who could not lead an active outdoor life. Moreover, the death of his father the year before had severed the last strong tie with his boyhood home.

Hudson's earliest years in England were marked by poverty and loneliness. For a time, he became secretary to an eccentric archaeologist, who often lacked money to pay him. In 1876, he married Emily Wingreave, a gentle woman fifteen years older than Hudson; she admired her husband unreservedly, though never completely understanding his peculiar gifts and qualities. After two experiments in running a boardinghouse failed, the Hudsons settled in a dreary house near Westbourne Park that had been left to Emily Hudson by her sister.

Though he had been writing steadily since arriving in England, literary recognition came to Hudson only slowly. His novel *The Purple Land*, which came to be regarded as one of his best works, appeared in 1885, and in 1887 came his utopian ro-

> *The species now being exterminated, not only in South America but everywhere on the globe are, so far as we know, untouched by decadence. They are links in a chain, and branches on the tree of life, with their roots in a past inconceivably remote; and but for our action they would continue to flourish. . . .*
>
> —from *The Naturalist in La Plata*

mance, *A Crystal Age.* Neither book created much stir, but in 1892 *The Naturalist in La Plata* received favorable attention; thereafter, Hudson's books won increasing, though still modest, circulation. In 1918 came the history of his childhood, *Far Away and Long Ago;* though highly regarded, it has probably been less read than *Green Mansions,* a brightly colored romance of the bird-girl Rima, set against the background of Venezuelan forests. Especially popular in America, it effectively combines Hudson's gifts as a storyteller with his deep feeling for nature.

After Hudson died in London in 1922, his literary reputation grew, possibly because an increasingly urban civilization had learned to value nature more than in the author's own time. Hudson's style is simple and direct. At its best, it embodies the author's almost mystical sense of natural beauty. Very appropriately, Hudson's London memorial is a bird sanctuary, established in Hyde Park in 1925.

Learn More

Arocena, Felipe. *William Henry Harrison: Life, Literature, and Science.* Translated by Richard Manning. Jefferson, N.C.: McFarland, 2003. Biography examining Hudson's life and his writings on art and science. Arocena maintains Hudson created an original literature because of his experiences visiting and living in various cultures; these experiences inform the theme of crossing boundaries and frontiers that is common to his work.

Frederick, John T. *William Henry Hudson.* New York: Twayne, 1972. A standard biography from Twayne's English Authors series. Includes a bibliography.

Miller, David. *W. H. Hudson and the Elusive Paradise.* New York: St. Martin's Press, 1990. Contains chapters on all of Hudson's major prose fiction, exploring such themes as the supernatural, the imagination, symbolic meaning, immortality, and ideology. Includes detailed notes and a bibliography.

Payne, John R. *W. H. Hudson: A Bibliography.* Hamden, Conn.: Archon Books, 1977. With a foreword by Alfred A. Knopf. Includes an index.

Reeve, N. H. "Feathered Women: W. H. Hudson's *Green Mansions.*" In *Writing the Environment: Ecocriticism and Literature,* edited by Richard Kerridge and Neil Sammells. London: Zen, 1998. Reeve explores the treatment of nature in Hudson's novel.

Ronner, Amy D. *W. H. Hudson: The Man, the Novelist, the Naturalist.* New York: AMS Press, 1986. A much-needed recent addition to critical studies on Hudson, examining Hudson's work in relationship to his contemporaries, his immigration to England, and his development as a naturalist and writer. Concludes with an interesting account of Charles Darwin's influence on Hudson and consequently on his writing. A useful bibliography is provided.

Shrubsall, Dennis. *W. H. Hudson: Writer and Naturalist.* Tisbury, England: Compton Press, 1978. Provides much useful background on Hudson's early years in Argentina and traces his development as a naturalist and his integrity as a writer on nature.

Tomalin, Ruth. *W. H. Hudson: A Biography.* London: Faber & Faber, 1982. A lively biography that has been thoroughly and painstakingly researched. Highly recommended for any serious study of Hudson. Contains excerpts of the letter which Hudson wrote in an attack on Charles Darwin and of Darwin's response.

Jorge Icaza

Ecuadoran novelist

Born: Quito, Ecuador; July 10, 1906
Died: Quito, Ecuador; May 26, 1978

LONG FICTION: *Huasipungo*, 1934, revised 1951 (*The Villagers*, 1964); *En las calles*, 1934; *Cholos*, 1938; *Huairapamushcas*, 1948; *El Chulla Romero y Flores*, 1958.
SHORT FICTION: *Seis relatos*, 1952; *Viejos Cuentos*, 1960.
DRAMA: *El intruso*, pb. 1929; *Flagelo*, pb. 1936.

Of the many novelists of Ecuador, perhaps the best known internationally is the social realist Jorge Icaza (HOR-hay ee-KAH-sah), whose works denounce the shameless exploitation of the Indians. While still a university student, Icaza and several classmates, with his wife Marina Moncayo as leading lady, barnstormed the nearby villages with a repertory of old Spanish farces and Icaza's own comedies. His popularity diminished in 1931 when he began writing serious plays. When he announced the completion of a dramatization of Jules Romains's *Le Dictateur* (1926) in 1933, the performance was forbidden by the government. Only then did Icaza turn to writing novels.

> *The day greeted Alfonso Pereira with enormous contradictions. He had just left in the hands of his wife and daughter, and to their women's intuition and instinct, the unresolved problem of "honor at stake," as he called it. As usual in a situation like this—from which he had to emerge blameless—he had banged the door on his way out, muttering a series of oaths under his breath.*
>
> —from *The Villagers* (trans. Bernard M. Dulsey)

W H A T   T O   R E A D

The Villagers

In *The Villagers* (1934), Alfonso Pereira is an Ecuadoran landowner plagued by domestic and financial troubles. His wife, Blanca, nags him, and he worries about his daughter Lolita, who wants to marry a man who is part Indian. Don Julio, his uncle, adds to his difficulties by demanding repayment of a loan of ten thousand *sucres*, a debt already three months overdue.

When Pereira confesses that he is unable to pay the loan, Don Julio suggests that his nephew try to interest Mr. Chapy, a North American promoter, in a timber concession on Pereira's mountain estate. Privately, the old man suspects that Mr. Chapy and his associates are on the lookout for oil and used their lumber-cutting activities in the region as a blind. In order to interest the North Americans, however, it will be necessary to build fifteen miles of road and to get possession of two forest tracts. Furthermore, the Indians must be driven off their *huasipungos*, the lands supplied to them in return for working on the master's estate.

The great success of his first attempt, *The Villagers*, confirmed him in his choice of genre. The work was translated into six languages, including Russian and Chinese. After that, though he did such dramatic sketches as *Flagelo* (the scourge), his chief work was novel writing and running a bookstore in Quito.

Huasipungo, the original title of *The Villagers*, is a Quechua term for a plot of land that the indigenous Andean Indian farm workers received for their own use. In his novel, Icaza denounces the suffering and exploitation of these dispossessed people. The didactic work became one of the best-known examples of the early *indigenista* literature and of Latin American social realism.

Icaza's first novel was followed by *En las calles* (in the streets),

Pereira agrees, and the road is built, but the Indians receive none of the benefits promised them, and many fall into lives of criminal activity and prostitution. The road makes it easier to get to the capital, Quito, where Pereira sells his grain rather than distribute it among the remaining Indians. Hunger stalks the region and babies and old people perish. When Mr. Chapy's orders the Indians to sacrifice their homes again to make room for company houses and a sawmill, they rebel, killing six white men. Mr. Chapy and the other white men flee, but soon return—along the road the Indians built—and slaughter all the Indians.

In *The Villagers*, the countryside is depicted as backward, isolated, and uncomfortable; the city is cultured and far superior. Nature is unattractive, and its dangers are stressed. The novel is almost devoid of color, a deliberate stylistic device to strengthen the novel's feeling of dismal hopelessness.

Intended as a tirade against the social injustice that then blighted Ecuador, *The Villagers* was initially better received and lauded abroad than it was in Icaza's own country, though eventually it helped launch the cycle of so-called indianista novels, which are devoted to telling the story of the Indians.

— *William Freitas*

which won a national prize. *Cholos* (half-breeds) is characterized by stark realism, and *Huairapamushcas* (children of the wind) depicts the Indians as scarcely above the level of animals, debased by their white overlords. His later work, *Seis relatos* (six tales), is told naturalistically and shows dramatic incidents building to a savage climax.

— *Emil Volek*

Learn More

Dulsey, Bernard. "Jorge Icaza and His Eduador." *Hispania* 44 (March, 1961). Dulsey, who has translated Icaza'a works into English, examines the author's relationship to his native country.

González-Perez, Armando. *Social Protest and Literary Merit in "Huasipungo" and "El mundo es ancho y ajeno."* Milwaukee: University of Wisconsin-Milwaukee, 1988. An analysis of political and sociological themes in two of Icaza's works.

Jones, C. A. *Three Spanish American Novelists, a European View: A Lecture Delivered on 10th February, 1966.* London: Hispanic and Luso Brazilian Councils, 1967. Provides an analysis of *Huasipungo* by Icaza, *Doña Bárbara* by Rómulo Gallegos, and *Muerte de Artemio Cruz* by Carlos Fuentes.

Spell, Jefferson Rea. *Contemporary Spanish-American Fiction.* 1944. Reprint. New York: Biblo and Tannen, 1968. Icaza is one of the authors whose work is examined in this literary overview.

Vetrano, Anthony J. "Imagery in Two of Jorge Icaza's Novels: *Huasipungo* and *Huairapamushcas.*" *Revista de estudios hispánicos* 6 (1972). In this article, Vetrano, an Icaza scholar who has written a Spanish-language book about the author, analyzes two of Icaza's works.

Wishnia, Kenneth J. A. *Twentieth-Century Ecuadorian Narrative: New Readings in the Context of the Americas.* Lewisburg, Pa.: Bucknell University Press, 1999. Places Icaza's work within the context of Ecuadorian literature.

José Lezama Lima

Cuban poet, novelist, and essayist

Born: Havana, Cuba; December 19, 1910
Died: Havana, Cuba; August 9, 1976
Also known as: José María Andres Fernando
Lezama Lima

LONG FICTION: *Paradiso*, 1966 (English translation, 1974); *Oppi-ano Licario*, 1977.

POETRY: *Muerte de Narciso*, 1937; *Enemigo rumor*, 1941; *Aventuras sigilosas*, 1945; *La fijeza*, 1949; *Dador*, 1960; *Poesía completa*, 1970; *Fragmentos a su imán*, 1977.

SHORT FICTION: *Cuentos*, 1987, 1999.

NONFICTION: *Analecta del reloj*, 1953; *La expresión americana*, 1957; *Tratados en La Habana*, 1958; *La cantidad hechizada*, 1970; *Imagen y posibilidad*, 1981; *La Habana*, 1991; *Fragmentos irra-diadores*, 1993.

EDITED TEXT: *Antología de la poesía cubana*, 1965.

MISCELLANEOUS: *Orbita*, 1964; *Obras completas*, 1975-1977 (2 vol-umes); *Cartas, 1939-1976*, 1978.

José Lezama Lima (hoh-SAY lay-ZAH-mah LEE-mah) is gener-ally considered one of the most influential Cuban poets, nov-elists, and essayists of the twentieth century. He was born to a well-to-do military family, where old patrician and immigrant traditions blended into a true creole spirit. His father was a colo-nel in the Cuban army, and the family moved frequently with him. During the time they lived in the old damp fortress of Ha-vana, Lezama Lima developed asthma, a condition from which he suffered for the rest of his life and which marked the rhythm of his poetry and prose. During World War I Lezama Lima's fa-ther volunteered for war service on the Allied side, but he died in training in the United States during the influenza epidemic when Lezama Lima was only eight years old. Until her death in

> *How certain is the mule's step in the abyss.*
> *Slow is the mule. He does not sense his mission.*
> *His fate is facing the stone, stone that bleeds*
> *creating the open laughter of pomegranates.*
> *His cracked skin, tiniest triumph now in the dark,*
> *tiniest blind-winged clod.*
>
> —from "Rhapsody for the Mule"
> (trans. José Rodríguez Feo,
> Dudley Fitts,

1964, Lezama Lima's mother was the biggest influence on his life. It was she who urged her son, when he was already a successful young poet, to take up the family history in a novel. The suggestion eventually led to the novel *Paradiso*, on which Lezama Lima worked for almost twenty years. His mother's death threw him into a deep depression, which he overcame by completing the novel.

As a student of law, Lezama Lima participated in the protest against the dictatorship of General Machado that led to the university's being shut down for years. Lezama Lima spent that time reading, accumulating the often quite arcane erudition that underlies his poetry. In his personal response to the crises of literary *Modernismo*, his poetic work followed the transformation of Symbolism into "pure poetry." The encounter with the Spanish poet Juan Ramón Jiménez after his arrival in Cuba in 1936 from war-torn Spain was of lasting influence on Lezama Lima. He became interested in the mystical line of "pure poetry" and pushed it in the direction both of hermetic, heterodox philosophy and of orthodox Catholic theology. When his exuberant baroque images overflowed the marked intellectualism and exquisiteness of postsymbolist poetry, he developed in his *Muerte de Narciso* (death of Narcissus) the drama of the Fall of man that can only be overcome by artistic creation.

Lezama Lima became the intellectual leader of the emerging Cuban post-avant-garde generation, whom he represented in

Jesse A. Fernandez

411

W H A T   T O   R E A D

Paradiso

José Lezama Lima's masterpiece, *Paradiso* (1966), combines the poetry and mythology that pervade many of Latin America's literary traditions. The narrative is dense and complex and portrays a young Creole man whose success as an artist depends on the completion of his quest to understand his cultural, sexual, and individual identity. *Paradiso* consistently returns to several themes: the Fall of humanity and its resurrection in art, death, transcendence, and the importance of family unity. Many readers will recognize the title as a reference to Dante Alighieri's description of Hell, Purgatory, and Paradise in *The Divine Comedy* (1320), and both works rely heavily on the use of allegory, religious symbols and Baroque images in the construction of their complex and multi-layered narratives.

The novel opens with its protagonist, José Cemí, whose family name comes from the great god of the Taino Indians, the inhabitants of Cuba at the time of the Conquest. The first name identifies the protagonist with the author, whose life story the novel loosely follows. Through José, Lezama Lima assumes as his own

the journals he edited. Among these were *Verbum* in 1937, *Espuela de plata* in 1939-1941, and, most particularly, *Orígenes* from 1944 to 1956, which came to be considered one of the leading Latin American literary journals of its time. Lezama Lima declared that he wrote poetry when he felt obscure, and essay when he felt clear, but it is revealing that he also said, "only what is difficult is stimulating."

Lezama Lima's reputation gradually transcended the small group of initiated acolytes that had gathered around him in Cuba. Much of his fame was connected with what was known of his persona. His aesthetic and philosophical struggle with his

the cultural heritage accumulated in his country from pre-Columbian times to the twentieth century. José is also an Everyman plotting his steps on an allegorical world stage.

The novel continues with the sudden death of the boy's father. Making sense of the loss becomes an obsession for the family and for the protagonist. Allegorical characters appear at decisive points in the protagonist's life, such as Oppiano Licario, a symbol of Icarus, of initiation, and a surrogate father figure for the orphan. The next hurdle for the protagonist is his sexual initiation and his fall into the chaos of worldly temptations. Homosexual experience is joyfully described; only later does it seem that homosexuality is philosophically (or rather, theologically) disavowed, leaving some perplexity about the author's intentions. Finally, Oppiano Licario reappears to pass the flame of artistic inspiration to the protagonist, who is, at the end of the novel, ready to start.

Paradiso is a family saga, an artistic autobiography, an allegorical *Bildungsroman*, a long Baroque poem in prose, and a summation of Lezama Lima's poetic philosophy. The homoerotic episode and the discussion of homosexuality in the novel caused some consternation among the revolutionary establishment in Cuba, and the novel went out of print in Cuba soon after its first limited edition.

— *Emil Volek*

homoerotic tendencies, which became part of the novel *Paradiso*, caused a controversy in his Cuba, as did the moral stance he adopted during the Stalinization of the Cuban culture in the 1970's, which led to his ostracism from the revolutionary regime.

It is surprising that such a cultivated man as Lezama Lima practically never left his native Havana. Only in 1949 and 1950 did he make two brief trips to Mexico and Jamaica. He used this experience to create his aesthetics of the "American expression" as something essentially baroque, which he expressed in the lectures and essays *La expresión americana*. Later, after *Paradiso* had brought him international fame and recognition, he was prevented from leaving Cuba by the government, which blocked his requests for a passport.

Lezama Lima had welcomed the triumph of the Cuban revolution in 1959 and even worked it into his visionary scheme of "imaginary eras," by which means he characterized certain periods of world cultures. His enthusiasm was short-lived, however. Although he held an important nominal position in the writers' union, he worked all his life in obscure jobs in Cuban literary research institutions; for that reason he sought an early retirement.

Paradiso is an amalgam of Caribbean and Latin American culture. The autobiographical line of the novel provides a framework for baroque imagistic descriptions and arcane philosophical discussions that offer a dense, poetic, and mythical portrayal of a young man in search of his family and an individual, sexual, and cultural identity on which to set the foundation for his manifest artistic vocation. Family cohesion, death and epiphany, the Fall of humankind and its resurrection through artistic creation, are some of *Paradiso*'s underlying themes. The title relates the narrative to Dante's story of a man's journey through Hell, Purgatory, and Paradise, and Lezama Lima's *Paradiso* builds heavily on allegory, Christian symbolism, Baroque imagery, and arcane cultural allusions, creating an immensely complex whole. The novel is a family saga, an autobiography, a *Bildungsroman* of a young artist, a long poem in prose, and a philosophical summation of Lezama Lima's mythopoiesis.

Lezama Lima spent the last years of his life in internal exile; his bitter isolation is reflected in many of his personal letters, some of which are collected in *Cartas, 1939-1976*. He left unfinished a sequel to *Paradiso*, the novel *Oppiano Licario*, and a book of poetry, *Fragmentos a su imán*.

— *Emil Volek*

Learn More

Bejel, Emilio. *Gay Cuban Nation*. Chicago: University of Chicago Press, 2000. Explores how Lezema Lima and other Cuban writers have treated the topic of homosexuality, placing their work within a social and political context leading to the Cuban Revolution.

_____. *Lezama Lima: Poet of the Image.* Gainesville: University of Florida, 1990. Focuses on criticism and interpretation of Lezama Lima's works. Includes bibliography and index.

Heller, Ben A. *Assimilation/Generation/Resurrection: Contrapuntal Readings in the Poetry of José Lezama Lima.* Lewisburg, Pa.: Bucknell University Press, 1997. A specialized and scholarly study of Lezama Lima's poetry. Bibliography and index.

Levinson, Brett. *Secondary Moderns: Mimesis, History, and Revolution in Lezama Lima's "American Expression."* Lewisburg, Pa.: Bucknell University Press, 1996. Examines Lezama Lima's notion of "American express" in detail. Bibliography and index.

Pellón, Gustavo. *José Lezama Lima's Joyful Vision: A Study of "Paradiso" and Other Prose Works.* Austin: University of Texas Press, 1989. A study of Lezama Lima's prose works and *Paradiso* in particular. Index.

Salgado, César Augusto. *From Modernism to Neobaroque: Joyce and Lezama Lima.* Lewisburg, Pa.: Bucknell University Press, 2001. A comparative study that provides criticism and interpretation. It also addresses the influence of these two authors on literary history. Bibliography and index.

Souza, Raymond D. *The Poetic Fiction of José Lezama Lima.* Columbia: University of Missouri Press, 1983. Lezama Lima's writing is analyzed. Bibliography and index.

Ulloa, J. C. "José Lezama Lima." In *Modern Latin-American Fiction Writers, First Series,* edited by William Luis. Vol. 113 in *Dictionary of Literary Biography.* Detroit: Gale Group, 1992. A good basic introduction to Lezama Lima's life and work.

Osman Lins

Brazilian novelist

Born: Vitória de Santo Antão, Brazil; July 5, 1924
Died: São Paulo, Brazil; July 8, 1978

LONG FICTION: *O visitante*, 1955; *O fiel e a pedra*, 1961; *Avalovara*, 1973 (English translation, 1979); *A rainha dos cárceres da Grécia*, 1976 (*The Queen of the Prisons of Greece*, 1995).

SHORT FICTION: *Os gestos*, 1957; *Nove, novena*, 1966 (*Nine, Novena*, 1995).

DRAMA: *Lisbela e o prisioneiro*, pb. 1964; *Santa, automóvel e soldado*, pb. 1975.

NONFICTION: *Guerra sem testemunhas*, 1969.

Osman Lins (AHS-mahn leens) was born in the state of Pernambuco in northeastern Brazil, a region whose cultural heritage is often elaborated in his fiction. Lins was the son of a tailor and was reared by his grandmother; he never knew his mother, and the author himself has speculated that his exploratory fiction may be psychologically linked to that loss. Lins went to high school in the state capital, Recife, where he also studied economics at the university. During this period he published his first stories. In addition, Lins studied dramaturgy at the university. He later wrote and published several plays, some of which were staged in Rio de Janeiro and São Paulo. Lins moved to metropolitan São Paulo to work for the Banco do Brasil. After retiring from the banking profession and completing a doctoral degree, Lins taught literature at a private college. He soon resigned his position, both to dedicate himself to writing and in protest of the precarious conditions of higher education in Brazil, a topic he addresses in essays and fiction. When he died, Lins was in the process of finishing another novel.

Lins's early work is largely introspective but also has some regionalist features. *O visitante* (the visitor) concerns moral questions and the relationship of personal awareness to behavioral codes. These preoccupations are also evident in the individual stories of *Os gestos* (gestures) and in *O fiel e a pedra* (the faithful and the stone), which is set in the author's home state. This novel has an epic design (derived from Vergil's *Aeneid*) and a clear moral intent. The hero, moved by passion and compassion, struggles to oppose injustice and to resist intimidation. In his mature works Lins reveals intense interest in the creative process, in authorial conscience, and in human consciousness. His later fiction is notably cerebral and revolves around structural experimentation. Lins avoids standard omniscient narrators and constructs intricate, at times hermetic, symbolic systems. Reflecting a complex vision of society, each of the nine "narratives" of *Nine, Novena* has a unique technique of narration or presentation, including use of graphic signs to identify narrators. The dense expression often embodies special codes or particular rhetorical constructions, as in "Retabulo de Santa Joana Carolina" (retable of St. Joan Caroline), which is based on the didactic model of medieval miracle plays. The complicated approaches of *Nine, Novena* and subsequent fiction are better grasped in the light of Lins's speculative *Guerra sem testemunhas* (war without witnesses). This essay contains elements of memoir and fiction as well and is a key to understanding the evolution of Lins's work.

The street we live on is one of the oldest in town. It has risen in status over the years. The original tiled sidewalk, almost buried, has retreated little by little over a long period, and street pavement and sidewalk merge. What month can it be? The end of August? The beginning of September? . . . Across from our house there lives a woman. She makes up for everything old and drab around.

—from *Hahn's Pentagon*
(trans. Gregory Rabassa)

W H A T   T O   R E A D

Avalovara

The structure of Osman Lins's *Avalovara* (1973) is at once astonishingly complex and altogether transparent. The sequence of events is predetermined by a geometric design which appears before the first page of text, consisting of a Latin palindrome of five five-letter words with a spiral superimposed on it. To visualize this palindrome, envision a large square subdivided into twenty-five smaller squares—five across and five down. In the first row of squares place the letters S-A-T-O-R; in the second, A-R-E-P-O; in the third, T-E-N-E-T; in the fourth, O-P-E-R-A; and in the fifth, R-O-T-A-S. The entire square is centered over a fourteen-ring spiral.

Each letter of the palindrome represents one plot line, and when the spiral touches a letter, a passage of that plot line appears. Since some letters are more frequent than others, plot segments vary in number of episodes from twenty-four (letter "O") to two (letter "N," which is in the center of the design). In addition, episodes increase in length each time that particular plot line reappears—most are ten lines long in the first epi-

The ambitious postmodern novel *Avalovara* is Lins's major contribution. In characteristic fashion, the novel is an interwoven network of narrative lines. The work constitutes a synthesis of all the author's fiction and an allegory of the art of the novel. Sexual relations and the instinct to reproduce are symbolic of writing as a necessary and natural regeneration of a moribund world. In the interplay of reality and fiction the main character's love life is revealed to be a pretext to show the author's translation of the outside world into words of fiction. Lins's last novel, *The Queen of the Prisons of Greece*, challenges readers to unravel a system of representation. It takes the form of a diary analyzing an imaginary work of fiction about a problematic life in north-

sode, twenty lines long in the second, and so on. Exceptions are the themes corresponding to the letters "P" and "T."

Six of the eight plot divisions directly involve Abel, the protagonist. Two deal with his love affairs, and the other four are all in some way concerned with the enigmatic ♀, with whom Abel lives a consuming passion and in whose arms he dies. One of the other remaining plot lines deals with the Pompeiian Publius Ubonius, who offers to free his slave Loreius if the slave can construct a magic sentence. The final subplot is the story of the obsessed clockmaker Julius Heckethorn, who designs a clock with a complex triple sound system which will some day play Domenico Scarlatti's Sonata in F Minor.

As the reader approaches the end of the book, the spiral approaches the center of the square, and the various narratives, separated in time and space, draw together as Abel approaches something like an erotic transcendence in the arms of his mysterious and oddly polymorphous lover. The moment of this epiphany coincides with the beginning of a solar eclipse, which is precisely the second that the intricate clock, now in the same room with Abel, begins the sonata.

— *Jon S. Vincent*

eastern Brazil. The novel is a layered critique of the hopelessly inadequate Brazilian welfare system and of the academic profession, particularly the branch of literary studies. In this way Lins reveals his abiding concerns with concrete realities and their reflections in works of imagination.

Osman Lins was a leading exponent of a new fiction of vitalization that followed the mid-twentieth century advances of João Guimarães Rosa and Clarice Lispector. His fiction is important for its depth of introspection and for speculation about writing itself, and his writing reflects the efforts in Brazilian literature to integrate ethical and aesthetic perspectives.

— *Charles A. Perrone*

Learn More

Andrade, Ana Luiza. "Osman Lins." In *Modern Latin-American Fiction Writers, Second Series*, edited by William Luis and Ann Gonzalez. Vol. 145 in *Dictionary of Literary Biography*. Detroit: Gale Group, 1994. A good introductory essay on Lins's life and works.

Frizzi, Adria, ed. *Review of Contemporary Fiction* 15, no. 3 (Fall, 1995): 155-222. In this issue, Lins's wife, Julieta Goloy Ladiera, collects various interviews, commentary, recollections and articles on and by Osman Lins. Some of the articles are an interview by Edla Van Steen; an introduction to Lins by Dria Frizzi; critiques of several of his works; Lins's essay "Of Idealism and Glory," in which he discusses what it means to be a writer; and an essay by his wife about his career.

Moisés, Massaud. "Osman Lins's *Avalovara*: A Novel of Love?" In *Tropical Paths: Essays on Modern Brazilian Literature*, edited and translated by Randal Johnson. New York: Garland, 1993. Analyzes the narrative structure of the novel and its relation to eroticism.

Simas, Rosa. *Circularity and Visions of the New World in William Faulkner, Gabriel Garcia Marquez, and Osman Lins*. Lewiston, N.Y.: Edwin Mellen Press, 1993. The specialized work focuses on the exploration theme. Lins's *Avalovara* is specifically discussed. Bibliography.

José Lins do Rego

Brazilian novelist

Born: Pilar, Paraíba, Brazil; June 3, 1901
Died: Rio de Janeiro, Brazil; September 12, 1957
Also known as: José Lins do Rego Cavalcanti

LONG FICTION: *Menino de Engenho*, 1932 (*Plantation Boy*, 1966); *Doidinho*, 1933 (English translation, 1966); *Bangüê*, 1934 (English translation, 1966); *O moleque Ricardo*, 1935; *Usina*, 1936; *Pureza*, 1937 (English translation, 1948); *Pedra bonita*, 1938; *Água-mãe*, 1941; *Fogo morto*, 1943; *Eurídice*, 1947; *Plantation Boy*, 1966 (includes *Plantation Boy*, *Doidinho*, and *Bangüê*).

Northeast Brazil, like the Deep South of the United States, at one time depended on slaves to work its plantations. Born at Pilar, Paraíba, on June 3, 1901, José Lins do Rego (hoh-SAY leenz doh reh-GEW) Cavalcanti was brought up in this region at a time when the plantation system was declining before the disrupting forces of modern society. When his mother died shortly after his birth, his father left him in the care of aunts and an old grandfather who owned a string of sugar plantations ex-

> *From time to time Old Totonha happened along at the plantation. And that was a red-letter day for the small fry. She lived by her fairy stories. Tiny and shriveled, so light that a puff of wind could have carried her away, she walked miles and miles on foot, from one plantation to another. . . . Without a tooth in her head, but with a voice that gave every shade of tone to her words.*
>
> —from *Plantation Boy* (trans. Harriet de Onís)

tending from the ocean to the *sertão*, a region plagued by alternating drought and floods.

Educated for the legal profession in Paraíba and Pernambuco, Lins do Rego became a professor of law, the prosecuting attorney in the small town of Minas Gerais in 1925, and a bank inspector. In 1932 he undertook to portray in his "sugar cane cycle" the economic and social conflicts of his native region; these five novels were built around Carlos de Mello, who embodied autobiographical details drawn from Lins do Rego's memory. The series follows Carlos as he grows up, goes to school, circulates among his friends of color in the city, and witnesses the de

W H A T   T O   R E A D

Plantation Boy

Plantation Boy (1932) tells the story of Carlos de Mello, who at the age of four sees the bloody body of his dead mother shortly after his father killed her in an insane rage. The boy is taken from his city home to live with his maternal grandfather and aunts and uncles at the family sugar plantation, Santa Rosa. His father is interned in an asylum for the insane where he dies, completely paralyzed, ten years later; Carlos never sees him again. At Santa Rosa, Carlos begins a new life, and, upon his grandfather's death, he ultimately inherits the plantation.

Initially, he is full of plans to restore the dilapidated estate to its former glory. But crops fail and workers desert, and instead of caring for the land, Carlos develops the paranoid belief that his uncle Juca and the black worker Marreira (whose success is representative of the rise of the working class in Brazil) are conspiring to kill him and take over the plantation. Eventually, the factory that refines the plantation's sugar refuses to extend credit, and Carlos runs out of money. Faced with the

cline of the plantation aristocracy. *Plantation Boy, Doidinho*, and *Bangüê* are the best known of the sugar cane novels. Lins do Rego was already well known when he moved to Rio de Janeiro to enter the newspaper world. He married Filomena Massa, and they had three daughters.

Lins do Rego was an uneven writer. He stands out among the increasing number of excellent Brazilian novelists for his character drawing and his simple, direct language, but most critics find his writing flawed by a lack of dialogue. Part of the problem may have been the speed with which he wrote, producing a novel a year. His defenders see in his preference for narrative so-

prospect of disposing of land at public auction, Carlos instead sells it to Uncle Juca and leaves the plantation without having learned anything of value from his experience. As he speeds away in a train, Carlos glimpses Marreira's prosperous mansion, a symbol of the new social environment in which he had been unable to compete.

Lins do Rego was involved in the Region-Tradition movement founded by Gilberto Freyre, who is considered his most profound intellectual influence. The result in *Plantation Boy* is a regionalism that fuses a lively view of local life and history with a submerged critique of the patriarchal plantation system. Unlike his grandfather, Carlos is sympathetic to the workers' poverty, and his observations weave among his longings for maternal love, his morbid fear of death and disease, and his ever-present pessimism.

Lins do Rego's creation of a decadent post-slavery Brazilian Northeast has been compared to William Faulkner's decadent rural American South. Certainly both writers are regionalists who describe crumbling plantation societies based on a single-crop economy that is ruled by a formerly slave-holding aristocracy. *Plantation Boy* is enjoyable reading, but its major strength lies in its vivid documentation of a time and place long since gone.

— *Linda Ledford-Miller*

liloquy the influence of professional oral storytellers he heard as a boy.

Among his later works, *Pedra bonita* (wondrous or beautiful rock), with its picture of fanaticism in the *sertão*, is founded on actual happenings. *Água-mãe* (mother-water) is a ghost story of eerie moods that won the Felipe d'Oliveira award as the best novel of the year in 1941. *Fogo morto* (dead fires), a novel with excellent dialogue and characters (such as the Don Quixote-like Captain Vitorino Carneiro da Cunha, quite different from the morbid Carlos de Mello), returns to the sugar plantations to follow the rise and fall of the epileptic Lula de Hollanda, aristocratic master of Santa-Fe. Another departure from Lins do Rego's earlier style is *Eurídice*, a psychological novel about sex, in which he experimented with new themes.

In 1956, elected to the Academia Brasileira de Letras, Lins do Rego was supposed to eulogize his predecessor in his acceptance speech, but instead he shocked the members by declaring that

Manchette

the man never wrote anything remotely resembling literature. The same statement could not be made about José Lins do Rego.

— *Linda Ledford-Miller*

Learn More

Chamberlin, Bobby J. "José Lins do Rêgo." In *Latin American Writers*, edited by Carlos A. Solé and Maria Isabel Abreu. New York: Charles Scribner's Sons, 1989. A fine introduction for the beginning reader of Lins do Rego. Notes the autobiographical elements of his work along with its regional and folkloric influences.

Ellison, Fred P. *Brazil's New Novel: Four Northeastern Masters.* Berkeley: University of California Press, 1954. Provides an excellent introduction to the new Brazilian regionalism of the 1930's and 1940's. One chapter is devoted to an examination of Lins do Rego's works. A classic in the field.

Hulet, Claude L. "José Lins do Rêgo." In *Brazilian Literature 3, 1920-1960: Modernism.* Washington, D.C.: Georgetown University Press, 1975. An anthology of Brazilian literature in Portuguese with introductions in English. Short biography of Lins do Rego followed by critical commentary. Discussion of Lins do Rego's style and techniques.

"José Lins do Rêgo (Cavalcanti)." In *World Authors, 1950-1970*, edited by John Wakeman. New York: H. W. Wilson, 1975. Gives an overview of Lins do Rego's life and summarizes each of the novels of the Sugar Cane Cycle. Includes a brief discussion of Lins do Rego's detailed naturalism and simple, direct style.

Marotti, Giorgio. *Black Characters in the Brazilian Novel.* Translated by Maria O. Marotti and Harry Lawton. Los Angeles: Center for Afro-American Studies, University of California, 1987. Includes a discussion of the relationship between slaves and slave holders.

Vincent, Jon. "José Lins do Rêgo." In *Dictionary of Brazilian Literature*, edited by Irwin Stein. New York: Greenwood Press, 1988. Provides an overview of Lins do Rego's life and work and discusses his involvement in the Region-Tradition school of thought and writing founded by the great Brazilian sociologist, Gilberto Freyre.

Clarice Lispector

Brazilian novelist and short-story writer

Born: Chechelnik, Ukraine, Soviet Union;
December 10, 1925
Died: Rio de Janeiro, Brazil; December 9, 1977

SHORT FICTION: *Alguns contos*, 1952; *Laços de família*, 1960 (*Family Ties*, 1972); *A legião estrangeira*, 1964 (*The Foreign Legion*, 1986); *Felicidade clandestina: Contos*, 1971; *A imitação da rosa*, 1973; *Onde estivestes de noite*, 1974; *A via crucis do corpo*, 1974; *A bela e a fera*, 1979; *Soulstorm*, 1989 (includes stories from *Onde estivestes de noite* and *A via crucis do corpo*).

LONG FICTION: *Perto do coração selvagem*, 1944 (*Near to the Wild Heart*, 1990); *O lustre*, 1946; *A cidade sitiada*, 1949; *A maçã no escuro*, 1961 (*The Apple in the Dark*, 1967); *A paixão segundo G. H.*, 1964 (*The Passion According to G. H.*, 1988); *Uma aprendizagem: Ou, O livro dos prazeres*, 1969 (*An Apprenticeship: Or, The Book of Delights*, 1986); *Água viva*, 1973 (*The Stream of Life*, 1989); *A hora da estrela*, 1977 (*The Hour of the Star*, 1986); *Um sopro de vida: Pulsações*, 1978.

NONFICTION: *Para não esquecer*, 1978; *A descoberta do mundo*, 1984 (*Discovering the World*, 1992).

CHILDREN'S LITERATURE: *O mistério do coelho pensante*, 1967; *A mulher que matou os peixes*, 1968 (*The Woman Who Killed the Fish*, 1982).

MISCELLANEOUS: *Seleta de Clarice Lispector*, 1975.

Clarice Lispector (klah-REES leh-SPEHKT-ur) is considered not only one of Brazil's most innovative writers but also one of the giants of twentieth century fiction. Born in 1925 in the Ukraine, she emigrated to Brazil with her parents and two older sisters when she was two months old. The family settled first in the Northeast of Brazil but moved to Rio de Janeiro in 1937. From the time she was a child, Lispector read widely, starting with Brazilian classics such as José de Alencar, Joaquim Maria Machado de Assis, and Graciliano Ramos, and gradually adding such foreign writers as Fyodor Dostoevski, Hermann Hesse, James Joyce, Katherine Mansfield, and Virginia Woolf. While attending the National Faculty of Law, she began a career in journalism, developed close friendships with several of Brazil's leading writers, and started work on the novel *Near to the Wild Heart*, which was published in 1944 and was awarded the Brazilian PEN Club's prestigious Graça Aranha Prize. A surprisingly mature first novel, this probing, anguished tale centering on a woman's search for self-identity set the direction that the author's fiction was to follow for the next thirty years.

In 1943, the year before she finished law school, Lispector married her classmate Mauri Gurgel Valente, who joined the Brazilian diplomatic corps upon their graduation. For the next fifteen years, Lispector accompanied her diplomat husband to posts in Europe and the United States. During that time, Lispector wrote two more novels and turned her attention increasingly to the short story, a genre in which she was to set new standards of excellence. After she was separated from her husband in 1959, Lispector returned with the couple's children to Rio de Janeiro, her home for the rest of her life. The late 1950's and the early 1960's were extremely creative periods, during which Lispector produced perhaps her most accomplished work. Two thematically complex and stylistically innovative nov-

---

And she had returned at last from the perfection of the planet Mars. She, who had never had any ambitions except to be a wife to some man, gratefully returned to find her share of what is daily fallible. With her eyes closed she sighed her thanks. How long was it since she had felt tired?

—from "The Imitation of the Rose"
(trans. Giovanni Pontiero)

Courtesy of New Directions

els, *The Apple in the Dark* and *The Passion According to G. H.*, date from these years. Written in a slow-moving, poetic prose, they are evidence that, by this time, Lispector had achieved a thorough command of narrative technique and had matured into one of the most sophisticated practitioners of the "lyrical novel." It was also during this period that Lispector published what are arguably her two finest volumes of short fiction, *Family Ties*, which includes some of her most frequently anthologized pieces, such as "Love" and "The Imitation of the Rose," and *The Foreign Legion*, a collection of short stories, chronicles, and several nonfiction pieces, including a few in which she discusses her ideas about what literature is and what writing means to her.

By the late 1960's, Lispector's reputation was firmly established in Brazil. As her works were translated into several languages, she quickly gained international recognition. Although in general her fiction grew more hermetic, some of her late work is quite accessible. Such is the case with *Soulstorm,* a collection of stories revolving around erotic themes and written in a subtly ironic and at times humorous style. Lispector's novel *The Hour of the Star,* published shortly before her death from cancer in 1977, can be interpreted, at least in part, as an answer to those who accused the writer of being indifferent to Brazil's social problems. Centering on the pathetic Macabéa, the novel alludes to the plight of migrants from the impoverished Northeast, who are attracted to the richer cities of the South. Nevertheless, even in this novel Lispector's primary interest lies not in social issues at large but in the questions of human suffering and failure. An overtly self-conscious narrative, *The Hour of the Star* can be considered an example of metafiction and can be read as Lispector's personal statement about the relationship between life and literature.

Influenced by the existentialist philosophy of Søren Kierkegaard, Martin Heidegger, and Jean-Paul Sartre, Lispector returned again and again to the question of human beings' place in an indifferent, contingent, and absurd universe. Lispector's work revolves around a relatively small number of obsessive themes, including the quest for self-identity, humankind's ontological loneliness, human beings' difficulty in establishing connections with one another, and the conflict between the inauthentic existence imposed by social constraints and the individual's search for an authentic existence. Most of her protagonists are middle-class women living in an urban environment. Nevertheless, although Lispector displays great talent in depicting the specific situation of women, her fiction is not only about the female condition but about the human condition as well. It is not surprising, then, that the issues confronting her male protagonists, such as Martim in *The Apple in the Dark*, are not significantly different from those confronting her female protagonists.

Lispector developed an original narrative style that was perfectly suited to her themes. Lispector was not overly concerned with plot and character development; her novels have an open-ended quality and rely on a delicate, rhythmic pattern of im-

WHAT TO READ

Family Ties

Family Ties (1960), the high point of Lispector's work in short fiction, is truly one of the masterpieces of Brazilian literature, regardless of period or genre. It is composed of thirteen enigmatic stories, six of which had already appeared in *Alguns contos* (1952), and the stories focus on the act of epiphany.

For example, in "Preciosidade" ("Preciousness"), a girl going through puberty experiences both fear and confusion after an ambiguous encounter with some boys. This story is particularly interesting in that the event that triggers the protagonist's reaction is never fully described to the reader. The reader sees the character's reaction to the event, however, and it is that reaction, full of anxiety and uncertainty, that constitutes the story, demonstrating that Lispector is not as concerned with the central event of her stories as she is with her characters' reactions to the event. By not providing details concerning the event in this particular story, she assumes that her reader's concerns are the same as her own.

Another interesting story included in this collection is "O crime do professor de matemática" ("The Crime of the Mathematics Professor"), which recounts the story of a man who buries a stray dog he has found dead in a desperate attempt to relieve himself of the guilt he feels for having once abandoned his own dog.

Finally, "Feliz aniversário" ("Happy Birthday") tells the story of an old woman surrounded by her family on her eighty-ninth birthday. Rather than celebrate, she observes with disdain the offspring she has produced and, much to the shock of those in attendance, spits on the floor to show her lack of respect. All the stories in this collection present individual characters in turmoil and the way in which each deals with this turmoil from the inside out.

— *Keith H. Brower*

ages, designed to represent the fluidity of consciousness and to record an ineffable, deeper dimension of existence. Her best short stories evolve from an outwardly insignificant occurrence, which functions, nevertheless, as a catalyst for an existential crisis. Borrowing from Woolf and Joyce, Lispector makes consistent use of stream of consciousness and the epiphany. Together with her contemporary João Guimarães Rosa, Lispector is responsible for moving Brazilian fiction away from a somewhat parochial dependence on regionalism. Since the late 1970's, Lispector has attracted much attention from feminist critics, particularly in Europe and the United States, who have hailed her texts as representing the best in "feminine writing." Nevertheless, as the extensive bibliography on Lispector demonstrates, her work can be successfully approached from a variety of critical perspectives. A master of the modern narrative, Lispector possesses a well-deserved reputation as one of the most original writers in the twentieth century.

— *Luiz Fernando Valente*

Learn More

Alonso, Cláudia Pazos, and Claire Williams. *Closer to the Wild Heart: Essays on Clarice Lispector.* Oxford, England: Legenda, European Humanities Research Centre, 2002. Collection of twelve essays examining Lispector's novels, stories, chronicles, and children's books.

Barbosa, Maria José Somerlate. *Clarice Lispector: Spinning the Webs of Passion.* New Orleans: University Press of the South, 1997. A good study of Lispector's works. Includes bibliographical references and an index.

Cixous, Hélène. *Reading with Clarice Lispector.* Minneapolis: University of Minnesota Press, 1990. Chapters on *The Stream of Life, The Apple in the Dark,* "The Egg and the Chicken," and *The Hour of the Star.* The book includes an introduction by Verena Andermatt Conley, carefully explaining Cixous's playfully profound deconstructionist reading of Lispector. Recommended for advanced students.

Fitz, Earl F. *Clarice Lispector.* Boston: Twayne, 1985. A useful introduction that includes a chapter of biography, a discussion of

Lispector's place in Brazilian literature, and a study of the style, structure, and point of view in her novels and short stories. Also contains a chronology, detailed notes, and a well-annotated bibliography.

————. *Sexuality and Being in the Poststructuralist Universe of Clarice Lispector: The Différance of Desire.* Austin: University of Texas Press, 2001. Fitz provides a poststructural analysis of Lispector's work, explaining how her characters struggle over, and humanize, their desires for the unattainable.

Marting, Diane E., ed. *Clarice Lispector: A Bio-bibliography.* Westport, Conn.: Greenwood Press, 1993. A full-length bibliographical resource.

Peixoto, Marta. *Passionate Fictions: Gender, Narrative, and Violence in Clarice Lispector.* Minneapolis: University of Minnesota Press, 1994. Written with a decidedly feminist bias, *Passionate Fictions* analyzes Lispector's frequently violent subject matter, juxtaposing it with her strange and original use of language. Special attention is paid to the nexus with Hélène Cixous and to the autobiographical elements of *The Stream of Life* and *A via crucis do corpo.*

Santos, Cristina. *Bending the Rules in the Quest for an Authentic Female Identity: Clarice Lispector and Carmen Boullosa.* New York: Peter Lang, 2004. Analyzes the female characters in works by Lispector and Boullosa, describing how the authors use an innovative narrative voice to depict women characters seeking their true voices and real life experiences.

Eduardo Machado

Cuban American playwright

Born: Havana, Cuba; June 11, 1953

DRAMA: *Worms*, pr. 1981; *Rosario and the Gypsies*, pr. 1982 (one-act musical; book and lyrics by Machado, music by Rick Var-toreila); *The Modern Ladies of Guanabacoa*, pr., pb. 1983; *There's Still Time to Dance in the Streets of Rio*, pr. 1983; *Broken Eggs*, pr., pb. 1984; *Fabiola*, pr. 1985, pb. 1991; *When It's Over*, pr. 1987 (with Geraldine Sherman); *Why to Refuse*, pr. 1987 (one act); *Across a Crowded Room*, pr. 1988; *A Burning Beach*, pr. 1988; *Don Juan in New York City*, pr. 1988 (two-act musical); *Once Removed*, pr., pb. 1988, revised pr. 1994; *Wishing You Well*, pr. 1988 (one-act musical); *Cabaret Bambu*, pr. 1989 (one-act musical); *Related Retreats*, pr. 1990; *Stevie Wants to Play the Blues*, pr. 1990, revised pr. 1998 (two-act musical); *In the Eye of the Hurricane*, pr., pb. 1991; *The Floating Island Plays*, pb. 1991, pr. 1994 as *Floating Islands* (cycle of four plays; includes *The Modern Ladies of Guanabacoa, Fabiola, In the Eye of the Hurricane,* and *Broken Eggs*); *1979*, pr. 1991; *Breathing It In*, pr. 1993; *Three Ways to Go Blind*, pr. 1994; *Between the Sheets*, pr. 1996 (music by Mike Nolan and Scott Williams); *Cuba and the Night*, pr. 1997; *Crocodile Eyes*, pr. 1999; *Havana Is Waiting*, pr. 2001 (originally pr. 2001 as *When the Sea Drowns in Sand*).
SCREENPLAY: *Exiles in New York*, 1999.
TRANSLATION: *The Day You'll Love Me*, pr. 1989 (of José Ignacio Cabrujas's play *El día que me quieras*).

Eduardo Machado (eh-DWAHR-doh mah-CHAH-doh) arrived from Cuba in 1961, at age eight, with his brother Jesús, five years younger, as a "Peter Pan" child. The Peter Pan Project, a collaboration between a United States-based Roman Catholic bishop and the United States Central Intelligence Agency, brought fourteen thousand Cuban children to the

W H A T   T O   R E A D

Machado's Gender-Bending Plays

Although Machado's early works often examine issues of immigrant identity, he leaves his immigrant theme behind with such major works as *Stevie Wants to Play the Blues* (1990), a musical about a female singer who transforms herself into a man, and *Don Juan in New York City* (1988), which is chiefly about sexual ambivalence in the age of AIDS. The latter play, a work that is operatic in scope and amplitude, centers on D. J. (Don Juan), an experimental filmmaker. Apparently bisexual, D. J. is torn between a female singer-celebrity, Flora, and his trashy male lover, Steve. His conflict is enacted against the backdrop of the AIDS epidemic: D. J.'s good friend, Paul, a female impersonator, has taken refuge in the guise of Carole Channing and is preparing first for a concert of Channing's songs and subsequently for a successful suicide, as he eludes the depredations of AIDS. The baroque action is further complicated by actual film clips from D. J.'s creations and by passionate songs performed by two mysterious figures, Abuelo and Mujer, representatives of the world of traditional heterosexual love for which the classic Don Juan was known.

Machado has called *Stevie Wants to Play the Blues* a "gender-bender," a genre in which he examines premises about sexuality and takes the characters through surprising and unconventional revelations about their gender identifications. Other plays in which he toys with the notion of sexual identity are *Related Retreats* (1990), about the lives of writers at an arts colony under the tutelage of a female guru, and *Breathing It In* (1993), about a motley band of lost souls who congregate around a male/female guru couple. It at once satirizes groups such as Werner Erhard's individual, social transformation technique (EST) and the women's liberation movement of the 1970's and 1980's and concocts a string of variations on sexual transformation among its characters.

— *David Willinger*

United States without their parents, ostensibly to "save" them from communism and from the governmental policies under Fidel Castro. Arriving with no knowledge of English and undergoing major culture shock, the brothers were sent to an aunt and uncle in Hialeah, Florida, who had their own children as well as other immigrant relatives living with them. Machado's first memory of the United States is celebrating Halloween by trick-or-treating, believing that they had been sent out truly begging, as the children had moved from an economically privileged childhood in Cuba to poverty in the United States. His parents came a year later.

The house in which Machado had lived in Cuba was taken by the government and transformed into a school. His father, a self-professed "professional rich man's son," initially could not find work in United States. Machado finished growing up in Canoga Park, a suburb of Los Angeles. By the time Machado was sixteen, his father had succeeded economically as an accountant. Machado's parents later divorced, reportedly due to his father's infidelity, which has been an item in his dramatic work.

Machado began his acting career in 1978 at the Padua Hills Playwrights Festival, where he met Maria Irene Fornes, a Cuban immigrant playwright who would become a major influence on his work. He became her assistant on her *Fefu and Her Friends* (1977) at the Ensemble Studio Theater. Machado began writing plays at the suggestion of a therapist, who recommended writing an imaginary letter forgiving his mother for sending him away.

By 2002, Machado had written twenty-seven plays, all but seven dealing with his family or Cuba in some way. In New York City, as part of INTAR (International Arts Relations) Hispanic American Arts Center, he wrote *The Floating Island Plays* (*The Modern Ladies of Guanabacoa, Fabiola, Broken Eggs*, and *In the Eye of the Hurricane*) between 1983 and 1991. He has been commissioned to write plays for The Public Theater, the Roundabout Theatre Company, and Wind Dancer Productions. He took his first trip back to Cuba in December, 1999, followed in rapid succession by two more visits to his homeland. Machado says he has

> *"No, nobility has to do with caring about the ugly things, seeing trash and loving it. It has to do with compassion, not table manners. It has to do with thought, not what people think about you."*
>
> —from *Broken Eggs*

always been at the mercy of politics. Critics say his works show his conflicts: capitalism versus communism, heterosexuality versus homosexuality, Cuban identity versus Cuban American identity.

Machado has taught at Sarah Lawrence College, New York University, the Mark Taper Forum, The Public Theater, and the Playwrights Center in Minneapolis. He has headed Columbia University's graduate playwriting program in the School of Arts since 1997 and has been an artistic associate of the Cherry Lane Alternative, the Off-Broadway Cherry Lane Theatre's nonprofit wing.

Machado received a 1995 National Theater Artist Residency to be playwright in residence at Los Angeles's Mark Taper Forum. He has been awarded grants from the National Endowment for the Humanities, the Rockefeller Foundation, and the City of Los Angeles for his works. He received a National Endowment for the Arts grant for a one-act play at Ensemble Studio Theatre. He first debuted *When the Sea Drowns in Sand* at the twenty-fifth annual Humana Festival of New American Plays. It has since been rewritten and performed as the autobiographical *Havana Is Waiting*.

— Debra D. Andrist

Learn More

Conde, Yvonne. *Operation Peter Pan: The Untold Exodus of Fourteen Thousand Forty-eight Cuban Children*. New York: Routledge, 1999. A history of the Peter Pan Project, written by one of the children who was sent to the United States.

Muñoz, Elias Miguel. "Of Small Conquests and Big Victories: Gender Constructs in *The Modern Ladies of Guanabacoa.*" In *The Americas Review* 20, no. 2 (Summer, 1992): 105-111. Examines the treatment of sexual roles in Cuban society in the work of Machado and other Cuban American dramatists.

Ortiz, Ricardo L. "Culpa and Capital: Nostalgic Addictions of Cuban Exile." *Yale Journal of Criticism* 10, no. 1 (Spring, 1997): 63-84. Analyzes the treatment of coffee and its relationship to Cuban exiles in the United States in Machado's *The Floating Island Plays;* compares this treatment to works by other Cuban American playwrights.

Torres, María de Los Angeles. *The Lost Apple: Operation Pedro Pan, Cuban Children in the United States and the Promise of a Better Future.* Boston: Beacon Press, 2003. Torres, one of the children sent to the United States, chronicles the history of the Peter Pan Project.

Joaquim Maria Machado de Assis

Brazilian novelist

Born: Rio de Janeiro, Brazil; June 21, 1839
Died: Rio de Janeiro, Brazil; September 29, 1908

LONG FICTION: *Resurreicão*, 1872; *A mão e a luva*, 1874 (*The Hand and the Glove*, 1970); *Helena*, 1876; *Yayá Garcia*, 1878 (English translation, 1977); *Memórias póstumas de Brás Cubas*, 1881 (*The Posthumous Memoirs of Brás Cubas*, 1951; better known as *Epitaph of a Small Winner*, 1952); *Quincas Borba*, 1891 (*Philosopher or Dog?*, 1954; also as *The Heritage of Quincas Borba*, 1954); *Dom Casmurro*, 1899 (English translation, 1953); *Esaú e Jacob*, 1904 (*Esau and Jacob*, 1965); *Memorial de Ayres*, 1908 (*Counselor Ayres' Memorial*, 1972).

SHORT FICTION: *Contos fluminenses*, 1870; *Histórias da meia-noite*, 1873; *Papéis avulsos*, 1882; *Histórias sem data*, 1884; *Várias histórias*, 1896; *Histórias românticas*, 1937; *The Psychiatrist, and Other Stories*, 1963; *What Went on at the Baroness'*, 1963; *The Devil's Church, and Other Stories*, 1977.

DRAMA: *Desencantos*, pb. 1861; *Quase ministro*, pb. 1864; *Os deuses de casaca*, pb. 1866; *Tu só, tu, puro amor*, pb. 1880; *Teatro*, pb. 1910.

POETRY: *Crisálidas*, 1864; *Falenas*, 1870; *Americanas*, 1875; *Poesias completas*, 1901.

NONFICTION: *Páginas recolhidas (contos ensaios, crônicas)*, 1899; *Relíquias de Casa Velha (contos crônicas, comédias)*, 1906; *Crítica*, 1910; *A semana*, 1910; *Crítica por Machado de Assis*, 1924; *Crítica literária*, 1937; *Crítica teatral*, 1937; *Correspondência*, 1938.

MISCELLANEOUS: *Outras relíquias*, 1908; *Obra completa*, 1959.

A lifelong resident of Rio de Janeiro, Joaquim Machado de Assis (zhwah-KEEM mah-SHAH-doh thay ah-SEES) was the son of a Portuguese mother and a mulatto father. Despite humble origins, epilepsy, and a speech defect, this self-taught intellectual not only attained the highest civil service position open to him but also founded the Brazilian Academy of Letters and served as its president until his death in 1908. While still living, Machado de Assis saw himself acknowledged as Brazil's greatest writer.

At the time of his death, in 1908, Joaquim Maria Machado de Assis was revered as Brazil's most important and influential man of letters, a distinction many critics feel he deserves. An innovator in such areas as the use of irony and of self-conscious but unreliable narrator/protagonists, Machado de Assis was instrumental in leading Brazilian literature toward an appreciation of both technical sophistication and authenticity of expression. Although he did outstanding work in all the literary genres, including poetry, drama, translation, and critical theory, it was in narrative—the novel and short-story forms especially—that he achieved his greatest successes. His extraordinary work *Epitaph of a Small Winner* can, for example, be regarded as the first modern novel of either North or South America, while the text widely held to be his supreme achievement, *Dom Casmurro*, ranks as one of the outstanding novels of its time. Perhaps even more brilliant as a writer of short fiction, however, Machado de Assis is credited with having originated the modern short-story

> *There went my father and my holiday! A day away*
> *from school without any fun! No, it was not a day*
> *but* eight, *eight days of mourning, during which*
> *the thought of returning to school sometimes*
> *occurred to me. Between condolence visits, my*
> *mother cried and sewed the mourning clothes. I cried*
> *too. . . .*
>
> —from *The Holiday*
> (trans. William L. Grossman)

WHAT TO READ

"Midnight Mass"

The narrator of "Midnight Mass," Mr. Nogueira, is of indeterminate age as he tells his tale, but he was a young man of seventeen when the events occurred. A country boy, he has come to Rio de Janeiro to stay with Mr. Menezes, a notary whose first wife was Nogueira's cousin, in order to prepare for his college entrance examinations. The Menezes household is composed of the notary, his wife, Madame Conceição, her mother, and two female slaves. Nogueira spends some months living quietly with the family, which he refers to as old-fashioned. The only exception to the nightly routine of a ten o'clock bedtime is the weekly visit that Menezes makes to the theater. Nogueira would like to join him, as he has never been to the theater, but he discovers that going to the theater is a euphemism that allows Menezes to spend one night a week with a married woman who is separated from her husband. Conceição accepts her husband's mistreatment of her passively, as she seems to respond to everything.

form in Brazil, where tales such as "The Psychiatrist," "Midnight Mass," "A Singular Event," "The Companion," and "Dona Paula" are still judged to be masterpieces of his laconic, metaphoric art.

To some modern readers it may appear lamentable that Machado de Assis's works bear neither overt references to his racial heritage nor arguably even oblique ones. In this regard the Brazilian mulatto will be seen to be fully integrated with the concerns and priorities of the European-leaning dominant bourgeois society in late nineteenth century Brazil. Nevertheless, Machado de Assis wrote on the fringes of "polite" society in a way that did not specifically derive from race, although a sense of social inferiority may well have contributed to his develop-

The events of the story occur on Christmas Eve, which coincides with the notary's weekly theater outing. Nogueira has remained in the city to see the special midnight Mass. He sits reading in the silent house when Conceiçao appears, dressed in her negligee. Nogueira notes that she does not appear to have slept. A conversation ensues, and Nogueira gradually realizes that the passive, thirty-year-old wife of Menezes is a very beautiful woman. The next day, Conceiçao expresses no interest in him, despite the seeming intimacy of the previous evening. He goes home a few days later. When he returns to Rio in March, the notary has died of apoplexy, and Conceiçao has moved to another district and married her husband's apprentice clerk.

In "Midnight Mass," Machado tells two stories in one: a sketch of the period, and the story of a woman who eventually finds happiness despite her present circumstances. Although each detail alone seems unambiguous, their accumulation results in an ambiguous narrative that leaves both the narrator and the reader in a quandary, wondering if Conceiçao was unfaithful, if her husband did die of shock, why Conceiçao married so soon after being widowed, why she moved, and if she was pregnant.

— *Linda Ledford-Miller*

ment of a cynical and biting stance toward the higher spiritual aspirations of the socially dominant Brazilian of his day.

Specifically, this stance can be seen in his critical analyses of the ambiguities of the human soul (his "Jamesian" quality) and in his dissection of the pious self-sufficiency of the ignorant bourgeoisie (his "Flaubertian" and "Tolstoian" qualities). Like many of the great realists, Machado de Assis lends himself to a Lukacsian or Marxist analysis. His works bespeak, beneath the surface of the comings and goings of polite, ordered society, the tremendous conflicts, passions, and irreconcilable tensions of a society that fragments human experience and strives to metaphorize, in terms of a myth of spiritual transcendence, humans' carnal and materialistic nature. The patterned texture of an ordered society remains permanently at odds with fundamental aspects of the human soul which it chooses to ignore or metaphorize.

— David W. Foster, updated by Earl E. Fitz

Learn More

Caldwell, Helen. *Machado de Assis: The Brazilian Master and His Novels.* Berkeley: University of California Press, 1970. A concise survey of Machado de Assis's nine novels and his various narrative techniques. Also includes discussions of his primary themes, a useful bibliography, and some comments on his plays, poems, and short stories.

Dixon, Paul. *Retired Dreams: "Dom Casmurro," Myth and Modernity.* West Lafayette, Ind.: Purdue University Press, 1989. Describes how Machado de Assis cultivated a radically new style of writing, featuring ambiguity as the most "realistic" aspect of language. Dixon also suggests that Machado de Assis was critical of his society's patriarchal codes and that, as evidenced in the relationship between the novel's two major characters (Bento and Capitu), he implies the virtues inherent in a more matriarchal approach to sociopolitical organization.

Fitz, Earl E. *Machado de Assis.* Boston: Twayne, 1989. The first English-language book to examine all aspects of Machado de Assis's writing. Includes information on his life, his place in Brazilian and world literature, his style, and his themes.

Graham, Richard, ed. *Machado de Assis: Reflections on a Brazilian Master Writer.* Austin: University of Texas Press, 1999. Part of the Critical Reflections on Latin America series, this volume has essays by John Gledson, Daphne Patai, and Sidney Chalhoub.

Jackson, K. David. "The Brazilian Short Story." In *The Cambridge History of Latin American Literature.* Vol. 3, edited by Robert González Echevarria and Enrique Pupo-Walker. Cambridge, England: Cambridge University Press, 1996. Discusses Machado de Assis's technique of suggestion and implication within an ironic frame of reference. Suggests that Machado de Assis's humor and irony underline the futility of human conflict in a world in which the nature of reality is illusory.

Maia Neto, José Raimundo. *Machado de Assis, the Brazilian Pyrrhonian.* West Lafayette, Ind.: Purdue University Press, 1994. Part 1 explores Machado de Assis's first phase (1861-1878)—from writing essays to stories to his first novels. Part 2 concentrates on his second phase (1879-1908), with separate chapters on *The Posthumous Memoirs of Brás Cubas, Dom Casmurro,* and later fiction.

Nunes, Maria Luisa. *The Craft of an Absolute Winner: Characterization and Narratology in the Novels of Machado de Assis.* Westport, Conn.: Greenwood Press, 1983. An excellent study of Machado de Assis's novelistic techniques, characterization, and primary themes. Argues that the essence of Machado de Assis's genius, like that of all great writers, lies in his singular ability to create powerful and compelling characters.

Schwarz, Roberto. *A Master on the Periphery of Capitalism: Machado de Assis.* Translated by John Gledson. Durham, N.C.: Duke University Press, 2001. A Marxist analysis of *Memórias póstumas de Brás Cubas,* including an examination of the novel's style and its historical and sociological aspects.

Eduardo Mallea

Argentine novelist and short-story writer

Born: Bahía Blanca, Argentina; August 14, 1903
Died: Buenos Aires, Argentina; November 12, 1982

LONG FICTION: *Nocturno europeo*, 1935; *Fiesta en noviembre*, 1938 (*Fiesta in November*, 1942); *La bahía de silencio*, 1940 (*The Bay of Silence*, 1944); *Todo verdor perecerá*, 1941 (*All Green Shall Perish*, 1966); *El vínculo, Los Rembrandtes, La rosa de Cernobbio*, 1946 (novellas); *Los enemigos del alma*, 1950; *Chaves*, 1953 (English translation, 1966); *Simbad*, 1957 (novella); *El resentimiento*, 1966 (three novellas); *La penúltima puerta*, 1969 (novella); *Gabriel Andaral*, 1971 (novella); *Triste piel del universo*, 1971 (novella).

SHORT FICTION: *Cuentos para una inglesa desesperada*, 1926; *La ciudad junto al río inmóvil*, 1936; *La sala de espera*, 1953; *Posesión*, 1957; *La barca de hielo*, 1967.

NONFICTION: *Conocimiento y expresión de la Argentina*, 1935; *Historia de una pasión argentina*, 1937 (*History of an Argentine Passion*, 1983); *El sayal y la púrpura*, 1946; *Notas de un novelista*, 1954; *La vida blanca*, 1960; *Las Travesías*, 1961-1962; *La guerra interior*, 1963; *Poderío de la novela*, 1965.

MISCELLANEOUS: *Obras completas*, 1961, 1965 (2 volumes); *La red*, 1968.

A descendant of the diplomat, author, and educator Sarmiento, Eduardo Mallea (eh-DWAHR-doh mah-YAH-ah) was born on August 14, 1903, in desolate, wind-swept Bahía Blanca, Argentina, the setting for much of his writing. After his primary instruction by an Australian woman, his physician father took him to Buenos Aires, where he studied law until the sale of some children's stories turned him to literature as a career. Some of his short stories were published in journals in the 1920's. In 1926 his first collection of stories, the fantastic and

frantic *Cuentos para una inglesa desesperada* (stories for a desperate Englishwoman), opened the way for a voyage to Europe and brought him in 1931 the literary editorship of *La nación*, Argentina's most influential newspaper, in Buenos Aires. A lecture trip to Italy later resulted in *Nocturno europeo*, an example of his technique of using a slim fictional plot to tie together his ideas. It won for him the first of many literary prizes, which included the Primer Premio Nacional de Letras in 1945, the Forti Glori Prize in 1968, and the Gran Premio Nacional de las Artes in 1970. Mallea married Helena Muñóz Larreta in 1944.

His "History of an Argentine Passion," probably his most important essay, is the cornerstone of his credo. It includes many

445

W H A T   T O   R E A D

Chaves

A brief, intense character study of a withdrawn saw-mill worker whose taciturnity is the result of profound grief and frustration, *Chaves* (1953) concentrates upon its grave, aloof, self-sufficient protagonist, who sometimes seems almost an allegorical figure. His refusal to socialize and participate in the pettiness of the primitive society of the sawmill community in Argentina's south-western mountains arouses hostility and alienates him. Although he is cast as an outsider, Chaves's behavior is not calculated arrogance or intellectual withdrawal, for he is rather a simple man.

Chaves's psychological formation is reconstructed from flashbacks. Born, like the author, in Bahía Blanca, he grew up with nature and the ocean, amid sand dunes, without developing ambition or a competitive spirit. A change ensues when he meets the woman who becomes his wife, Pura (whose name means "pure"), and decides to compromise his ethical values to support her better: He sells worthless real estate while they live in a rented room. A daughter born to the couple dies

autobiographical elements, and its hero Adrian seeks relief for his tormented soul in the *Confessions* of Saint Augustine and in Spanish mysticism. Mallea's confessed admiration for Marcel Proust, James Joyce, and Franz Kafka explains Mallea's *The Bay of Silence*, the work which firmly established him as a modern novelist who expresses philosophical implications in a pungently lyrical style and who excels in descriptions of the city. The novel describes Martin Tregua as a student in Buenos Aires and portrays his relationship in Europe with the disillusioned, frustrated, married Gloria, with whom he finds solace. In *Fiesta in November* Mallea presents three complicated and temperamental women in a literary feat inspired by the execution of the

at age four, underlining their failure and inability to conquer the sterile, dead environment. Moving from the hills of Córdoba to Tucumán, they settle in a small town where they live uneventfully for years, until fate intervenes and Pura dies of typhoid fever. Chaves's last attempt to communicate with other human beings is part of the futile effort to save Pura, but his recourse to the long-unused spoken word is to no avail. His silence deepens, and coworkers' attempts to force him to speak nearly degenerate into violence. Rescued by the foreman from an attack by coworkers, Chaves responds to his benefactor's request that he terminate his alienation with one word, "No." He is the existential outsider, a prototype of the hero so popular among French existentialists during the 1940's.

Some critics have suggested parallels between Chaves and Meursault in Albert Camus's *The Stranger* (1942). Both refuse to play by the rules and as a result become pariahs, but with certain differences. At the end of *The Stranger,* Meursault rises to denounce man's inhumanity to man and to point to the fact that humanity is eagerly awaiting his death. Chaves, by contrast, refuses to speak, and his alienation is prolonged beyond the novel's end because he is not released by death.

— *Genaro J. Pérez*

Spanish poet Federico García Lorca at the outbreak of the Civil War. Between chapters about the useless rich of Buenos Aires, fearing suppression of liberty and thought, are sections of another story about soldiers murdering the liberal poet for having different ideas.

Stefan Zweig insisted that Mallea's *All Green Shall Perish* should be published in Europe, and José Lins do Rego translated it into Portuguese for Brazilian readers. Ernest Hemingway and others recognized Mallea's skill with words and ideas by including one of his representative works in the anthology *The Best of the World* (1950). Mallea tried to create a style typically Argentine; his portrayal of his characters, solitary souls in pain

> *This was the thousandth time that I had seen you. You had never seen me, except vaguely. You did not see me now until you raised your eyes in a distant way, realized that the florist was busy attending to me, and smiled at your own discourtesy. There was a harsh and blighted look in your eyes, even in your smile.*
>
> —from *The Bay of Silence*
> (trans. Stuart Edgar Grummon)

seeking freedom and self-expression, reveals his patriotic belief that his native land is a paradise even if the inhabitants possess many weaknesses.

— Emil Volek

Learn More

Chapman, Arnold. "Terms of Spiritual Isolation in Eduardo Mallea." *Modern Language Forum* 37 (1952): 21-27. An insightful study of Mallea's use of metaphor.

Dudgeon, Patrick. *Eduardo Mallea: A Personal Study of His Work.* Buenos Aires: Agonia, 1949. Brief but useful for its discussions of *Fiesta in November* and *The Bay of Silence.*

Lewald, H. Ernest. *Eduardo Mallea.* Boston: Twayne, 1977. A sound introduction covering Mallea's formative period, his handling of passion, his cosmopolitan spirit, his national cycle, and his last fictional works. Includes chronology, notes, and annotated bibliography.

Lichtblau, Myron I. Introduction to *History of an Argentine Passion,* by Eduardo Mallea. Translated by Lichtblau. Pittsburgh, Pa.: Latin American Literary Review Press, 1983. This introduction to the first English translation of a Mallea essay provides an excellent overview of his place in Spanish American fiction. Lichtblau includes an excellent bibliography.

Polt, John H. *The Writings of Eduardo Mallea.* Berkeley: University of California Press, 1959. Polt discusses Mallea's essays and fiction through the mid-1950's. A thorough study.

Shaw, Donald L. Introduction to *Todo verdor perecerá*, by Eduardo Mallea. Edited by Shaw. Oxford, England: Pergamon Press, 1968. Cited as an outstanding interpretation.

————. "Narrative Technique in Mallea's *La bahía de silencio*." *Symposium* 20 (1966): 50-55. One of the few studies of this kind in English.

Stabb, Martin S. *In Quest of Identity: Patterns in the Spanish American Essay of Ideas, 1890-1960*. Chapel Hill: University of North Carolina Press, 1967. Although Stabb devotes a section mainly to Mallea's essays, his comments provide helpful background for the fiction as well.

José Julián Martí
Cuban poet and revolutionary

Born: Havana, Cuba; January 28, 1853
Died: Dos Ríos, Cuba; May 19, 1895

POETRY: *Ismaelillo,* 1882; *Versos sencillos,* 1891 (*Simple Verses,* 1997); *Versos libres,* 1913; *José Martí, Major Poems: A Bilingual Edition,* 1982; *The Complete Poems of José Martí,* 2003.

DRAMA: *Amor con amor se paga,* pr. 1875; *Patria y libertad: Drama indio,* pr. 1877; *Adúltera,* pr. 1936; *Abdala,* pr. 1940.

LONG FICTION: *Amistad funesta,* 1911.

NONFICTION: *El presidio político en Cuba,* 1871; *La república española ante la revolución cubana,* 1873; *The America of José Martí: Selected Writings,* 1954; *Diarios,* 1956; *Diario de campaña,* 1962; *Del 95 al 62: Darios de Martí, el declaración de la Habana,* 1964; *Inside the Monster: Writings on the United States and American Imperialism,* 1975; *Our America: Writings on Latin America and the Struggle for Cuban Independence,* 1977; *On Education: Articles on Educational Theory and Pedagogy, and Writings for Children from the Age of Gold,* 1979; *On Art and Literature: Critical Writings,* 1982; *Political Parties and Elections in the United States,* 1989; *José Martí, Reader: Writings on the Americas,* 1999; *Selected Writings,* 2002.

MISCELLANEOUS: *Obras completas,* 1963-1973 (28 volumes).

José Martí (hoh-SAY mar-TEE) has become known worldwide for his wide-ranging abilities and monumental contributions to Latin American literature and history. His unswerving devotion to the cause of Cuban independence from Spain and his heroic death in battle have made him a much-revered symbol of Latin American independence. Both of Martí's parents were from Spain, and even in childhood Martí's strong sense of his identity as a Cuban and his resentment toward Spain's colonial rule made for tense family relations. This situation was exemplified by Martí's 1862 trip to the province of Matanzas, where he and his father watched hundreds of Africans arriving as slaves. That same day, Martí observed a slave who had been lynched. Horrified, the nine-year-old vowed to spend his life fighting for justice.

He enrolled in school in Havana and soon met Fermín Valdés Domínguez; the two would remain best friends for the rest of their lives. Also crucial to Martí's development was the influence of his principal and mentor, the poet Rafael María Mendive, who helped pay for Martí's education and encouraged his student's political and artistic penchants. By the time he turned fifteen, Martí had published several poems, including the dramatic poem *Abdala*, which appeared in the first and only issue of *La Patria Libre* (the free homeland) on January 23, 1869. The newspaper, which Martí founded, was created to take advantage of the single month of free press (January 9-February 11, 1869) granted to the Cubans by their Spanish rulers. The play, in which an East African soldier dies while fighting for his nation's independence, introduces two of the most dominant themes in Martí's work: the evils of colonialism and the

Cuban students march in Havana on January 28, 2005, to celebrate the birthday of poet and national hero José Martí.
AP/Wide World Photos

W H A T   T O   R E A D

Simple Verses

Many readers will recognize the first poem from Martí's *Versos sencillos* (1891; *Simple Verses*, 1997) as the lyrics from the popular song "Guantanamera," and the book's collective influence has been widely acknowledged as fundamental to the canon of Latin American Modernist literature. Martí was the consummate Cuban patriot, and *Simple Verses* provides a window into the author's struggle to reconcile the worlds of poetry and politics and to locate his own role in the developing world of postcolonial Latin America. Even in the book's first lines, Martí hints at this sense of inner conflict, of being torn in more than one direction:

> I am an honest man
> From where the palms grow;
> Before I die I want my soul
> To shed its poetry.
> I come from everywhere,
> To everywhere I'm bound:
> An art among the arts,
> A mountain among mountains.

---

conflict created when devotion to country runs counter to family expectations and obligations. It should be noted that even during this month of free press all mentions of slavery—legal in Cuba until 1886—were prohibited, and so Martí's use of African characters made a particularly bold statement.

In late 1869, a police search of Valdés Domínguez's home uncovered a letter signed by him and Martí accusing a classmate of being disloyal to Mendive and the struggle for independence. Martí was convicted of sedition and sentenced to six years' hard labor in the rock quarries of Havana's San Lázaro prison. When he was released in 1870 he was immediately deported to Spain and spent the next three years in Madrid and Saragossa, where

Themes of pain and conflict (both inner and exterior) are consistently present in these poems. Martí's life was full of emotional anguish (his family relations, both with his parents and his wife and son, were generally characterized by geographical and emotional distance) and sickness (as a result of his years of hard labor in a Cuban rock quarry), but his mother had taught him to think of pain as a necessary and even vital force. The influence of this lesson and others are apparent in the folksong-like tone adopted in his verses, distinguishing him from Rubén Darío and other Modernist poets who were more accepting of the movement's stylistic restrictions. *Simple Verses* was written in 1890, as Martí recuperated from illness in the Catskill Mountains of upstate New York. Each poem is numbered, and some deal with individual events in the writer's life, providing a kind of poetic autobiography. Martí also draws heavily from the natural world, emphasizing Cuba's lush vegetation and its dramatic, exotic landscapes. However, the most important theme in this volume—and in Martí's work in general—is the power of poetry and revolution in the creation of a utopian world. Poetry, says Martí, is the tool best suited for the construction of this ideal community; revolution is the act of turning the ideal into reality.

— *Anna A. Moore*

he earned degrees in philosophy and law. Political debate was permitted in Spain, and Martí devoted much of his energies to advocating Cuban independence in the Spanish press. He returned to the Americas in 1874—his family had settled in Mexico—and became an active participant in the Mexican literary scene, writing for the magazine *Revista Universal,* founding the Alarcón Society, and writing his well-received play *Amor con amor se paga* (love is repaid with love). He also met (and later married) Carmen Zayas Bazán, the daughter of a fellow Cuban exile.

The installation of Porfirio Díaz's dicatorship forced Martí to leave Mexico in 1876, and though he tried to return to Cuba he found that he could not do so without being recognized. Convinced that the Cuban independence movement still lacked sufficient momentum, Martí and his new wife settled in Guatemala, where Martí taught literature and philosophy. The political climate in Guatemala became inhospitable after only one year, but by this time the Ten Years' War had ended in Cuba and Martí was able to return in 1879. He found work in a law office, but his continued political outspokenness resulted in another deportation to Spain in late 1879. His wife was frustrated by his political activity, and the pair later separated. Martí would always remain devoted to their son, José Francisco Martí Zayas Bayan, the Ismaelillo to whom Martí's 1882 book—which many consider to be the earliest example of *Modernismo*—is dedicated.

This exile was not nearly as arduous as the first. After two months, Martí eluded Spanish police and went briefly to Paris before sailing on to New York City. He remained in New York for a full fifteen years—until 1895—as he completed the development of his artistic and political philosophies. For Martí, art and politics cannot be separated: Art is the means through which freedom is achieved, and the struggle for freedom is itself a form of art. Personal relationships, love, and pain are equally fundamental; Martí's work often reflects the lessons he learned from his mother, who taught her son to bear life's misfortunes without self-pity.

> *I know the unfamiliar names*
> *Of grasses and of flowers,*
> *Of fatal deceptions*
> *And exalted sorrows.*
> *On darkest nights I've seen*
> *Rays of the purest splendor*
> *Raining upon my head*
> *From heavenly beauty.*
>
> —from "Simple Verses" (trans. Elinor Randall)

While living in New York, Martí worked as a correspondent for American and Latin American newspapers and completed another book of poems, *Versos libres* (free verses) that remained unpublished until 1913. This book covers a wider range of subjects than its predecessors and carries a heavier emphasis on death, especially as a metaphor for exile. Fulfillment, Martí says, can only come from a return to his homeland, an idea that is also present in *Simple Verses*. Martí felt increasingly conflicted about life in the United States through the 1890's; he valued the freedom America offered but was alarmed by its expansionist policies and overtures toward Cuba. He traveled along the United States' East Coast in an attempt to inspire a pro-independence movement among Cuban tobacco workers and, while serving as the consul for Uruguay in 1887, he took a public stand against the U.S. Secretary of State James G. Blaine, who wanted to strengthen North American influence by moving Latin American countries onto a silver standard. The foreword to *Simple Verses* reflects many of these concerns, making the book a valuable contribution to Latin America's history as well as to its literature.

Martí had founded the Cuban Revolutionary Party in 1892, and by April of 1895 he was back in Cuba and ready for battle. Appointed to the rank of major general in the Liberating Army, he wrote a letter to the *New York Herald* explaining the motives behind Cuba's independence movement before leading his troops into the fighting. He was killed by Spanish soldiers in the battle of Dos Ríos on May 19, 1895, and his already mythic status among Cubans caused his body to be reburied five times before finally coming to rest in Santiago de Cuba.

— *Anna A. Moore*

Learn More

Belnap, Jeffrey, and Raul Fernandez, eds. *José Martí's "Our America": From National to Hemispheric Cultural Studies*. Durham, N.C.: Duke University Press, 1998. This volume focuses on Martí's career as a journalist, concentrating on his belief in the universality of events; namely, that the Cuban struggle for independence was a reflection of a larger global movement towards increased freedom.

Laraway, David. "José Martí and the Call of Technology in 'Amor de ciudad grande.'" *MLN* 119, no. 2 (March, 2004): 290-302. This article centers on the poem "Amor de ciudad grande," in which Martí explores the technology of his era and its role in Latin American society.

Rabin, Lisa M. "Marble Heroes and Mortal Poets: José Martí's Dream of Statuary." *Romance Quarterly* 47, no. 4 (Fall, 2000): 227-239. A case study of Poem 45 in Martí's book *Simple Verses*. Rabin sees this poem, which focuses on a dream about statues, as representative of Martí's desire to link visual art and politics through poetry.

Rodriguez-Luis, Julio, ed. *Re-reading José Martí (1853-1895): One Hundred Years Later.* Albany: State University of New York Press, 1999. Thoroughly examines Martí's impact on Latin American literature and statehood and places his writings in a modern context.

Gabriela Mistral

Chilean poet

Born: Vicuña, Chile; April 7, 1889
Died: Hempstead, New York; January 10, 1957
Also known as: Lucila Godoy Alcayaga

POETRY: *Desolación*, 1922; *Ternura*, 1924, enlarged 1945; *Tala*, 1938; *Antología*, 1941; *Lagar*, 1954; *Selected Poems of Gabriela Mistral*, 1957; *Poesías completas*, 1958; *Poema de Chile*, 1967; *A Gabriela Mistral Reader*, 1993.

It is speculated that Lucila Godoy Alcayaga's pen name, Gabriela Mistral (gah-bree-EHL-ah mee-STRAHL), comes from the names of two earlier poets, Gabriele D'Annunzio and Frédéric Mistral. "Gabriela" also recalls the angel Gabriel and "Mistral," the Mediterranean wind. Spiritual and natural forces pervade her work, which generally displays the virtues of simplicity and clarity. Long considered a leading poet of Latin America, she saw her international recognition crowned when she became the recipient of the Nobel Prize in Literature in 1945.

Mistral came from a humble background. Her father, Jerónimo Godoy, was a village schoolteacher in northern Chile when she was born; he was also known locally as a writer and singer of songs. He abandoned the family when she was three years old. Her childhood was spent in her small town, where she also later attended the local *liceo*, or high school. Her career as a schoolteacher began early, first by example. Like Mistral's father, her mother, Petrolina Alcayaga de Molina, was a rural schoolteacher. The future teacher was once expelled from school for having pagan ideas, although she is universally recognized as one of the most spiritual poets of her time. Later she was a student at the pedagogical college at Santiago.

Mistral thought of herself primarily as a teacher rather than a poet. Her teaching career began at the age of fifteen, instructing small children in a rural school. Later she became a teacher in secondary schools. For a short time she was the mentor of young Neftalí Ricardo Reyes Basoalto, who adopted the pen name of Pablo Neruda and was in 1971 the second Chilean to win the Nobel Prize in Literature. In 1911 Mistral received the post of inspector-general and professor of history at the *liceo* in Antofagasta. A year later she was appointed inspector and professor of Castilian at the Liceo de los Andes, where she remained for six years.

By that time she had achieved some fame for her "Sonetos de la muerte" ("sonnets of death," appearing in *Desolación*), which had won first prize in a national contest. The sonnets grew out of her love for a railroad worker, Romelio Ureta. Their love did not end happily; he left her and later shot himself fatally over a financial debt. The sonnets include such imagery as the poet's taking and walking with the urn containing her love's ashes, feeling a sense of contentment because no woman now contends with her for him. In another sonnet she asks Christ to forgive the suicide (the kind of thinking that resulted in her expulsion from school) and asserts that only Christ can judge her. *Desolación* (desolation) was first published in the United States, appropriately at the initiative of students who read her poetry in the classroom.

Mistral loved children, but she never married or had any of her own, although she adopted a nephew, Juan Miguel Godoy. *Ternura* (tenderness), especially, is devoted to the spiritual bond

Little fleece of my flesh
that I wove in my womb,
little shivering fleece,
sleep close to me!
The partridge sleeps in the clover
hearing its heart beat.
My breathing will not wake you.
Sleep close to me!

—from "Close to Me" (trans. Doris Dana)

and the spiritual greatness of motherhood and childhood. It contains numerous poems that one may call literary works or that may be called lullabies or children's poems. Children throughout Latin America have sung Mistral's poems. *Ternura* also was published at the urging of readers of Mistral's poetry; Mistral, modest about her art, favored publishing in periodicals.

From 1922 to 1924, already famous as a poet and educator, Mistral was in Mexico, at the invitation of the Mexican government, to assist in the reorganization and development of libraries and schools. She also lectured there on Latin American literature. After travel in Europe, she returned to her native Chile to receive many honors.

As is common in South American culture, she was given, as a leading author, a series of diplomatic posts abroad. One of her assignments was as the Chilean delegate to the Institute of Intellectual Cooperation of the League of Nations. She also served in

WHAT TO READ

Tala

Tala (1938) was compiled as a gesture to the Spanish children uprooted during the Spanish Civil War (1936-1939). Mistral was disappointed and ashamed that Latin America had not appeared to share her grief for the plight of these homeless children, and the proceeds from the sale of this volume went to the children's camps. The title of the book refers to the felling of trees and applies to both the poems themselves and the purpose for which the author compiled them. The limbs are cut from the living trunk and offered as a gift, a part of oneself. From within the poet, there remains the assumption of the growth of a new forest.

In *Tala*, happiness, hope, and peace flow in songs that speak of the beauties of America, and Mistral humanizes, spiritualizes, and orders the creatures of the continent around the presence of man. She gathers all things together, animate and inanimate, nourishes them like children, and sings of them in love, wonder, thanksgiving, and happiness. Far from America, she has felt the nostal-

her country's consular service at a number of cities, including Madrid, Lisbon, Genoa, and Nice. In addition, she taught for some months in the United States, at Barnard College and at Middlebury College. She worked diligently at these jobs.

By the time she received the Nobel Prize her fame had been spread by way of the many translations of her work into other languages. The proceeds from *Tala* (felling of trees), which contains poems honoring the natural beauty of her native region in Chile, were donated to the cause of children left homeless by the Spanish Civil War.

From 1946 to 1948 the poet lived in Santa Barbara, California. Then, at the invitation of Mexican president Miguel Alemán Valdés, she lived for two years in Mexico. In the early 1950's

gia of the foreigner for home, and hopes to inspire the youth of her native soil.

Mistral sees Latin America as one great people. She employs the sun and the Andes Mountains as binding physical elements, and she calls for a similar spiritual kinship. She believes that governments should emphasize education, love, respect for manual labor, and identification with the lower classes. She declares that there is much in the indigenous past that merits inclusion in the present, and invokes pre-Columbian history with nostalgia, feeling remorse for the loss of the Indian's inheritance and his acceptance of destiny.

Maternal longing is the mainspring of Mistral's many lullabies and verses for children. The other constant, implicitly present in all the poems of *Tala*, is God. She approaches God along paths of suffering, self-discipline, and a deep understanding of the needs of her fellow people. In God, she seeks peace from her suffering, comfort in her loneliness, and perfection. Her ability to humanize all things grows from her desire to find God everywhere. Thus these objects and the wonder derived from them infuse religion into the poet's creation. Her imagery derives from the contemplation of nature and its relationship with the divine.

— *Alfred W. Jensen*

she served as the Chilean consul at Naples. She had, by a special law, become a "lifetime consul" for her native country wherever she chose to live. *Lagar* (winepress) includes some of the grief she felt after the suicides of her friends, the Austrian writer Stefan Zweig and his wife, and of her adopted son. From 1953 until her death from cancer, she lived in the United States.

— *Eric Howard*

Learn More

Arce de Vázquez, Margot. *Gabriela Mistral: The Poet and Her Work.* Translated by Helene Masslo Anderson. Ann Arbor: University of Michigan Press, 1990. Biography and critical study of Mistral's life and poetry. Includes bibliographical references.

Agosín, Marjorie, ed. *Gabriela Mistral: The Audacious Traveler.* Athens: Ohio University Press, 2003. Collection of essays examining Mistral's legacy and how her work continues to define Latin America.

Brevard, Lisa Pertillar. *Womansaints: The Saintly Portrayal of Select African-American and Latina Cultural Heroines.* New Orleans, La.: University Press of the South, 2002. Brevard analyzes the public images of Mistral, Frida Kahlo, and other women, drawing parallels between the stereotypes of Latinas and African American women.

Castleman, William J. *Beauty and the Mission of the Teacher: The Life of Gabriela Mistral of Chile, Teacher, Poetess, Friend of the Helpless, Nobel Laureate.* Smithtown, N.Y.: Exposition Press, 1982. A biography of Mistral and her life as a teacher, poet, and diplomat. Includes a bibliography of Mistral's writing.

Fiol-Matta, Licia. *A Queer Mother for the Nation: The State and Gabriel Mistral.* Minneapolis: University of Minnesota Press, 2002. Explains how Mistral became a symbol of motherhood to Latin Americans and what her image, life, and poems say about race, gender, and the sexual politics of her time.

Marchant, Elizabeth. *Critical Acts: Latin American Women and Cultural Criticism.* Gainesville: University Press of Florida, 1999. This reevaluation of Latin American women writers during the first half of the twentieth century includes a chapter about Mistral's representation of nation and motherhood. Marchant reconsiders some representative poems, focusing on the dichotomy between Mistral's theories and practices and the female intellectual's alienation from the public sphere. While Mistral refused a traditional societal role for herself, she advocated it for her readership.

Mistral, Gabriela. *This America of Ours: The Letters of Gabriela Mistral and Victoria Ocampo.* Edited and translated by Elizabeth Horan and Doris Meyer. Austin: University of Texas Press, 2003. The correspondence between Mistral and Argentine writer Ocampo provides a glimpse into their private lives and their opinions of the political and intellectual climate of their times. The appendix contains essays by the two writers.

Nicholasa Mohr

Puerto Rican
fiction writer and visual artist

Born: New York, New York; November 1, 1935

SHORT FICTION: *El Bronx Remembered: A Novella and Stories*, 1975; *In Nueva York*, 1977; *Rituals of Survival: A Woman's Portfolio*, 1985; *The Song of El Coquí, and Other Tales of Puerto Rico*, 1995; *A Matter of Pride, and Other Stories*, 1997.

LONG FICTION: *Nilda*, 1973 (juvenile); *Felita*, 1979 (juvenile); *Going Home*, 1986 (sequel to *Felita*); *All for the Better: A Story of El Barrio*, 1992; *Isabel's New Mom*, 1993; *The Magic Shell*, 1994.

NONFICTION: *Growing Up Inside the Sanctuary of My Imagination*, 1994.

RADIO PLAY: *Inside the Monster,* 1981.

TELEVISION PLAY: *Aquí y ahora*, 1975.

The daughter of Puerto Rican immigrants, Nicholasa Mohr (nih-koh-LAH-sah mohr) documents life in New York City's barrios. Mohr examines the Puerto Rican experience from the perspective of girls and young women. Her female characters face multiple social problems associated with the re-

---

"You know he went to P.R. to get a wife, don't you? Because he knew he's not gonna find nothing like that here, right? My mother says he works her to death. You know, they could use some more help with the business he's got, but. . . ." Lillian shrugged. "Poor Lali, she's a little jibarita, a hick, from the mountains, so I guess to her this is living."

—from "I Never Even Seen My Father"

WHAT TO READ

El Bronx Remembered

Nicholasa Mohr's *El Bronx Remembered* (1975) is a collection of short stories depicting life in a Puerto Rican barrio in New York City during the 1960's and 1970's, in which Mohr portrays Puerto Rican urban life by concentrating on subjects of particular importance to young adults. Her narratives do not offer a denunciation of the troubled lives of immigrants and children of immigrants. Instead, her stories bring forward voices of female characters of several age groups and social backgrounds.

Mohr writes from autobiographical memories. In her hands, the barrio is a strong presence that affects the lives of characters in myriad ways. City life and traditional Puerto Rican family values are set against each other, producing the so-called Nuyorican culture, or Puerto-Rican-in-New-York culture. The clashes within that hybrid culture are the thematic center of Mohr's short stories.

The introduction to the collection sets a strong historical context for the stories. The 1940's saw an increase in Puerto Rican migration to New York, changing the ethnic constitution of the city, especially of Manhattan's Lower East Side and the South Bronx. El Bronx, as it is called by the Puerto Ricans, became home to new generations of Puerto Rican immigrants. The center of Nuyorican culture, El Bronx challenges the Nuyorican characters in their struggle to survive in a world of rapid economic and technological changes.

The short stories in *El Bronx Remembered* speak openly about struggles with linguistic and other cultural barriers and with racist attitudes within institutions. Mohr's stories, however, attempt to go beyond social criticism. Puerto Rican characters challenge such obstacles, and although some characters succumb to tragedy because they are ill prepared to face adversity, others around them survive by learning from the plight of the weak.

— *Rafael Ocasio*

strictions imposed upon women by Latino culture. The struggle for sexual equality makes Mohr's literature central to Latina feminism.

Mohr's characters are an integral part of her realistic portrayal of life in a barrio. The parallels between her characters and her experience are evident. Nilda Ramírez, for example, is a nine-year-old Puerto Rican girl who comes of age during World War II. She also becomes an orphan and is separated from her immediate family. There are close parallels between these events and those of Mohr's life. In other stories, girls must also face social adversity, racism, and chauvinistic attitudes, and they must do so alone. Gays also frequently appear in her work. Gays and girls or young women (especially those who have little or no family) have often been subjected to mistreatment in the male-dominated Puerto Rican culture.

Mohr, a graphic artist and painter, studied at the Brooklyn Museum Art School from 1955 to 1959. Her advocacy to the social underclass is visible in her visual art, which includes elements of graffiti. Her use of graffiti in her art attracted the attention of a publisher who had acquired several of her paintings. Believing that Mohr had a story to tell, the publisher convinced her to write a short autobiographical piece on growing up Puerto Rican in New York. Many changes later, that piece became *Nilda*, her first novel, which has earned several prizes. Mohr has also drawn pictures for some of her literary work.

New York City is as important to Mohr's writing as her Puerto Rican characters. The city, with its many barrios, provides a lively background to her stories. Her short-story collections *El Bronx Remembered* and *In Nueva York* stress the characters' relationship to New York. Mohr's work can be described as cross-cultural, being a careful and artistic portrait of Puerto Rican culture in New York City.

— *Rafael Ocasio*

Learn More

Delgado, Teresa. "Prophesy Freedom: Puerto Rican Women's Literature as a Source for Latina Feminist Theology." In *A Reader in Latina Feminist Theology: Religion and Justice*, edited by María Pilar Aquino, Daisy L. Machado, and Jeanette Rodríguez. Austin: University of Texas Press, 2002. Compares the treatment of spirituality and its relationship to feminist theology in short stories by Mohr, Judith Ortiz Coffer, Esmeralda Santiago, and Rosario Ferré.

Hernandez, Carmen Dolores. *Puerto Rican Voices in English: Interviews with Writers.* Westport, Conn.: Praeger, 1997. Mohr is interviewed in this collection of interviews with Puerto Rican writers who live in the United States and write in English. The writers discuss their lives, the experience of living in both the American and Puerto Rican cultures, and their literary tradition.

Mohr, Nicholasa. "An Interview with Author Nicholasa Mohr." Interview by Nyra Zarnowski. *The Reading Teacher* 45, no. 2 (October, 1991): 106.

Rivera, Carmen S. *Kissing the Mango Tree: Puerto Rican Women Rewriting American Literature.* Houston, Tex.: Arte Público Press, 2002. One of the chapters is an analysis of Mohr's work, locating it within the framework of feminist theory and literature. Includes a bibliography of primary and secondary sources.

Sanchez-Gonzalez, Lisa. *Boricua Literature: A Literary History of the Puerto Rican Diaspora.* New York: New York University Press, 2001. Mohr is one of the writers discussed in this comprehensive survey of literature written by Puerto Ricans living in the United States.

Alejandro Morales

Mexican American
novelist and short-story writer

Born: Montebello, California; October 14, 1944

LONG FICTION: *Caras viejas y vino nuevo*, 1975 (*Old Faces and New Wine*, 1981; also known as *Barrio on the Edge*, 1998); *La verdad sin voz*, 1979 (*Death of an Anglo*, 1988); *Reto en el paraíso*, 1983; *The Brick People*, 1988; *The Rag Doll Plagues*, 1992.

Alejandro Morales (ah-lay-HAHN-droh moh-RAL-ehs) is a leading Chicano writer and professor at the University of California, Irvine (UCI). Born in Montebello, California (locally considered "East L.A."), Morales grew up in a secure and loving working-class home, though in the midst of a more turbulent barrio. Witnessing the gang fights, drug deals, homelessness, and chaos on the streets of his neighborhood while still in high school, Morales decided to become a writer who would chronicle his community. He recorded his neighborhood experiences in his journals and then set out for college, first to earn a B.A. from California State University, Los Angeles, and then an M.A. (1971) and Ph.D. (1975) in Spanish from Rutgers University. Morales became a professor in the Department of Spanish and Portuguese, with an appointment in film studies at UCI, where he teaches courses on Latin American literature. He married Rohde Teaze on December 16, 1967, and they had two children, Alessandra Pilar and Gregory Stewart.

After finishing his Ph.D., Morales pursued publication of his first novel, *Old Faces and New Wine*, which was based on his youthful journal writings. Offers from American publishing companies proved elusive because of his challenging, experimental prose style and because the journals were initially written in Spanish. His early fiction reflects Morales's anger at the exploitation of his parents, who worked in manufacturing, his despair

W H A T   T O   R E A D

The Rag Doll Plagues

The Rag Doll Plagues (1992) is a collection of stories that offer an absorbing panoramic view of the continuing encounter of European and Native American and of English- and Spanish-speaking cultures in the Americas. It is divided into three books. In book 1, Gregorio Revueltas, sent by his king to improve health conditions in seventeenth century Mexico, encounters a plague that threatens to depopulate the colony and weaken Spain's empire. Revolted by the primitive savagery and amorality of the colonials, Revueltas nevertheless grows to care for them and eventually sees himself as a Mexican. Important to this transformation is his vision of two men who often appear to guide his efforts.

In book 2, a young California doctor, Gregory Revueltas, falls in love with Sandra Spear, a hemophiliac actress. As a result of a transfusion, she develops AIDS during the first years after its identification. Seeking help, he returns with her to Old Mexico, where he and Sandra rediscover the ancient Mexican/Indian spiritual traditions that help her to think of death as a positive transformation, traditions that seem verified in Gregory's guiding visions of his ancestor, Gregorio.

Book 3 takes place at the end of the twenty-first century in Lamex, an extrapolated administrative region that comprises most of western Mexico and the southwestern United States. Gregory Revueltas, state doctor, deals with frequent plagues that erupt from centers of organic pollution that have become living entities. He discovers that Mexicans from the highly polluted Mexico City area have developed a genetic mutation that makes their blood, given in transfusion, a cure for most lung ailments. He too is led by the visionary presence of his ancestor, Gregorio. At the end of this book, Revueltas, as narrator, reflects upon the multiple ironies of Mexicans' new place in American civilization.

— *Terry Heller*

over the conditions of the barrio, and his struggles against the racism, subtle and overt, he experienced in the academic world early in his teaching career. The result is an arresting prose style; readers of Morales's early fiction have to work to make connections between events and their meanings and must also learn to comprehend the peculiar dialect he constructs to describe his subject. Often criticized by reviewers, especially for the way he bends both Spanish and English, Morales has written substantial literature that, because it is not easily accessible, has received less attention than other Mexican American literature of his generation.

Morales wrote two more novels in Spanish, but then, seeking a wider audience in the United States, he wrote *The Brick People* and *The Rag Doll Plagues* in English. The critical success of these two works has positioned Morales as a leading Chicano novelist. Since the late 1980's, he has become a noted spokesman for Chicano writers—and Chicano culture—writing reviews and essays on Mexican American literature and Latino films and conducting interviews with other Chicano writers and poets.

Besides his stylistic innovations, Morales's early publications demonstrate his interest in local history and biography. For example, his most popular novel, *The Brick People*, is based on the lives of his parents, who emigrated to California from Mexico and lived and worked at the Simmons Brick Plant in Pasadena, California. *The Brick People* chronicles the emigration to California of an entire generation of Mexican Americans at the turn of the twentieth century and describes how their labor helped build the growing metropolis of Los Angeles in the early 1930's. It narrates the Mexican laborers' exploitation by the paternalistic brick manufacturer. In interviews, public conversations, and symposia, Morales is fond of describing the Simmons brick, which graces the landscaping of his Southern California home, remarking that, like the brick, the lives and labors of Mexican Americans are embedded in the history and geography of California.

Morales's later works, such as *The Rag Doll Plagues*, evince a strong interest in science, medicine, and technology. In these works, plots revolve around technological change and the effects of science on social evolution. This turn toward science

> *Arcadia made her decision. "Abel Stearns, you are the ugliest man I have ever seen. I will marry you and I will be yours to the last moment of your life." Stearns's broken lips formed a smile. He kissed her hand and went off full of excitement to explore the Bandini estate.*
>
> —from "Cara de caballo"

and its social implications reflects Morales's interest in how history is shaped and recorded and how it thus guides the present and future. Furthermore, writing about science and technology gives Morales a metaphorical language for describing the ongoing evolution of Mexican American culture, as Mexican Americans, or Chicanos, increasingly integrate with Anglos, Asian Americans, and African Americans, especially in California. In Morales's allegorical fiction is a mixture of two compelling literary styles which reflect both his realism and his optimism. A gritty depiction of the racism, oppression, and violence that afflict the poor and minority cultures of America sits side by side on the page with fantastic or "magically real" interventions such as ghosts and the mythic powers of culture. Morales's continuing experimentation reflects his often stated devotion to developing his mastery of the craft of writing.

— *Dean Franco and Adrienne Pilon*

Learn More

Gurpegui, José Antonio, ed. *Alejandro Morales: Fiction Past, Present, Future Perfect.* Tempe, Ariz.: Bilingual Review/Press, 1996. Comprising essays on Morales's fiction, this collection includes biographical background, an interview, an essay by Morales, and family photos. Essays are in Spanish and English.

Gutiérrez-Jones, Carl. "Rancho Mexicana: USA Under Siege." In *Rethinking the Borderlands: Between Chicano Culture and Legal*

Discourse. Berkeley: University of California Press, 1995. Set in the context of a longer, theoretical analysis of the influence of the judicial system on Chicano identity, this chapter offers an analysis of the implications of both the American and the Mexican legal system in Morales's *The Brick People.*

Kaup, Monika. "From Hacienda to Brick Factory: The Architecture of the Machine and Chicano Collective Memory in Alejandro Morales's *The Brick People.*" In *U.S. Latino Literatures and Cultures: Transnational Perspectives,* edited by Francisco A. Lomelí and Karin Ikas. Heidelberg, Germany: Carl Winter Universitätsverlag, 2000. Examines the novel's treatment of industrialization and its relationship to the collective memory of Mexican Americans.

Lee, James Kyung-Jin. "Fictionalizing Workers, or The Abuse of Fiction: Violence, Reading, and the Staging of Barrio-Space in Alejandro Morales's *The Brick People.*" In *Re-Placing America: Conversations and Contestations: Selected Essays,* edited by Ruth Hsu, Cynthia Franklin, and Suzanne Kosanke. Honolulu: College of Languages, Linguistics, and Literature, University of Hawaii, with East-West Center, 2000. Analyzes the treatment of the barrio, violence, and Mexican American workers in Morales's novel.

_____. *Urban Triage: Race and the Fictions of Multiculturalism.* Minneapolis: University of Minnesota Press, 2004. Examines *The Brick People* and three other novels written in the 1980's to determine how they address the decade's racial, economic, and ethnic inequities.

Libretti, Tim. "Forgetting Identity, Recovering Politics: Rethinking Chicano/a Nationalism, Identity Politics, and Resistance to Racism in Alejandro Morales's *Death of an Anglo.*" *Post Identity* 1, no. 1 (Fall, 1997): 66-93. This article analyzes *Death of an Anglo* for its description of nationalism and identity-based community in both Chicano and Anglo culture.

Pablo Neruda

Chilean poet

Born: Parral, Chile; July 12, 1904
Died: Santiago, Chile; September 23, 1973
Also known as: Neftalí Ricardo Reyes Basoalto

POETRY: *Crepusculario*, 1923; *Veinte poemas de amor y una canción desesperada*, 1924 (*Twenty Love Poems and a Song of Despair*, 1969); *Tentativa del hombre infinito*, 1926; *El hondero entusiasta*, 1933; *Residencia en la tierra*, 1933, 1935, 1947 (3 volumes; *Residence on Earth, and Other Poems*, 1946, 1973); *España en el corazón*, 1937 (*Spain in the Heart*, 1946); *Alturas de Macchu Picchu*, 1948 (*The Heights of Macchu Picchu*, 1966); *Canto general*, 1950 (partial translation in *Let the Rail Splitter Awake, and Other Poems*, 1951; full translation as *Canto General*, 1991); *Los versos del capitán*, 1952 (*The Captain's Verses*, 1972); *Odas elementales*, 1954 (*The Elemental Odes*, 1961); *Las uvas y el viento*, 1954; *Nuevas odas elementales*, 1956; *Tercer libro de odas*, 1957; *Estravagario*, 1958 (*Extravagaria*, 1972); *Cien sonetos de amor*, 1959 (*One Hundred Love Sonnets*, 1986); *Navegaciones y regresos*, 1959; *Canción de gesta*, 1960 (*Song of Protest*, 1976); *Cantos ceremoniales*, 1961; *Las piedras de Chile*, 1961 (*The Stones of Chile*, 1986); *Plenos poderes*, 1962 (*Fully Empowered*, 1975); *Memorial de Isla Negra*, 1964 (5 volumes; *Isla Negra: A Notebook*, 1981); *Arte de pájaros*, 1966 (*Art of Birds*, 1985); *Una casa en la arena*, 1966; *La barcarola*, 1967; *Las manos del día*, 1968; *Aún*, 1969 (*Still Another Day*, 1984); *Fin de mundo*, 1969; *La espada encendida*, 1970; *Las piedras del cielo*, 1970 (*Stones of the Sky*, 1987); *Selected Poems*, 1970; *Geografía infructuosa*, 1972; *New Poems, 1968-1970*, 1972; *Incitación al Nixonicidio y alabanza de la revolución chilena*, 1973 (*Incitement to Nixonicide and Praise of the Chilean Revolution*, 1979; also known as *A Call for the Destruction of Nixon and Praise for the Chilean Revolution*, 1980); *El mar y las campanas*, 1973 (*The Sea and the Bells*, 1988); *La rosa separada,* 1973 (*The Separate Rose,* 1985); *El corazón amarillo,* 1974 (*The Yellow Heart,* 1990); *Defectos escogidos,* 1974; *Elegía,* 1974; *Pablo Neruda: Five Decades, a Selection (Poems, 1925-1970),* 1974; *2000,* 1974 (English translation, 1992); *Jardín de invierno,* 1974 (*Winter Garden,* 1986); *Libro de las preguntas,* 1974 (*The Book of Questions,* 1991); *El mal y el malo,* 1974; *El río invisible: Poesía y prosa de juventud,* 1980; *The Poetry of Pablo Neruda,* 2003 (Ilan Stavans, editor).

LONG FICTION: *El habitante y su esperanza,* 1926.

DRAMA: *Romeo y Juliet,* pb. 1964 (translation of William Shakespeare); *Fulgor y muerte de Joaquín Murieta,* pb. 1967 (*Splendor and Death of Joaquin Murieta,* 1972).

NONFICTION: *Anillos,* 1926 (with Tomás Lago); *Viajes,* 1955; *Comiendo en Hungría,* 1968; *Confieso que he vivido: Memorias,* 1974 (*Memoirs,* 1977); *Cartas de amor,* 1974 (letters); *Lo mejor de Anatole France,* 1976; *Para nacer he nacido,* 1978 (*Passions and Impressions,* 1983); *Cartas a Laura,* 1978 (letters); *Correspondencia durante "Residencia en la tierra,"* 1980 (letters; with Héctor Eandi).

Pablo Neruda (PAH-bloh nay-REW-duh) is one of the greatest South American poets of the twentieth century. He was born Neftalí Ricardo Reyes Basoalto in Parral, a small frontier town in Chile, to José del Carmen Reyes, a railway worker, and Rosa Basoalto, who died of tuberculosis shortly after Neruda's birth. The family eventually moved to Temuco, where Neruda attended school and met, at the age of twelve, the poet Gabriela Mistral, who introduced him to the great classical writers. "In this frontier—or 'far west'—of my country," Neruda later wrote, "I was born to life, land, poetry, and rain." At the age of seventeen, honoring his father's wish that he be educated for a profession, Neruda left Temuco to study French at the University of Chile in Santiago. In October, 1921, he won first prize in the Federacíon de Estudiantes poetry contest and subsequently began publishing poetry in *Claridad,* the organization's magazine. One year later, initiating a long career that united poetry and politics, Neruda abandoned his studies, declared himself a poet and political activist, and took the pen name Pablo Neruda, af-

ter the Czech writer Jan Neruda. In 1923 Neruda published his first book, *Crepusculario*, at his own expense, and the following year he published *Twenty Love Poems and a Song of Despair*, his most widely read book.

As a result of meeting the Chilean minister of external affairs, Neruda entered into a long career in his country's diplomatic service. After his first consular post in Rangoon, Burma, other Chilean diplomatic positions took him to Ceylon, Jakarta, Java, and Singapore. During his travels in the Far East, Neruda wrote most of the poems in the first volume of *Residence on Earth, and Other Poems*, a book that shows its lonely author attempting to assimilate eternal images of time and place. In 1933 he was named Chilean consul to Buenos Aires, Argentina, where he befriended the visiting Spanish poet Federico García Lorca. In 1934 Neruda was transferred to Barcelona, Spain, and later to Madrid. Still a diplomat in Spain when the Spanish Civil War began in 1936, Neruda witnessed widespread violence, the imprisonment of friends, and the execution of Lorca. "The world changed," Neruda wrote, "and my poetry has changed. One drop of blood falling on these lines will remain alive in them, indelible like love." Published during the Spanish Civil War, *Spain in the Heart* showed that Neruda had turned from purely personal themes toward political causes. His Communist sympathies led him to organize support for Spanish Republicans, and he helped find asylum in Chile for refugees of the war. After

Poetry is rebellion. The poet was not offended when he was called subversive. Life transcends all structures, and there are new rules of conduct for the soul. The seed sprouts anywhere; all ideas are exotic; we wait for enormous changes every day; we live through the mutation of human order avidly: spring is rebellious.

—from *Memoirs* (trans. W. S. Merwin)

serving in another diplomatic post in Mexico, Neruda returned to Chile, where he wrote one of his best-known epic poems, *The Heights of Macchu Picchu*. His political activity ended when the Chilean government moved to the right, forcing Neruda and other Communists into hiding. He fled the country in February, 1948, and did not return until 1952, when the Chilean govern-

WHAT TO READ

Twenty Love Poems and a Song of Despair

One year after the publication of *Crepusculario* (1923), Neruda's collection *Twenty Love Poems and a Song of Despair* (1924) appeared. It would become the most widely read collection of poems in the Spanish-speaking world. In it, Neruda charts the course of a love affair that progresses from passionate attraction to despair and indifference. In these poems, Neruda sees the whole world in terms of the beloved:

> The vastness of pine groves, the sound of
> beating wings,
> the slow interplay of lights, a solitary bell,
> the evening falling into your eyes, my darling, and
> in you
>   the earth sings.
> Love shadows and timbres your voice in the dying
> echoing
>   afternoon
> just as in those deep hours I have seen
> the field's wheat bend in the mouth of the wind.

Throughout these twenty poems, Neruda's intensity and directness of statement function to universalize his private experiences, in the process establishing another constant throughout his work: the effort to create a community of feeling through the expression of the common experiences that define the human condition.

— *Kenneth A. Stackhouse*

ment withdrew its order to arrest all leftist writers and political figures.

Always a prolific writer, Neruda completed sixteen books of poetry in the final thirteen years of his life, including *The Separate Rose* and *Winter Garden*, two of several posthumously published volumes. In 1971 he won the Nobel Prize in Literature. A poet of many themes and styles, Neruda has been referred to as the "Picasso of poetry." Although each of his volumes projects a distinct voice and persona, his work is often divided into three periods: the early period up to the time of the Spanish Civil War, characterized by the first volume of *Residence on Earth, and Other Poems*; the middle period, from the time of *Spain in the Heart* through *Canto General*, which was written during his exile and before his return to Chile in 1952; and the final, longest, and most prolific period, from 1952 until his death in 1973.

If there are consistent themes running through Neruda's opus, they are those of love and death. In his earliest work Neruda identifies woman with nature; he uses nature imagery to describe woman, yet he also sees in woman a hopeful return to nature and the eternal life cycles. Later, in the middle period of his epic political poems, Neruda shows that life, corrupted by a world in disintegration, is only redeemed through love. In his epic vision, culminating in *The Heights of Macchu Picchu*, Neruda first sees human beings as weak and transitory against the eternal verities of nature; however, as his vision unfolds, Neruda defines impermanence not as death but as the individual's isolation among the living. Thus he calls for love to transcend both the great deaths of civilizations, symbolized by the Inca ruins of Macchu Picchu, and the petty deaths each individual dies daily. In the last two decades of his life, although writing on a wide spectrum of themes in equally various styles, Neruda mainly returned to a personal expression of love. Throughout this final period Neruda expressed the wonder, play, nostalgia, and joy of passionate, romantic intimacy, what he calls "the entanglements of the genitals."

The style of Neruda's early work, especially that of the three *Residence on Earth, and Other Poems* volumes, is often compared with Walt Whitman's "Song of Myself." Yet Neruda is a Surrealist of the natural world. Fascinated with simple objects, animals, and plants, Neruda turns these into ambiguous symbols that, as translators have noted, are difficult to render in English, given that they are parts of larger patterns of association.

— *Bill Hoagland*

Learn More

Agosín, Marjorie. *Pablo Neruda.* Translated by Lorraine Roses. Boston: Twayne, 1986. A basic critical biography.

Durán, Manuel, and Margery Safir. *Earth Tones: The Poetry of Pablo Neruda.* Bloomington: Indiana University Press, 1982. An excellent critical overview of Neruda's life and work.

Feinstein, Adam. *Pablo Neruda: A Passion for Life.* New York: Bloomsbury, 2004. Comprehensive, detailed and accurate biography. Recounts Neruda's experiences as a diplomat, his political activism in Chile, his years in exile, his marriages and love life, among other subjects. Well illustrated with photographs.

Longo, Teresa, ed. *Pablo Neruda and the U.S. Culture Industry.* New York: Routledge, 2002. A collection of essays examining the process by which Neruda's poetry was translated into English and the impact of its dissemination on American and Latino culture.

Méndez-Ramírez, Hugo. *Neruda's Ekphrastic Experience: Mural Art and "Canto general."* Lewisburg, Pa.: Bucknell University Press, 1999. The book focuses on the interplay between verbal and visual elements in Neruda's masterpiece *Canto general.* It demonstrates how mural art, especially that practiced in Mexico, became the source for Neruda's ekphrastic desire, in which his verbal art paints visual elements.

Nolan, James. *Poet-Chief: The Native American Poetics of Walt Whitman and Pablo Neruda.* Albuquerque: University of New Mexico Press, 1994. A comparative study of Whitman and Neruda, and how they were influenced by the theme of Native American culture and the practice of oral poetry.

Sayers Pedén, Margaret. Introduction to *Selected Odes of Pablo Neruda,* by Pablo Neruda. Translated by Sayers Pedén. Berkeley: University of California Press, 2000. Sayers Pedén is among the most highly regarded translators of Latin American poetry. Her introduction to the translations in this bilingual edition constitutes an excellent critical study as well as providing biographical and bibliographical information.

Teitelboim, Volodia. *Neruda: A Personal Biography.* Translated by Beverly J. DeLong-Tonelli. Austin: University of Texas Press, 1991. A biography written by a close friend and fellow political exile.

Urrutia, Matilde. *My Life with Pablo Neruda.* Translated by Alexandria Giardino. Stanford, Calif.: Stanford General Books, 2004. Urrutia, Neruda's muse and widow, recalls her life with the poet.

Juan Carlos Onetti

Uruguayan
novelist and short-story writer

Born: Montevideo, Uruguay; July 1, 1909
Died: Madrid, Spain; May 30, 1994

LONG FICTION: *El pozo*, 1939, 1965 (*The Pit*, 1991); *Tierra de nadie*, 1941 (*No Man's Land*, 1994; also known as *Tonight*, 1991); *Para esta noche*, 1943; *La vida breve*, 1950 (*A Brief Life*, 1976); *Los adioses*, 1954 (novella; *Goodbyes*, 1990); *Una tumba sin nombre*, 1959 (novella; better known as *Para una tumba sin nombre*; *A Grave with No Name*, 1992); *La cara de la desgracia*, 1960 (novella; *The Image of Misfortune*, 1990); *El astillero*, 1961 (*The Shipyard*, 1968); *Tan triste como ella*, 1963 (novella); *Juntacadáveres*, 1964 (*Body Snatcher*, 1991); *La muerte y la niña*, 1973; *Dejemos hablar al viento*, 1979 (*Let the Wind Speak*, 1997); *Cuando ya no importe*, 1993 (*Past Caring?*, 1995).

SHORT FICTION: *Un sueño realizado, y otros cuentos*, 1951; *El infierno tan temido*, 1962; *Jacob y el otro: Un sueño realizado, y otros cuentos*, 1965; *Cuentos completos*, 1967, revised 1974; *La novia robada, y otros cuentos*, 1968; *Cuentos*, 1971; *Tiempo de abrazar*, 1974 (short stories and fragments of unpublished novels); *Tan triste como ella, y otros cuentos*, 1976; *Goodbyes, and Other Stories*, 1990.

NONFICTION: *Réquiem por Faulkner, y otros escritos*, 1975; *Confesiones de un lector*, 1995.

MISCELLANEOUS: *Obras completas*, 1970; *Onetti*, 1974 (articles, interview).

Juan Carlos Onetti (hwahn KAHR-lohs oh-NEHT-tee) was born in Montevideo, Uruguay, in 1909, the second of three children. He grew up in a stable, middle-class family, and he remembered his childhood as a happy one. His father, Carlos Onetti, was a customs official, and his mother, Borges de Onetti, was a descendant of wealthy Brazilian landowners. In 1930, he married his cousin, María Amalia Onetti, and left for Buenos Aires, Argentina. His first job in Buenos Aires was that of a salesman for a firm selling calculators. In 1933, he published his first short story, "Avenida de Mayo-Diagonal-Avenida de Mayo" ("May Avenue-Diagonal-May Avenue") in *La Prensa* of Buenos Aires. While he was making some headway in his literary career, however, his personal life was not going well. After the breakup of his first marriage, he returned to Montevideo. He remarried; his second wife was María Julia Onetti, the sister of his first wife.

In 1939 he helped to found and became chief editor of *Marcha*, which went on to become one of the most prestigious cultural weeklies in Latin America. Under the enlightened direction of luminaries such as Emir Rodríguez Monegal, Ángel Rama, and Jorge Ruffinelli, its cultural section established Uruguay as a cultural center in the Third World. In December, 1939, Onetti published *The Pit*. This novella constituted a break with the previous conventions of the genre. It is narrated by a middle-aged man who is disillusioned with life. He lives in squalor and loneliness, separated from his wife, and his isolation is made all the worse by his sense that his country, Uruguay, lacks a cultural tradition able to sustain the individual spiritually. The novel offers a jaundiced view of the fragmentation of life in a modern urban environment; it may well be seen as a projection of Onetti's own experience of city life.

> *Equally far—now that they call him Robert and he gets drunk on anything, shielding his mouth with a dirty hand when he coughs—from the Bob who drank beer, never more than two glasses during the longest of evenings, a pile of ten-piece coins on his table in the club's bar to spend in the juke box.*
>
> —from "Welcome, Bob"

Vincenzo Flore

In 1941, Onetti moved back to Buenos Aires (where he was to remain until 1954) and began working for the British news agency Reuters. He subsequently went on to become editor of various periodicals. In 1941, his novel *No Man's Land* was published by the prestigious publishing house Losada of Buenos Aires. Like his previous work, this novel focuses on the disjointed, and ultimately aimless, lives of people struggling to find some dignity for themselves in a hostile urban environment.

Onetti's second marriage also ended, and in 1945, he was married for the third time, to Elizabeth María Pekelhering. In 1950, he published his masterpiece, *A Brief Life*, which won him international fame. Like most of his fiction, it expresses in poignant fashion the spiritual anguish of life in the modern city. The following year, his wife gave birth to a daughter, Isabel María. In 1954, Onetti's novella *Goodbyes* appeared; the following year, he returned to Montevideo to live. There, he worked for a publicity firm and later for the periodical *Acción*. In 1957, largely as a result of his literary success, he was elected director of the municipal library system in Montevideo. In the same year, he became a member of the board of directors of the Comedia Nacional.

In 1961, he published *The Shipyard*, which offers a grim view of life in midcentury Uruguay. The narrator is Larsen, who had appeared in *No Man's Land*; Larsen describes his desperate attempts to breathe new commercial life into a shipyard. Yet there are no ships, no work, and no orders. As the novel progresses, it becomes clear that the shipyard symbolizes the futility of humanity's attempt to make sense of life.

In 1963, Onetti was awarded the Premio National de Literature, Uruguay's national literary prize. In the same year, *The Shipyard* was distinguished by receiving the William Faulkner Foundation Certificate of Merit. His novel *Body Snatcher* was published in 1964 and three years later was runner-up in competition for the prestigious Rómulo Gallegos Prize, which is given every five years to the best novel written in Spanish. Like *The Shipyard*, it is set in the imaginary city of Santa María and features the same character, Larsen. It focuses on the plan entertained by a number of the residents to establish a brothel in Santa María; the project eventually ends in failure as a result of the opposition of a number of women. More important than the plot itself is the opportunity it provides for the narrative voice to provide a violently satiric vision of the sordidness of people's lives. In 1968 a translation of *The Shipyard* was published in New York and brought Onetti's work a great deal of international recognition. In 1970 an edition of his complete works was published, although his career as a novelist was by no means over.

In 1974 Onetti was involved in a literary scandal, made all the more painful since he was by then a public figure on the Uruguayan literary scene. Uruguay had been witness to an alarming growth of political radicalization in the late 1960's and 1970's; the terrorist organization Tupamaros, named after the sixteenth century Indian leader Túpac Amaru, had been involved

---

W H A T   T O   R E A D

"Welcome, Bob"

In this early Onetti story, popular with anthologists, a middle-aged narrator gets sadistic pleasure from observing the aging of Bob; it is his revenge for Bob's preventing his marriage several years earlier to his sister Inez, because he was too old for her. At that time Bob told the narrator that he was a finished man, washed up, "like all men your age when they're not extraordinary." Bob tells the narrator that the most repulsive thing about old age, the very symbol of decomposition, is to think in terms of concepts formed by second-rate experiences. For the old, Bob says, there are no longer experiences at all, only habits and repetitions, "wilted names to go on tagging things with and half make them up."

After the sister rejects the narrator and Bob grows older, the narrator begins a friendship with him so that he can more closely watch Bob's aging process. He delights in thinking of the young Bob who thought he owned the future and the world as he watches the man now called Robert, with tobacco-stained fingers, working in a stinking office, married to a fleshy woman. "No one has ever loved a woman as passionately as I love his ruin," says the narrator, delighting in the hopeless manner in which Bob has sunk into his filthy life. The story ends with the narrator's final sad and ironic triumph: "I don't know if I ever welcomed Inez in the past with such joy and love as I daily welcome Bob into the shadowy and stinking world of adults."

— *Charles E. May*

---

in a bitter and ruthless war with the state. In 1973 the military toppled the civilian government, which had by then been discredited, and seized power. *Marcha*, which had been founded by Onetti many years before and had been a forceful independent cultural voice of Uruguay for more than thirty years, was closed down by the military establishment in 1974. Journal archives were burned, historical research was prohibited, and many of the country's works of literature, as well as works by contemporary European and U.S. writers, were banned from library bookshelves. These were shocking events, especially in a country that had prided itself on being the "Switzerland of Latin America."

Onetti, understandably, became embroiled in these events. In 1974 when the military repressiveness was at its height, a literary prize was awarded to a work that was critical of the military regime, and Onetti was unlucky enough to be one of the judges who voted for the award to be made. He was imprisoned as a result; however, because of his poor health and the public and international outcry that followed the decision to imprison him, he was released. In 1975 *The Shipyard* was awarded Italy's prize for best foreign work translated into Italian that year. Onetti, who had been under increasing pressure from the military authorities, was refused leave to attend the awards ceremony. At this point Onetti felt that he had no choice but to leave his native country. He resigned his library post and traveled to Europe. He subsequently took up residence in Madrid with his wife, and he remained in self-imposed exile until his death; he eventually became a Spanish citizen. Onetti was awarded the Cervantes Prize, Spain's most prestigious literary honor, in 1980. He died in Madrid in the spring of 1994.

— *Stephen M. Hart*

Learn More

Adams, M. Ian. *Three Authors of Alienation: Bombal, Onetti, Carpentier.* Austin: University of Texas Press, 1975. Includes an extended discussion of Onetti's novella *The Pit*, showing how Onetti's artistic manipulation of schizophrenia creates a sensation of participating in an alienated world.

Clark, Draper. "Juan Carlos Onetti (1909-1994): An Existential Allegory of Contemporary Man." In *Twayne Companion to Contemporary World Literature: From the Editors of World Literature Today,* edited by Pamela A. Genova. New York: Twayne/Thomson Gale, 2003. Analyzes the treatment of the individual and solitude in Onetti's novels.

Kadir, Djelal. *Juan Carlos Onetti.* Boston: Twayne, 1977. Offers one of the best introductions in English to Onetti's life and work, with separate chapters on the main phases of Onetti's life.

Maloof, Judy. *Over Her Dead Body: The Construction of Male Subjectivity in Onetti.* New York: P. Lang, 1995. Focuses on gender relations in Onetti's work.

Millington, Mark. *An Analysis of the Short Stories of Juan Carlos Onetti: Fictions of Desire.* Lewiston, N.Y.: Edwin Mellen Press, 1993. Looks at Onetti's short stories from a largely psychological perspective.

_____. *Reading Onetti: Language, Narrative and the Subject.* Liverpool, England: Francis Cairns, 1985. Discusses the development of Onetti's work under the "hegemony of international modernism." Drawing on stylistics, the structure of the narrative, and post-structuralism, Millington focuses on the status of Onetti's fiction as narrative discourse. Discusses how *Goodbyes* makes the art of reading problematic.

Murray, Jack. *The Landscapes of Alienation: Ideological Subversion in Kafka, Céline, and Onetti.* Stanford, Calif.: Stanford University Press, 1991. In his discussion of alienation in Onetti's fiction, Murray provides some background about how Uruguay has affected Onetti's ideological unconscious.

San Román, Gustavo, ed. *Onetti and Others: Comparative Essays on a Major Figure in Latin American Literature.* Albany: State University of New York Press, 1999. A collection of twelve essays written from a variety of perspectives. Several focus on gender relationships in Onetti's work; comparative studies relating Onetti to other Latin American writers also are prominent.

Judith Ortiz Cofer

Puerto Rican poet, short-story writer, and memoirist

Born: Hormigueros, Puerto Rico; February 24, 1952
Also known as: Judith Ortiz

LONG FICTION: *The Line of the Sun*, 1989; *The Meaning of Consuelo*, 2003.

SHORT FICTION: *Latin Women Pray*, 1980; *The Native Dancer*, 1981; *Among the Ancestors*, 1981; *An Island Like You: Stories of the Barrio*, 1995.

DRAMA: *Latin Women Pray*, pr. 1984.

POETRY: *Peregrina*, 1986; *Reaching for the Mainland*, 1987; *Terms of Survival*, 1987; *Reaching for the Mainland, and Selected New Poems*, 1995.

NONFICTION: *Silent Dancing: A Partial Remembrance of a Puerto Rican Childhood*, 1990; *Woman in Front of the Sun: On Becoming a Writer*, 2000.

EDITED TEXTS: *Letters from a Caribbean Island*, 1989; *Sleeping with One Eye Open: Women Writers and the Art of Survival*, 1999 (with Marilyn Kallet); *Riding Low on the Streets of Gold: Latino Literature for Young Adults*, 2003.

CHILDREN'S LITERATURE: *Call Me Maria*, 2004.

MISCELLANEOUS: *The Latin Deli: Prose and Poetry*, 1993; *The Year of Our Revolution: New and Selected Stories and Poems*, 1998.

Born in Hormigueros, near Mayagüez in southwest Puerto Rico, Judith Ortiz Cofer (JEW-dihth ohr-TEEZ KOH-fuhr) spent part of every year in Paterson, New Jersey, as she was growing up. Her father, Jesús Ortiz Lugo, who served in the U.S. Navy, was assigned to the Brooklyn Navy Yard during many of his service years. Although Ortiz's mother, Fanny Morot Ortiz, saw to it that the family spent part of every year in Puerto Rico, they lived for long periods in Paterson, which became the setting of a

> *My father was a quiet, serious man; my mother,*
> *earthy and ebullient. Their marriage, like my*
> *childhood, was the combining of two worlds, the*
> *mixing of two elements—fire and ice. This was*
> *sometimes exciting and life-giving and sometimes*
> *painful and draining.*
>
> —from "The Black Virgin"

great many of Ortiz's stories. Some of these stories center on El Building, as their apartment house was called when the Jewish tenants left and large numbers of Puerto Ricans moved in. Ortiz Cofer calls El Building a vertical barrio.

The young Judith Ortiz attended school in Puerto Rico, where she went to San José Catholic School in San Germán, and in New Jersey, where she attended public schools and later St. Joseph's Catholic School in Paterson. When she was sixteen, her father suffered a nervous breakdown and was forced to retire from the Navy. The family moved to Augusta, Georgia, where Judith completed high school and enrolled in Augusta College, from which she graduated in 1974. She received a master's degree from Florida Atlantic University in 1977 and that year also studied at Oxford University.

Her first book, a reflective collection of stories entitled *Latin Women Pray*, appeared in 1980. Ortiz Cofer turned this collection into a play, which was produced in Atlanta in 1984. In 1981, Ortiz Cofer received a fellowship from the Bread Loaf Writers' Conference in Vermont, where she subsequently served on the administrative staff during the summers of 1983 and 1984. During that time she published *The Native Dancer* and *Among the Ancestors*, and these works, as well as the poetry collection *Reaching for the Mainland*, appear to be a direct outcome of the Bread Loaf experience. Ortiz married Charles John Cofer during her sophomore year in college, and she taught bilingually from the time of her graduation until she completed the master's degree.

John Cofer

She thereupon taught English in various Florida colleges until 1984, when she joined the faculty of the University of Georgia at Athens, where she was appointed to teach creative writing.

Ortiz Cofer's first volume of poetry, *Reaching for the Mainland*, which she later revised and expanded, focuses on the conflicts inherent in Puerto Ricans' struggle to adapt to the mainland environment and to master the language, the history, and the customs of a new society. In *Terms of Survival* she explores some of the same problems but also hones in on the Puerto Rican dialect, emphasizing its ability to dictate the roles that males and females play in society simply through its linguistic conventions. The book is psychologically challenging and thought-provoking.

W H A T   T O   R E A D

Silent Dancing

Silent Dancing: A Partial Remembrance of a Puerto Rican Childhood (1990) is Judith Ortiz Cofer's collection of fourteen essays and accompanying poems looking back on her childhood and adolescence in Hormigueros, Puerto Rico, and Paterson, New Jersey. Her father joined the Navy before she was born, and two years later he moved them to Paterson, where he was stationed. When he went to sea for months at a time, he sent his wife and children back to Puerto Rico until he returned to New Jersey.

While her father urged the family to assimilate in America and even moved them outside the Puerto Rican neighborhoods in New Jersey, her mother remained loyal to the island, and her quiet sadness emerges throughout the book. The central theme in the book is the traditional Puerto Rican "script of our lives," which confines "everyone [to] their places." The narrator struggles with her family's expectations for her to become a traditional Puerto Rican woman: domestic, married, and fertile. This script allows little room for individual identity, so the

The Line of the Sun, Ortiz Cofer's first full-fledged novel, which is set both in Salud, Puerto Rico, and in Paterson, is concerned with immigration and with the problems of adjusting to a new society. This theme also pervades *Silent Dancing: A Partial Remembrance of a Puerto Rican Childhood,* a collection of autobiographical essays, many of which focus on the dynamics of the vertical barrio in which Ortiz Cofer spent major portions of her childhood years.

The Latin Deli, a collection of short prose pieces and poems, captures well the outlook of transplanted Puerto Ricans, most of whom harbor the dream of working on the mainland to assure their financial security but then returning to "The Island" to live out the rest of their lives. The principals in this book cling to

maturing narrator focuses on those characters who rewrite the script and extemporize their own lives ("Some of the Characters").

The embodiment of Puerto Rican tradition is Mamá, the grandmother who ironically gives Ortiz Cofer the tools that enable her to redefine her own role. In "More Room," for instance, Ortiz Cofer tells the story about Mamá expelling her husband from her bedroom to avoid giving birth to even more children, thus liberating herself to enjoy her children, her grandchildren, and her own life. Similarly, "Tales Told Under the Mango Tree" portrays Mamá's queenly role as the matriarchal storyteller surrounded by the young women and girls of the family as she passes on *cuentos* (stories) about being a Puerto Rican woman, such as the legend of the wise and courageous María Sabida who is not controlled by love and is "never a victim."

Silent Dancing is ultimately a *Künstlerroman,* the story of an artist's apprenticeship. Ortiz Cofer has revised the script for her life as a Puerto Rican woman by inheriting Mamá's role as storyteller; she redefines what it means to be a Puerto Rican woman and tells her stories to a wider audience.

— *Nancy L. Chick*

their old ways; the women, for example, cook the green plantains they buy at inflated prices in the neighborhood *bodegas,* where they also purchase the overpriced Bustelo coffee without which their afternoon coffee klatches would lack authenticity.

In this collection, especially in the story entitled "Not for Sale," Ortiz Cofer focuses on the clash of cultures. Ortiz Cofer broaches the conflict between Puerto Ricans and African Americans in the story "The Paterson Public Library," in which Lorraine, a black bully, intimidates the story's Puerto Rican protagonist for purely racial reasons.

— *R. Baird Shuman*

Learn More

Hernandez, Carmen Dolores. *Puerto Rican Voices in English: Interviews with Writers.* Westport, Conn.: Praeger, 1997. Ortiz Cofer is interviewed in this collection of interviews with Puerto Rican writers who live in the United States and write in English. The writers discuss their lives, the experience of living in both the American and Puerto Rican cultures, and their literary tradition.

Kanellos, Nicolas, ed. *The Hispanic American Almanac: A Reference Work on Hispanics in the United States.* 3d ed. Detroit: Gale Group, 1993. Includes a brief but useful sketch of the writer and her work.

Mujcinovic, Fatima. *Postmodern Cross-culturalism and Politicization in U.S. Latina Literature: From Ana Castillo to Julia Alverez.* Modern American Literature 42. New York: P. Lang, 2004. A literary and cultural analysis of the work of Mexican American, Puerto Rican, Cuban American, and Dominican American women writers, including Ortiz Cofer. Mujcinovic views these writers' work from a contemporary feminist, political, postcolonial, and psychoanalytical perspective.

Ortiz Cofer, Judith. "Judith Ortiz Cofer." http://www.english .uga.edu/~~jcofer/. Accessed March 22, 2005. This Web site contains a curriculum vitae and links to articles, interviews, and Web sites about the author.

_____. *Women in Front of the Sun: On Becoming a Writer.* Athens: University of Georgia Press, 2000. In this collection of poems and essays, Ortiz Cofer expresses her love of language, explains how she became a writer, and discusses the challenges of living between two cultures and meeting the demands of family and career.

Rivera, Carmen S. *Kissing the Mango Tree: Puerto Rican Women Rewriting American Literature.* Houston, Tex.: Arte Público Press, 2002. One of the chapters is an analysis of Ortiz Cofer's work, locating it within the framework of feminist theory and literature. Includes a bibliography of primary and secondary sources.

Sanchez-Gonzalez, Lisa. *Boricua Literature: A Literary History of the Puerto Rican Diaspora.* New York: New York University Press, 2001. Ortiz Cofer's novel *The Line of the Sun* is analyzed in this comprehensive survey of literature written by Puerto Ricans who live in the United States.

Nicanor Parra

Chilean poet

Born: Chillán, Chile; September 5, 1914

POETRY: *Cancionero sin nombre*, 1937; *Poemas y antipoemas*, 1954 (*Poems and Antipoems*, 1967); *La cueca larga*, 1958; *Versos de salón*, 1962; *Canciones rusas*, 1967; *Obra gruesa*, 1969; *Los profesores*, 1971; *Emergency Poems*, 1972; *Artefactos*, 1972; *Antipoems: New and Selected*, 1985; *Nicanor Parra: Biografía emotiva*, 1988; *Poemas para combatir la calvicie: Muestra de antipoesia*, 1993.

NONFICTION: *Pablo Neruda y Nicanor Parra: Discursos*, 1962; *Discursos de sobremesa*, 1997; *Pablo Neruda and Nicanor Parra Face to Face*, 1997.

N icanor Parra (NEE-kah-nohr PAH-rah) is the originator of the contemporary poetic movement in Latin America known as "antipoetry." The prefix notwithstanding, antipoetry, however unconventional, is poetry, and Parra himself willingly explains his concept of the form. It is, he says, traditional poetry enriched by Surrealism. As the word implies, the "antipoem" belongs to that tradition which rejects the established poetic order. In this case, it rebels against the sentimental idealism of Romanticism, the elegance and the superficiality of the *Modernistas*, and the irrationality of the vanguard movement. It is not a poetry of

---

A young man of scanty means doesn't know what's going on
He lives in a bell jar called Art
Or Lust or Science
Trying to make contact with a world of relationships
That only exist for him and a small group of friends.

—from "The Tunnel" (trans. W. S. Merwin)

Courtesy of New Directions

heroes, but of antiheroes, because man has nothing to sing to or celebrate. The antipoet, as this Chilean calls himself, is the absolute antiromantic, debasing all, even himself, while producing verses that are aggressive, wounding, sarcastic, and irritating.

One of eight children in a family plagued by economic insecurity, Parra, grew up in Chillán, in the south of Chile. His father was a schoolteacher whose irresponsibility and alcoholism placed considerable strain on the life and order of the family, which was held together by Parra's mother. Parra was in his early teens when his father died. The earlier antipathy he felt toward his father then turned toward his mother, and he left home. He began a process of identification with his father, toward whom he felt both attraction and repulsion, and to whom he attributes the basic elements of his inspiration for antipoetry.

During his youth, Parra composed occasional verses, so that when he went to the University of Chile in Santiago in 1933 he felt that he was a poet in addition to being a student of physics. He associated with the literary leaders at the student residence where he lived, and a year prior to being graduated in 1938, he had published his first volume of poetry, *Cancionero sin nombre.*

After completing studies in mathematics and physics at the Pedagogical Institute of the University, Parra taught for five years in secondary schools in Chile. Between 1943 and 1945, he

W H A T   T O   R E A D

La Cueca Larga and *Versos de salón*

Parra's third collection, *La cueca larga* (1958; the long *cueca*—the *cueca* is a native dance of Chile), exalts wine; written in the popular tradition of marginal literature, the book is an anti-intellectual contribution to Chilean folklore. It is similar to antipoetry—the style that Parra developed to reject sentiment in favor of creating an experience that stressed life's hopelessness and man's fallen condition—in its preference for the masses and its position on the periphery of established literature.

In *Versos de salón* (1962; salon verses), Parra returned to the antipoetic technique, but with some significant differences. The ironic attack on the establishments of society remains, but these poems are shorter than the earlier ones. They are fragments whose images follow one another in rapid fashion and mirror the absurd chaos of the world. The reader, forced to experience this confusion at first hand, is left restless, searching for a meaning that is not to be found. The chaotic enumeration of the Surrealists, a favorite technique with Parra, abounds, while the anecdotal poetry of *Poems and Antipoems* (1954), with its emphasis on dialogue, all but disappears. The sense of alienation is sharper, the bitterness and disillusion more deeply felt, the humor more pointed. The antihero changes from a victim into an odd creature who flings himself at the world in open confrontation. His introverted suffering is now a metaphysical despair.

— *Alfred W. Jensen*

studied advanced mechanics at Brown University in the United States. Returning home in 1948, he was named Director of the School of Engineering at the University of Chile. He spent two years in England studying cosmology at Oxford, and upon his return to South America he was appointed Professor of Theoretical Physics at the University of Chile.

The publication of Parra's second collection of poetry, *Poems and Antipoems,* formally introduced the antipoetry with which his name is associated. This new poetry shook the foundation of the theory of the genre in Latin America, winning for its author both condemnation and praise. In 1963, Parra visited the Soviet Union, where he supervised the translation into Spanish of an anthology of Soviet poets, and then traveled to the People's Republic of China. He visited Cuba in 1965 and the following year served as a visiting professor at Louisiana State University, later holding similar positions at New York University, Columbia, and Yale.

Parra has plowed new terrain in Latin American poetry using a store of methods which traditional poetry rejects or ignores. Nevertheless, his work has been attacked as boring, disturbing, crude, despairing, ignoble, inconclusive, petulant, and devoid of lyricism. The antipoet generally agrees with these points of criticism but begs the reader to lay aside what amounts to a nostalgic defense of worn-out traditions and join him in a new experience. Parra has established himself firmly in a prominent position in Latin American literature, influencing both his defenders and detractors.

— *Alfred W. Jensen*

Learn More

Carrasco, Iván. *Para leer a Nicanor Parra.* Santiago, Chile: Editorial Cuarto Propio, 1999. An insightful analysis of the perception of Parra's work as antipoetry. An expert on Parra's work analyzes the evolution of his poetry from its rejection of thematic and syntactic structures to the development of a unique yet mutable voice that responds to its social and political environment. In Spanish.

Grossman, Edith. *The Antipoetry of Nicanor Parra.* New York: New York University Press, 1975. One of the few books about

Parra that is written in English. Grossman analyzes Parra's poetic style and technique.

Neruda, Pablo. *Pablo Neruda and Nicanor Parra Face to Face.* Lewiston, N.Y.: Edwin Mellen Press, 1997. This is a bilingual and critical edition of speeches by both Neruda and Parra on the occasion of Neruda's appointment to the University of Chile's faculty, with English translations and a useful introduction by Marlene Gottlieb. Bibliographical references.

Parra, Nicanor. *Antipoems: How to Look Better and Feel Good.* Antitranslation by Liz Werner. New York: New Directions Books, 2004. Collection of fifty-eight poems, thirty-three of which have never before been published. The poems illustrate Parra's mocking humor and his ability to subvert conventions and pretentions in poetry and life. Werner, the "antitranslator" (Parra's word) of these poems, analyzes Parra's work in an introductory essay.

————. *Antipoems: New and Selected.* Translated by Frank MacShane, and edited by David Unger. New York: New Directions, 1985. This bilingual anthology focuses on representative antipoems in an attempt to demonstrate how Parra's poetry has revolutionized poetic expression globally as well as within the sphere of Latin American poetry. Notes by the editor enhance understanding for English-speaking readers.

Parrilla Sotomayor, Eduardo E. *Humorismo y sátira en la poesía de Nicanor Parra.* Madrid: Editorial Pliegos, 1997. This study identifies and discusses the elements of humor and satire in Parra's antipoetry. It analyzes the poet's technique as well as unique antirhetorical style and language that creates a direct link to contemporary Latin American society. In Spanish.

Sarabia, Rosa. *Poetas de la palabra hablada: Un estudio de la poesía hispanoaméricana contemporánea.* London: Tamesis, 1997. This study analyzes the oral nature of the literary production of several representative contemporary Latin American writers with roots in oral literature. In her chapter titled "Nicanor Parra: La antipoesía y sus políticas," the author explores the origins and consequences of antipoetry in its political and social milieus in contemporary Latin America. In Spanish.

Octavio Paz

Mexican poet and essayist

Born: Mexico City, Mexico; March 31, 1914
Died: Mexico City, Mexico; April 19, 1998

POETRY: *Luna silvestre*, 1933; *Bajo tu clara sombra, y otros poemas sobre España*, 1937; *Raíz del hombre*, 1937; *Entre la piedra y la flor*, 1941; *Libertad bajo palabra*, 1949, 1960; *Águila o sol?*, 1951 (*Eagle or Sun?*, 1970); *Semillas para un himno*, 1954; *Piedra de sol*, 1957 (*Sun Stone*, 1963); *La estación violenta*, 1958; *Agua y viento*, 1959; *Libertad bajo palabra: Obra poética, 1935-1957*, 1960, revised 1968; *Salamandra*, 1962; *Selected Poems*, 1963; *Blanco*, 1967 (English translation, 1971); *Discos visuales*, 1968; *Topoemas*, 1968; *La centena*, 1969; *Ladera este*, 1969; *Configurations*, 1971; *Renga*, 1972 (in collaboration with three other poets; *Renga: A Chain of Poems*, 1972); *Early Poems, 1935-1955*, 1973; *Pasado en claro*, 1975 (*A Draft of Shadows, and Other Poems*, 1979); *Vuelta*, 1976; *Poemas*, 1979; *Selected Poems*, 1979; *Airborn = Hijos del Aire*, 1981 (with Charles Tomlinson); *The Collected Poems of Octavio Paz: 1957-1987*, 1987; *Arbol adentro*, 1987 (*A Tree Within*, 1988); *Obra poetica (1935-1988)*, 1990; *Stanzas for an Imaginary Garden*, 1990 (limited edition); *Viento, agua, piedra/Wind, Water, Stone*, 1990 (limited edition); *A Tale of Two Gardens: Poems from India, 1952-1995*, 1997; "Snapshots," 1997; *Figuras y figuraciones*, 1999 (*Figures and Figurations*, 2002).

DRAMA: *La hija de Rappaccini*, pb. 1990 (dramatization of a Nathaniel Hawthorne story; *Rappacini's Daughter*, 1996).

NONFICTION: *Voces de España*, 1938; *Laurel*, 1941; *El laberinto de la soledad: Vida y pensamiento de México*, 1950, revised and enlarged 1959 (*The Labyrinth of Solitude: Life and Thought in Mexico*, 1961); *El arco y la lira*, 1956 (*The Bow and the Lyre*, 1971); *Las peras del olmo*, 1957; *Rufino Tamayo*, 1959 (*Rufino Tamayo: Myth and Magic*, 1979); *Magia de la risa*, 1962; *Cuatro poetas contemporáneos de Suecia*, 1963; *Cuadrivio*, 1965; *Poesia en movimiento*, 1966; *Puertas al campo*, 1966; *Remedios Varo*, 1966; *Claude Lévi-Strauss: O, El nuevo festín de Esopo*, 1967 (*Claude Lévi-Strauss: An Introduction*, 1970); *Corriento alterna*, 1967 (*Alternating Current*, 1973); *Marcel Duchamp*, 1968 (*Marcel Duchamp: Or, The Castle of Purity*, 1970); *Conjunciones y disyunciones*, 1969 (*Conjunctions and Disjunctions*, 1974); *México: La última década*, 1969; *Posdata*, 1970 (*The Other Mexico: Critique of the Pyramid*, 1972); *Las cosas en su sitio*, 1971; *Los signos en rotación y otros ensayos*, 1971; *Traducción: Literatura y literalidad*, 1971; *Apariencia desnuda: La obra de Marcel Duchamp*, 1973 (*Marcel Duchamp: Appearance Stripped Bare*, 1978); *El signo y el garabato*, 1973; *Solo a dos voces*, 1973; *La búsqueda del comienzo*, 1974; *Los hijos del limo: Del romanticismo a la vanguardia*, 1974 (*Children of the Mire: Modern Poetry from Romanticism to the Avant-Garde*, 1974); *El mono gramático*, 1974 (*The Monkey Grammarian*, 1981); *Teatro de signos/transparencias*, 1974; *Versiones y diversiones*, 1974; *The Siren and the Seashell, and Other Essays on Poets and Poetry*, 1976; *Xavier Villaurrutia en persona y en obra*, 1978; *In/mediaciones*, 1979; *México en la obra de Octavio Paz*, 1979, expanded 1987; *El ogro filantrópico: Historia y politica 1971-1978*, 1979 (*The Philanthropic Ogre*, 1985); *Sor Juana Inés de la Cruz: O, Las trampas de la fé*, 1982 (*Sor Juana: Or, The Traps of Faith*, 1989); *Sombras de obras: Arte y literatura*, 1983; *Tiempo nublado*, 1983 (*One Earth, Four or Five Worlds: Reflections on Contemporary History*, 1985); *Hombres en su siglo y otros ensayos*, 1984; *On Poets and Others*, 1986; *Convergences: Essays on Art and Literature*, 1987; *Primeras letras, 1931-1943*, 1988 (Enrico Mario Santi, editor); *Poesía, mito, revolución*, 1989; *La búscueda del presente/In Search of the Present: Nobel Lecture, 1990*, 1990; *La otra voz: Poesía y fin de siglo*, 1990 (*The Other Voice: Essays on Modern Poetry*, 1991); *Pequeña crónica de grandes días*, 1990; *Convergencias*, 1991; *Al paso*, 1992; *One Word to the Other*, 1992; *Essays on Mexican Art*, 1993; *Itinerario*, 1993 (*Itinerary: An Intellectual Journey*, 1999); *La llama doble: Amor y erotismo*, 1993 (*The Double Flame: Love and Eroticism*, 1995); *Un más allá erótico: Sade*, 1993 (*An Erotic Beyond: Sade*, 1998); *Vislumbres de la India*, 1995 (*In Light of India*, 1997).

EDITED TEXTS: *Antología poética,* 1956 (*Anthology of Mexican Poetry,* 1958; Samuel Beckett, trans.); *New Poetry of Mexico,* 1970.

MISCELLANEOUS: *Lo mejor de Octavio Paz: El fuego de cada día,* 1989; *Obras completas de Octavio Paz,* 1994; *Blanco,* 1995 (facsimiles of manuscript fragments and letters).

No Mexican writer did more to explore and celebrate the mysteries of Mexican life than poet and essayist Octavio Paz (ahk-TAH-vyoh pahz), considered to be the leading twentieth century interpreter of his country's complex civilization. Paz's poems explore life's illusions and fragmented realities, the problem of language, the innocent individual, humankind's loss of connection with nature and its rhythms, and the disordered, dislocated modern world. Known primarily as a poet, Paz also distinguished himself as a diplomat and essayist, delving into such areas as religion, philosophy, and politics in the course of his work.

Born into a family of intellectuals in Mexico City, Paz inherited a literary tradition through his grandfather, Irineo Paz, a newspaper publisher and novelist. His father practiced law and briefly published one of the first Spanish-language newspapers in Los Angeles, California, where the family lived for a year in the early 1920's as political exiles. Upon returning to Mexico, his father fell victim to a political assassination and Paz, an only child, was left alone with his widowed mother.

> *My steps along this street*
> *resound*
>   *in another street*
> *in which*
>   *I hear my steps*
> *passing along this street*
> *in which*
>
> *Only the mist is real*
>
>   —"Here" (trans. Charles Tomlinson)

By the 1930's Paz had become a leading voice of a new generation of Mexican intellectuals. After completing the course of study in law at the National University, he abruptly abandoned law and Mexico, failing to turn in his final thesis and traveling to Spain during the Spanish Civil War (1936-1939). There, he became part of the tragic intellectual venture that culminated in the fall of the Spanish Republic. As a witness to the deaths of fellow writers, exponents of the noblest expressions of language and culture, and the destruction of human values and ideals, Paz found his poetic voice and published his first two books. They received immediate recognition. Upon his return to Mexico, he collaborated in founding two important literary journals, *Taller* and *El hijo pródigo*.

During the 1940's Paz traveled to the United States on a Guggenheim Fellowship and studied at the University of California, Berkeley, in 1944 to 1945, then lived briefly in New York. The distance created by the English language and Anglo-American culture sowed the seeds for the introspective interpretation that marked the essays published in *The Labyrinth of Solitude*, in which Paz contrasts Mexico's long history to that of the United States, affording a hermeneutical view of the differences between these two neighboring countries.

It was in France, however, that Paz's love for his native land, combined with his fascination for Surrealist poetry's notions of spontaneity, movement, dislocation, and freedom, enabled him to develop his art to a new degree of strength. The culmination of his 1946 to 1951 stay in France with the Mexican diplomatic service was the much-praised poetry collection *Sun Stone*, which he wrote in a Surrealist vein after leaving France and published in 1957. Lessons learned from French colleagues stayed with Paz for the remainder of his life.

His diplomatic career from the 1940's to the 1960's serving at the Mexican embassies in France, Japan, and India afforded him the opportunity to expand his views—to look at the problems of existence and the capacity for creativity in worlds still connected to the sacred and the mythic while coming to terms with progress in an increasingly dehumanized world. In Japan, he adapted some of the formalized techniques of Japanese po-

W H A T T O R E A D

Eagle or Sun?

Eagle or Sun? (1951), a collection of short prose poems, was the first book of its kind in Spanish and has been
extremely influential. Each of its three parts, which are
tenuously connected only through their formal similarities, functions autonomously. Part 1, "Trabajos del poeta"
("The Poet's Works"), consists of sixteen brief sections,
each of which elaborates a narrative line, but usually in
strongly imagistic and even surrealistic language. The
surface concerns of these poems mask Paz's underlying
interest: the poet's relationship with his creation. This is
not allegory; here, the reader perceives the two levels simultaneously. The ubiquitous silence is interrupted by a
tapping: "it is the sound of horses' hooves galloping on a
field of stone. . . ." These are the words appearing, demanding articulation. They pour out uncontrollably, this
"vomit of words":

> The thistle whistles, bristles, buckles with chuckles. Broth
> of moths, charts of farts, all together, ball of syllables of
> waste matter, ball of snot splatter, ball of the viscera of

ets to his own writing. A new concern with structure, along with
his Surrealist impulses, enriched Paz's poems.

Paz was Mexico's ambassador to India during the 1960's, a
decade that left an indelible mark on the man and his work. In
literary terms, these changes are evident in *Ladera este* and
Blanco, works that explore the language and space of literature.
Here the work is symbol and sign; the text is an aesthetic (concrete) manifestation which simultaneously confers verbal meaning. In these works, Paz fully explored the "other," not only as a
manifestation of the self but also as an integral voice within his
poetic construct. The "other" is what lies beyond the parameters
of the ordinary; it is myth and dream, love and eroticism. Dur-

syllable sibyls, chatter, deaf chatter. I flap, I swing,
smashdunguided I flap.

Here, Paz conveys what it is like to be an artist, always at
the mercy of competing inner voices, of spontaneous creative demands.

The second part of *Eagle or Sun?*, "Arenas movedizas"
("Shifting Sands"), consists of nine sections; each is a self-
contained account couched in mundane, imageless
prose with occasional dialogue interspersed. Some of the
sections, such as "El ramo azul" ("The Blue Bouquet"),
recall the manner of Jorge Luis Borges; others, such as
"Un aprendizaje difícil" ("A Difficult Apprenticeship"),
are Kafkaesque; still others, such as "Mi vida con la ola"
("My Life with the Wave"), have the flavor of André
Breton: Together, they resemble a collection of very short
stories more than they do a series of prose poems.

The concluding part of *Eagle or Sun?*, the title section,
contains twenty-one pieces. Divided between investigations into the poetics of creation and metaphysical narratives—Paz thus attempts to combine the methodologies
developed in parts one and two—these pieces are ab-
stract and are therefore less accessible than the earlier
ones in the volume, but they are not meant to be hermetic conundrums.

— *Robert Hauptman*

ing his sojourn in India, Paz married Marie-José Tramini, who
became his lifelong soul mate and companion. Near the end of
the decade, Paz was faced with choosing between conformity
and principles. In October, 1968, the Mexican government ordered troops against the student demonstrations taking place
during the Summer Olympics in Mexico City. The result was a
massacre, and Octavio Paz resigned as ambassador to New Delhi
in protest.

Paz spent much of the 1970's and 1980's as a visiting professor at various academic institutions, including Cambridge University, where he was appointed to the Simón Bolívar Chair, and
later at Harvard University as Samuel Eliot Norton Professor of

Poetry. In Mexico he founded and directed the literary magazine *Plural* (later *Vuelta*). This was also a period of intense and prolific writing and of international recognition. By the 1990's, Paz had been honored with every important international prize, culminating with the Nobel Prize in Literature in 1990.

All these experiences, combined with a continued and acute awareness of the meaning of the Mexican historical and cultural legacy, informed Paz's writing. Juxtaposing dualities—such as the mythic timelessness of ancient Mexico and modern questions of temporality and human existence—and examining the larger questions that define human existence, his is a voice that constantly challenges the reader to probe and examine the tenets of the human condition.

—John D. Raymer and Margarita Nieto

Learn More

Bloom, Harold, ed. *Octavio Paz.* Philadelphia: Chelsea House, 2002. Bloom's introduction focuses on two prose works, *The Labyrinth of Solitude* and *Sor Juana: Or, The Traps of Faith.* The book's eleven essays primarily focus on Paz's poetry, describing his ideas, motifs, and style. The sophisticated nature and technical language of some of these essays may be difficult for some high school students.

Grenier, Yvon. *From Art to Politics: Octavio Paz and the Pursuit of Freedom.* Lanham, Md.: Rowman & Littlefield, 2001. Focuses on the ways in which Paz's social and political views surface in his poetry.

Hozven, Roberto, ed. *Otras voces: Sobre la poesía y prosa de Octavio Paz.* Riverside: University of California Press, 1996. A collection of critical essays in both English and Spanish. Includes bibliographical references.

Quiroga, José. *Understanding Octavio Paz.* Columbia: University of South Carolina Press, 1999. A critical study of selected poems by Paz. Includes a bibliography of the author's works, an index, and bibliographical references.

Roman, Joseph. *Octavio Paz.* New York: Chelsea House, 1994. A brief introduction, presenting the poet's life and career. Suitable for young adults.

Stavans, Ilan. *Octavio Paz: A Meditation.* Tucson: University of Arizona Press, 2001. Stavans, a noted critic of Latino culture, ponders Paz's ability to maintain his intellectual courage in an age of ideology.

Wilson, Jason. *Octavio Paz.* Boston: Twayne, 1986. A solid introduction in Twayne's World Authors series. Contains a bibliography and an index.

_____. *Octavio Paz: A Study of His Poetics.* New York: Cambridge University Press, 1979. Brief, useful biographical and analytical study of Paz and his poetry. Encomiums, texts, and articles concerning Paz on the occasion of his receiving the Neustadt Prize.

Miguel Piñero

Puerto Rican playwright and poet

Born: Gurabo, Puerto Rico; December 19, 1946
Died: New York, New York; June 17, 1988
Also known as: Miguel Antonio Gomez Piñero

DRAMA: *Short Eyes,* pr. 1974; *The Sun Always Shines for the Cool,* pr. 1976; *Eulogy for a Small-Time Thief,* pr. 1977; *A Midnight Moon at the Greasy Spoon,* pr. 1981; *Outrageous: One-Act Plays,* pb. 1986.
POETRY: *La Bodega Sold Dreams,* 1980.
SCREENPLAY: *Short Eyes,* 1977 (adaptation of his play).
TELEPLAY: "Smuggler's Blues," 1984 (episode of *Miami Vice*).
EDITED TEXT: *Nuyorican Poetry: An Anthology of Puerto Rican Words and Feelings,* 1975.

Miguel Piñero (mih-GEHL peen-YEHR-oh) is an important member of the Nuyorican (New York and Puerto Rican) literary and political movement that crystallized in the late 1960's and early 1970's in New York City. Born in Puerto Rico, Piñero moved to New York City with his parents when he was four. His father, Miguel Angel Piñero, abandoned the family four years later, and Piñero subsequently experienced the poverty, marginalization, and crime of New York's lower East Side. Piñero remained devoted to his mother, Adelina, as his poems and opening dedication to *Short Eyes* ("El Cumpleaños de Adelina" by Miguel Algarín) reveal.

At an early age, Piñero fell victim to his harsh environment: he began "hustling" and taking drugs and soon entered the world of petty crime that was to shape his future. A truant, shoplifter, and drug addict by his teenage years, Piñero never graduated from junior high. He was convicted of armed robbery at age twenty-four and was sent to Sing Sing, the notorious New York prison. Ironically, it was in prison that Piñero experienced his literary awakening, thanks to a theater workshop established at Sing Sing by Clay Stevenson. Like that of most Nuyorican authors, Piñero's experience as a marginalized Puerto Rican in America was to become the source for a significant portion of his literary output.

Through Stevenson's prison workshop, Piñero began his first and most recognized play, *Short Eyes*. In addition, while still in prison he came into contact with Marvin Felix Camillo, actor and activist, who had formed The Family, an acting troupe of former inmates, and who encouraged Piñero's writing and acting. Out of prison, Piñero worked with Camillo and The Family to develop *Short Eyes* for performance. The play moved from its opening in the Riverside Church to Off-Broadway, to the Public Theater with the help of producer Joseph Papp, and finally to the Vivian Beaumont Theater. Piñero received both an Obie Award and the New York Drama Critics Circle Award for best American play.

Piñero's success in playwriting put him in contact with the thriving Puerto Rican literary and political community. In the mid-1970's, as a member of the Nuyorican artistic community, Piñero cofounded the Nuyorican Poets Café with Miguel Algarín and edited a volume of Nuyorican poetry with Algarín as well. After a return to Puerto Rico, Piñero's work also reflected the displacement of the Puerto Rican experience in America: He and his fellow artists felt accepted neither in their native land nor in their land of adoption, and such alienation is a major tenet of Nuyorican literature. Like the dialogue of his characters, his poetry—and the poetry of the Nuyorican Poets

> *i was born on an island where to be puerto rican meant to be part of the land & soul & puertorriqueños were not the minority*
> *puerto ricans were first, none were second*
> *no, i was not born here . . .*
>
> —from "This Is Not the Place Where I Was Born"

Café—was characterized by oral performances of it, as poets performed their works in an apparently improvisational style, reflecting the influence of the Beat poets, of Puerto Rican street culture, and of the emerging African American rap and hip-hop styles. Piñero continued to write and see his plays performed, but none were to have the success of *Short Eyes*.

In 1977 Piñero wrote the screenplay and performed in the film version of his play *Short Eyes*. From the early 1970's into the 1980's, he began a long series of guest-starring appearances in television and cinema. Most notably, he played a series of drug smugglers and ne'er-do-wells in such television series as *Miami Vice* (1984), *The Equalizer* (1985), and *Kojak* (1973). On film, he appeared in *Breathless* (1983), *Exposed* (1983), and *Fort Apache, The Bronx* (1981).

In addition to working in Hollywood, Piñero also taught writing at Rutgers University and received a Guggenheim Fellowship for playwriting in 1982. Such activity and influence in his ethnic and literary community could not help in his battle against addiction, however, and Piñero continued to struggle with drugs and alcohol. Never married, Piñero had a series of serious relationships with both women and men, and an intense, although nonsexual, relationship with fellow Nuyorican poet Algarín. Piñero died in 1988 of cirrhosis of the liver.

Piñero's *Short Eyes* remains his most successful and enduring contribution to American playwriting and reveals his primary concerns with ethnic and racial alienation in the United States, the all-controlling power of violence, and the hope of individual triumph against such terror. In addition, it offers a window onto the language—a mixture of Spanish, English, street language, and profanity—that in many ways embodies the world of New York's lower East Side, where Nuyorican literature developed and thrived. His later works, although virtually ignored by literary critics, reveal Piñero's continued focus on the language, alienation, and perseverance of his community. Despite his close dealings with the New York and Hollywood elite, Piñero remained rooted in his lower East Side, Nuyorican experiences.

In December, 2001, *Piñero*, a film of the author's life directed by Leon Ichaso, opened in limited release and prompted re-

W H A T   T O   R E A D

Short Eyes

Short Eyes (1974) was Miguel Piñero's first and most famous play. After its debut, critics hailed the author as the first Puerto Rican playwright to enter theater's mainstream.

The play begins with a group of prisoners—mostly African American and Latino—struggling to maintain a sense of dignity under deplorable conditions. Early action focuses on Clark Davis, one of only two white members of the group, who is from a different socioeconomic background than most of the other inmates. Davis has been accused of child molestation, a crime that the other inmates consider especially shameful, and makes his situation worse by refusing to adapt to the prison's customs. Through the play's second act he is harassed constantly, and is ultimately murdered. The guilty prisoners are not punished—the guards look the other way—but must come to terms with their guilt and responsibility.

Only one of the inmates, an elderly Puerto Rican man named Juan, refused to participate in the murder. Paradoxically, he is the only one who knows that Davis is guilty. Critics have argued whether Juan abstained from the murder because of its immorality or because it was in the interest of his self-preservation to do so; perhaps both are true. Juan does not allow himself to take another's life, but neither does he make any attempt to relieve Davis's murderers of their guilt (the other prisoners have been told by a guard that Davis had been mistakenly identified and was innocent).

Piñero wrote *Short Eyes* after serving a jail sentence for armed robbery at Sing Sing prison. It draws heavily from his knowledge of life in jail, depicting the violence of prison life from the inmates' perspectives. The play's title comes from a slang term for pornography, "short heist." Piñero explained many Puerto Ricans had difficulty pronouncing the *h* in "heist," so the word sounded more like "eyes."

— *Anna A. Moore*

newed interest in the author and actor, particularly in his poetic performances. The film had the support and cooperation of Piñero's friends and family. Actor Benjamin Bratt's performance as Piñero, particularly in his "performance" of Piñero's poems at the Nuyorican Poets Café, suggests the intensity and immediacy of his poetry as performance that mere readings of Piñero's work cannot impart.

— Cami D. Agan

Learn More

Camillo, Marvin Felix. Introduction to *Short Eyes*, by Miguel Piñero. New York: Hill & Wang, 1975. Camillo's introduction is helpful in explaining the process by which Piñero moved from inmate at Sing Sing to author and performer, then to award-winning Broadway playwright. The introduction also contains an analysis of the play.

Deaver, William O. "Miguel Piñero (1946-1988)." In *Latino and Latina Writers*, edited by Alan West-Durán. Vol. 2. New York: Charles Scribner's Sons, 2004. The biographical article on Piñero provides information on his life, a detailed summary of his drama and poetry, and a bibliography of primary and secondary literature.

Fahy, Thomas Richard, and Kimball King, eds. *Captive Audience: Prison and Captivity in Contemporary Theater.* New York: Routledge, 2003. Analyzes works by Piñero and other dramatists to describe how incarceration is depicted in their plays.

Maffi, Mario. "The Nuyorican Experience in the Plays of Pedro Pietri and Miguel Piñero." In *Cross-Cultural Studies: American, Canadian and European Literatures, 1945-1985*, edited by Mirko Jurak. Bled, Slovenia: Symposium on Contemporary Literatures and Cultures of the United States of America and Canada, 1988. Although this essay is primarily a literary analysis of Pietri and Piñero's works, Maffi examines the environment of New York City in the 1970's, in which Puerto Rican authors developed and against which they constructed an identity. He explains the importance of language in Nuyorican works and the centrality of poetry and theater to the aesthetic.

"Miguel Piñero." In *Twentieth Century American Dramatists*, edited by Christopher J. Wheatley. Vol. 266 in *Dictionary of Literary Biography*. Detroit: Gale Group, 2003. The biographical entry on Piñero includes information on his life, works, and the production and reception of his plays.

Piñero, Miguel. "Miguel Piñero: 'I Wanted to Survive.'" Interview by Nat Hentoff. *The New York Times*, May 5, 1974, pp. 1, 8. Hentoff's interview with Piñero took place when *Short Eyes* was on stage at Joseph Papp's Public Theater. It provides helpful insight into Piñero's life in New York.

Saldivar, Jose David. "Miguel Piñero." In *Biographical Dictionary of Hispanic Literature in the United States: The Literature of Puerto Ricans, Cuban Americans, and Other Hispanic Writers*, edited by Nicolas Kanellos. New York: Greenwood Press, 1989. The dictionary's entry on Piñero contains a brief biography, a discussion of the major themes of his work, a survey of criticism, and a bibliography.

Mary Helen Ponce

Mexican American novelist, short-story writer, and memoirist

Born: Pacoima, California; January 24, 1938
Also known as: Maria Elena Ponce

LONG FICTION: *The Wedding*, 1989.

SHORT FICTION: *Recuerdo: Short Stories of the Barrio*, 1983; *Taking Control*, 1987.

NONFICTION: *Hoyt Street: An Autobiography*, 1993 (reprinted in 1995 in English as *Hoyt Street: Memories of a Chicana Childhood* and in Spanish as *Calle Hoyt: Memorias de una juventud chicana*).

A prolific author of Chicano prose, Mary Helen Ponce (POHN-say) was born and raised in the San Fernando Valley of Southern California. The youngest of ten children (seven girls and three boys), Ponce grew up in the security of her *barrio* (neighborhood) community, a blend of Mexicans and Mexican Americans for whom the family, the Catholic church, the school, and the little local grocery store provided stable landmarks for a world moving between languages and cultures. Writing in English and Spanish, or in English with brief shifts to Spanish, Ponce conjures the experiences of her childhood and youth in a bilingual and bicultural context, addressing the female experience in particular.

Ponce attended California State University at Northridge, earning a B.A. and an M.A. in Mexican American studies. She earned a second M.A. from the University of California at Los Angeles in history, minoring in anthropology and women's studies. She pursued course work toward a doctorate in American studies at the University of New Mexico, combining her twin interests in history and literature, receiving her Ph.D. in 1995.

The mother of four children, Ponce delayed the start of her writing career until she was in her forties, beginning to publish

> *The funeral mass was offered free of charge; the cemetery plot was paid for in installments. The mortuary bill, which included* la carroza *and the coffin, was also to be paid in installments. . . . Early on it was decided that Rito's wake would be held in our front room. My siblings and cousins put things in order. They cleaned and dusted, wanting the* sala *to look worthy of my brother.*
>
> —from "The Day Rito Died"

short stories in Spanish in the early 1980's. She soon wrote stories in English and translated some of her Spanish stories into English. She has published nonfiction essays on Latino topics ("Latinas and Breast Cancer," for example) and interviews of Latino figures ("Profile of Dr. Shirlene Soto: Vice Provost, CSU Northridge"). She has also given presentations on such topics as Spanish American pioneer women in California, Chicana literature, and oral history. She has read her fiction at college campuses and conferences in the United States and El Colegio de Mexico in Mexico City and has published in the largest Spanish-language newspaper in Southern California, *La Opinión.*

Recuerdo: Short Stories of the Barrio gathers a number of Ponce's earliest pieces, some of which begin with the Spanish word "Recuerdo," which may be translated as "I recall," "I remember," or simply "memory," suggesting the autobiographical element typical of Ponce's writing. Her early narratives are first-person, allowing Ponce to describe the experiences of Mexican women with an intimate tone. Later some of Ponce's stories would employ third-person narration.

Taking Control contains several short narratives. Though the characters of these stories are often subject to difficult circumstances, Ponce's title reflects her decision to emphasize the positive outcomes of even the most negative circumstances. Both *Recuerdo* and *Taking Control* are firmly anchored in the Mexican American experience, particularly as lived by women.

W H A T   T O   R E A D

The Wedding

The Wedding (1989) is dedicated to "the chicks and guys from the barrios who remember the big, fun weddings . . . and fights." The book follows the life of Blanca Munoz, who lives in Taconos, a poor Chicano neighborhood not far from Los Angeles. Like many of her peers, Blanca lives in a single-parent home and drops out of school to look for work. She is young and uneducated and finally has to take a job at a turkey-processing plant while she imagines a better life.

She meets Cricket, the leader of the local gang, the Tacones. Although she calls him honey, their relationship seems based more on proximity than on love. Blanca and Cricket focus much more on the impending wedding as a social symbol than as the symbol of their union. Each wants a splendid wedding for different reasons: Cricket wants to raise his status among the gang members with a wedding that "would outclass all others"; Blanca wants to salvage the family's pride, increase its social status and, consequently, please her mother.

Father Ranger, the parish priest, reluctantly agrees to perform the wedding. "Married men come and go at will," says Father Ranger. "They are free to find other women, abandon wives and children at whim, then return to claim their rights." Blanca constantly acquiesces to Cricket. She hopes for a single night of honeymoon at a hotel, but Cricket refuses, explaining that first he has to take care of the dance. On the way to the dance, as his new bride leans against him, Cricket admonishes her not to wrinkle his clothes. He knows he will be facing the rival gang and must look his best.

As the novel closes, Cricket is carried to the hospital in an ambulance after the rumble, and Blanca is taken to the hospital suffering a miscarriage. She still has hopes for a good future with Cricket. Her last words before passing out are "the best wedding, in all of Taconos."

— *Linda Ledford-Miller*

Ponce's novel *The Wedding* is set in a fictional small-town neighborhood near Los Angeles. It depicts the San Fernando Valley in the 1940's and 1950's while exploring women's place in Mexican American society of the time. Blanca is planning the wedding of her dreams, although the marriage is not necessarily to the man of her dreams. She has to work Saturdays plucking turkeys in order to pay for the fancy gown she wants, despite its reduced, factory-seconds price. Her fiancé is a *pachuco*, or zoot-suit-wearing member of a 1950's gang. Blanca does have her fancy wedding—but she also has a miscarriage and has to leave the party in an ambulance as two rival gangs fight in the background. Like many of Ponce's other works, *The Wedding* examines the stereotypes that seem to circumscribe the lives of Mexican American women, who are subject to their husband's whims, who endure multiple pregnancies, and who must rise to the social expectations inculcated in them by their families and the Catholic church. Nonetheless, Blanca, like other Ponce characters, is strong, tough, and essentially optimistic. A panorama of Mexican American life is presented in the book: the gangs; the hardworking women; the swaggering men; the influences of family, friends, and church; the financial struggle; and the changing culture.

Ponce's 1993 nonfiction work *Hoyt Street: An Autobiography* returns to the San Fernando Valley of the 1940's. (The book was reprinted in 1995 simultaneously in Spanish and English editions: *Hoyt Street: Memories of a Chicana Childhood* and *Calle Hoyt: Memorias de una juventud chicana.*) *Hoyt Street* leaves fiction behind to tell Ponce's own story of growing up Chicana in a bilingual, bicultural neighborhood whose population is gradually acculturating to the dominant Anglo culture. The book begins with Ponce as a preschooler and ends at the beginning of puberty, depicting the neighborhood and introducing friends and family as it goes. Though her memories are mostly happy ones, Ponce comments: "It seems that we Mexican-Americans, as we were called, had so many things wrong with us that I wondered why it was we were happy." The voice is Ponce's, but the vision is split between her own childhood recollections and the implied critique by Anglos.

It is in this matrix of identities (Mexican, Mexican American, Anglo-American, Spanish language, English language) and issues (the socialization of men and women, the church, school) that Ponce positions all of her writing. It has been remarked that minority writers usually begin their careers by writing their autobiography and only then move toward less personalized fictions. Ponce's fiction, however, has always had autobiographical elements, and she moved through fictional representation to the nonfiction autobiography itself.

— *Linda Ledford-Miller*

Learn More

Gonzalez, Maria C. *Contemporary Mexican-American Women Novelists: Toward a Feminist Identity.* New York: Peter Lang, 1996. Ponce is one of the authors included in this feminist critique of Chicana novelists.

Ikas, Karin Rosa, ed. *Chicana Ways: Conversations with Ten Chicana Writers.* Reno: University of Nevada Press, 2002. Lorna Dee Cervantes, Denise Chávez, Lucha Corpi, and Mary Helen Ponce are among the ten Chicana writers who describe their lives and work.

McCracken, Ellen. *New Latina Narrative: The Feminine Space of Postmodern Ethnicity.* Tucson: University of Arizona Press, 1999. Ponce's work is included in this analysis of writing by Cuban American, Puerto Rican American, Mexican American, and Dominican American writers. McCracken explains how these writers have redefined concepts of multiculturalism and diversity in American society.

Ponce, Mary Helen. *Hoyt Street: An Autobiography.* Albuquerque: University of New Mexico Press, 1993. Ponce recalls her life in Pacoima, California, from the age of eight through thirteen, describing the poverty and prejudice—as well as the joys—of her childhood.

Rochy, John. "A Pacoima Childhood." Review of *Hoyt Street*, by Mary Helen Ponce. *Los Angeles Times*, October 3, 1993. A favorable review.

Veyna, Angelina F. "Mary Helen Ponce." In *Chicano Writers, Second Series*, edited by Francisco A. Lomelí. Vol. 122 in *Dictionary of Literary Biography.* Detroit: Gale Group, 1992. Provides a bio-bibliographic overview of Ponce's work up to *The Wedding*.

Elena Poniatowska

Mexican journalist, novelist, and essayist

Born: Paris, France; May 19, 1933

NONFICTION: *Palabras cruzadas*, 1961; *Todo empezó el domingo*, 1963; *La noche de Tlatelolco*, 1971 (*Massacre in Mexico*, 1975); *Fuerte es el silencio*, 1980; *Domingo siete*, 1982; *¡Ay vida, no me mereces!*, 1985; *Nada, nadie: Las voces del temblor*, 1988 (*Nothing, Nobody: The Voices of the Mexico City Earthquake*, 1995); *Juchitán de las mujeres*, 1989; *Guerrero Viejo*, 1997 (bilingual); *Me lo dijo Elena Poniatowska*, 1997 (interviews); *Octavio Paz: Las palabras del árbol*, 1998; *Las mil y una: La herida de Paulina*, 2000; *Las siete cabritas*, 2000; *Mariana Yampolsky y la buganvillia*, 2001.

LONG FICTION: *Hasta no verte, Jesús mío*, 1969 (*Here's to You, Jesusa!*, 2001); *La "Flor de Lis,"* 1988; *Tinísima*, 1993 (*Tinisima*, 1996); *Paseo de la Reforma*, 1997; *La piel del cielo*, 2001 (*The Skin of the Sky*, 2004).

SHORT FICTION: *Lilus Kikus*, 1954; *Querido Diego, te abraza Quiela*, 1978 (*Dear Diego*, 1986); *De noche vienes*, 1979; *Tlapalería*, 2003.

Elena Poniatowska (eh-LAY-nah poh-nyah-TOW-skah) is best known for her journalistic work, a career launched by chance when, in 1954, she interviewed the U.S. ambassador the day after meeting him at a cocktail party. Poniatowska has dedicated her writing to recording a wide spectrum of Mexican life, from the country's power elite to marginalized peasant populations. In 1978 she became the first woman in Mexico awarded the Premio Nacional de Periodismo, the country's most prestigious prize in journalism.

Dialogue serves as a foundation for most of her literary production. Poniatowska's first collection of interviews, *Palabras cruzadas* (crossed words), includes such varied personalities as Spanish film director Luis Buñuel, Argentine writer Jorge Luis

Borges, and Cuban dictator Fidel Castro. By contrast, *Todo empezó el domingo* (everything started on Sunday) celebrates the mundane Sunday outings of working-class Mexicans. The attention Poniatowska gives to the cross-section of social classes in Mexico reflects aspects of her own background.

Poniatowska was born in Paris in 1933 of French-born parents whose families had been displaced by political upheaval. Her mother, Dolores de Amor, came from a Mexican family of hacienda owners who left for Europe when the government of Lázaro Cárdenas expropriated their land and instituted agrarian reform after the Mexican Revolution. Her paternal family of Polish aristocrats settled in France after fleeing Poland during World War II. When her own family moved to Mexico, Poniatowska was about nine years old and spoke only French. In fact, Poniatowska never studied Spanish in school and acquired the language from house maids. She attended French and English schools, one of which was a convent school in Pennsylvania. Since rigorous religious training instilled young women with self-sacrificing qualities, the fact that many nontraditional women populate her writing suggests the author's rejection of customary female roles.

Although Poniatowska grew up among the Mexican gentry, the household help exposed her to the problems of the working-class poor. Furthermore, since from an early age Poniatowska witnessed her parents' civic involvement and wartime service

> *Guerrero Viejo is a stone in the sun, a hard, implacable sun. The rocks in a row at the edge of the road like the earth's teeth. Stone, the men's heads, and stone, their bones, scattered there. Stone, their memory of themselves, of their lives that, for the uninitiated, leave no more of a trace than the rings in the water when a stone is dropped.*
>
> —from *Guerrero Viejo*

(her father fought in World War II, and her mother drove am-
bulances), it is not surprising that much of her journalistic work
documents national crisis. The October, 1968, clash between
police and student protesters at the Plaza de las Tres Culturas in
Mexico City prompted Poniatowska to record the bloodbath
in *Massacre in Mexico. Fuerte es el silencio* (silence is strong) incorporates other national concerns such as the influx of peasants
into the capital in search of work, the miserable shantytown
housing of these urban dwellers, the "disappeared" victims

521

of political repression, and the struggle of rural communities to improve living conditions. The very title suggests the voicelessness of the unrepresented poor, a social ill Poniatowska denounces in her writing. In *Nothing, Nobody* Poniatowska turns from social inequities to natural disaster by recording the aftermath of the 1985 earthquake in Mexico City. Typically her journalistic texts feature mixed media, including accounts from news clips, eyewitness accounts, interviews, author narrative, and photographs.

The interviews of the seven 1982 presidential candidates compiled in *Domingo siete* (Sunday the seventh) suggest the importance of politics in Mexican society. The country's intelligentsia also command a space in Poniatowska's writing. The essays in *¡Ay vida, no me mereces!* (oh, life, you do not deserve me!) delve into the work of prominent contemporary writers Rosario Castellanos, Juan Rulfo, and Carlos Fuentes. A feminist, Poniatowska shows a predilection for Castellanos's writing, which takes a stand on women's issues.

Themes relating to women's issues predominate in Poniatowska's fiction writing. Her first book, *Lilus Kikus*, consists of short vignettes about the protagonist's nonconformity with typical female socialization. Lilus likes to play outdoors and explore nature, but society dictates otherwise for girls. Fiction took a back seat to journalism until the publication of the testimonial novel *Here's to You, Jesusa!*, which is based on a year's worth of conversations with Josefina Bórquez, an extraordinary peasant woman. A staunch feminist by today's standards, Jesusa Palancares—as Poniatowska renames her in the novel—fought in the Mexican Revolution alongside her father and husband, stood up to their abuse, liberated herself from male tutelage, and led an independent life. Again drawing from real life to construct fiction, in *Dear Diego* Poniatowska writes the series of letters she imagines that émigré Russian artist Angelina Beloff would have written to her lover, Mexican muralist Diego Rivera, when he left Paris and returned to Mexico in 1921. The emotional dependence the heartbroken Quiela shows for Diego contrasts dramatically with the polygamous wife in the title story of *De noche vienes* (you come at night). Esmerald, a nurse by pro-

WHAT TO READ

Dear Diego

Dear Diego (1978) is based on one chapter of Bertram Wolfe's *The Fabulous Life of Diego Rivera* (1963). It is a fictionalized portrayal of the Russian painter Angelina Beloff as a broken-hearted lover waiting for the painter Diego Rivera to send for her from Mexico City.

At first Angelina, or Quiela (the Spanish name given to her by Diego), is confident that her lover will send for her. They share a ten-year union and the tragic memory of a child lost to a terrible fever. She continues to paint in his absence but cannot recapture the joys of creation that Diego's presence made possible.

In a desperate attempt to bring his spirit back, she turns her letters into monologues that review the comradeship and poverty of their life together. Because Diego's Mexican sensibility has, in a sense, replaced her Russian soul, she becomes almost crazed by loneliness and lost identity. Instead of losing him in the Paris crowds, she "recognizes" his face, with its warm smile, cresting the wave of faces pouring out of the Metro.

Diego finally sends money orders accompanied by impersonal messages that are more painful than was silence. To add to her suffering, Diego asks Angelina to pass on money to another former mistress, a promiscuous woman who has earned Angelina's disdain. Instead of succumbing to jealousy, Angelina throws herself into her painting and overcomes her despair through a rediscovery of her artistic independence and creative will.

Most of the novel is epistolary, but it ends with a short narrative that presents a curious paradox of reconciliation. Although Diego never sends for her, and years later does not even recognize her at a concert in Mexico City, Angelina has turned his rejection of her into a source of inspiration. Deprived of his companionship, she has internalized his power and enlarged her own capacities. He deserts her, but Diego—that genius with a "large belly"— has also given birth to her artist's soul.

fession, epitomizes the traditional caretaker role of females—so much so that she manages to keep five husbands until getting caught. Poniatowska applies a humorous feminist spin to machismo's double standard.

Autobiographical similarities abound in *La "Flor de Lis."* An aristocratic child, Mariana, lives in France surrounded by luxury and servants until World War II changes her family's lifestyle. Mariana's French father leaves for the war, while her Mexican mother sets off for exile in Mexico with two young daughters. The narrative focuses on the class and gender traditions that shape Mariana's cultural identity in the new country. Whether focusing on the uniqueness of one woman, as in *Tinísima*, the story of early twentieth century photographer and political militant Tina Modotti, or of village women, as in *Juchitán de las mujeres* (the women's Juchitán), Poniatowska's writings typically inscribe the cultural contributions of the underrepresented in Mexican society.

— *Gisela Norat*

Learn More

Amador Gómez-Quintero, Raysa Elena, and Mireya Pérez Bustillo. *The Female Body: Perspectives of Latin American Artists.* Foreword by Elena Poniatowska. Westport, Conn.: Greenwood Press, 2002. Examines the works of Poniatowska and other women writers to determine how they represent themselves and treat female identity and the female body.

Franco, Jean. "Rewriting the Family: Contemporary Feminism's Revision of the Past." In *Plotting Women: Gender and Representation in Mexico.* New York: Columbia University Press, 1989. Discusses the unconventionality of both protagonists and genre categories.

Hurley, Teresa M. *Mothers and Daughters in Post-Revolutionary Mexican Literature.* Rochester, N.Y.: Tamesis, 2002. Explores the myths about women that were prevalent in Mexico in the first half of the twentieth century and examines how women writers debunked those myths. Includes an analysis of the treatment of mother, country, and identity in Poniatowska's *La "Flor de Lis."*

Jörgensen, Beth Ellen. *The Writing of Elena Poniatowska: Engaging Dialogues.* Austin: University of Texas Press, 1994. A study of the whole range of Poniatowska's work, focusing on how Poniatowska's work as a journalist informs her fiction.

Medeiros-Lichem, María Teresa. *Reading the Feminine Voice in Latin American Women's Fiction: From Teresa de la Parra to Elena Poniatowska and Luisa Valenzuela.* New York: P. Lang, 2002. Focuses on Poniatowska's fiction, providing a feminist critique of her work.

Poniatowska, Elena. "How I Started Writing Chronicles and Why I Never Stopped." In *The Contemporary Mexican Chronicle: Theoretical Perspectives on the Liminal Genre,* edited by Ignacio Corona and Beth E. Jörgensen. Albany: State University of New York Press, 2002. An examination of the *crónica* or chronicle, a popular literary genre in Latin America that combines fiction and nonfiction, literature and journalism. The essays by Poniatowska and other authors describe the theory and practice of this genre in the twentieth century.

Schaefer, Claudia. *Textured Lives: Women, Art, and Representation in Modern Mexico.* Tucson: University of Arizona Press, 1992. Explores Poniatowska's use of the epistolary genre in reconstructing true-to-life protagonists.

Von Son, Carlos. *Deconstructing Myths: Parody and Irony in Mexican Literature.* New Orleans, La.: University Press of the South, 2002. Analyzes Poniatowska's *Querido Diego, te abraza Quiela* and works by three other writers to determine if these writers' use of parody and irony is unique to Mexican literature.

Manuel Puig

Argentine novelist

Born: General Villegas, Argentina;
December 28, 1932
Died: Cuernavaca, Mexico; July 22, 1990

LONG FICTION: *La traición de Rita Hayworth*, 1968 (*Betrayed by Rita Hayworth*, 1971); *Boquitas pintadas*, 1969 (*Heartbreak Tango*, 1973); *The Buenos Aires Affair: Novela policial*, 1973 (*The Buenos Aires Affair: A Detective Novel*, 1976); *El beso de la mujer araña*, 1976 (*Kiss of the Spider Woman*, 1979); *Pubis angelical*, 1979 (English translation, 1986); *Maldición eterna a quien lea estas páginas*, 1980 (*Eternal Curse on the Reader of These Pages*, 1982); *Sangre de amor correspondido*, 1982 (*Blood of Requited Love*, 1984); *Cae la noche tropical*, 1988 (*Tropical Night Falling*, 1991).

DRAMA: *Bajo un manto de estrellas*, pb. 1983 (*Under a Mantle of Stars*, 1985); *El beso de la mujer araña*, pb. 1983 (*Kiss of the Spider Woman*, 1986; adaptation of his novel); *Misterio del ramo de rosas*, pb. 1987 (*Mystery of the Rose Bouquet*, 1988).

SCREENPLAYS: *Boquitas pintadas*, 1974 (adaptation of his novel); *El lugar sin límites*, 1978 (adaptation of José Donoso's novel).

Manuel Puig (mah-NWEHL pweeg), one of Latin America's major writers and one of the most widely read, has been called the chronicler of middle-class Argentina. Born in the provincial town of General Villegas, where he spent his childhood and received his elementary education, Puig was the son of Baldomero Puig, who worked in commerce, and Elena Delledonne. He began learning English at the age of ten to enhance his enjoyment of the American films that he and his mother saw every afternoon. Within a year, Puig was at the top of his class and had added to his interest in American films new interests in literature, philosophy, psychology, and Italian films. His ambition as a teenager was to become a film director.

In 1957, after having studied philosophy, languages, and literature in Argentina, he traveled to Rome with a scholarship to study at the Experimental Film Center; however, he was dissatisfied with the school and moved on to Paris, and then to London, where he earned a living by giving Spanish and Italian lessons as well as by washing dishes at the theater restaurant. During this time, Puig began writing film scripts; he continued to do so in 1959, when he moved to Stockholm. A year later, upon his return to Argentina, he obtained a position as assistant director in the Argentine film industry. After a short stay in his native country, he moved to New York City to expose himself to Broadway musicals, and he worked as a ticket agent for Air France. In 1965 he completed his first novel, which he had begun in 1962 but which was not to be published in Buenos Aires until 1968, partly because of problems with censorship.

With the publication of *Betrayed by Rita Hayworth*, Puig was immediately heralded as one of Latin America's most gifted writers. Most critics still consider this first novel to be his masterpiece. In addition to its penetrating examination of the narrow world of alienated human beings (particularly the petit bourgeois and blue-collar Argentine people) who find refuge in the large-scale consumption of films and soap operas, the work was considered to be an attack on conventional or naïve realism as

---

—Mmm. . . . It must be a fear that you'll turn into a panther, like with the first movie you told me.
—I'm not the panther woman.
—It's true, you're not the panther woman.
—It's very sad being a panther woman; no one can kiss you. Or anything.
—You, you're the spider woman, that traps men in her web.

—from *Kiss of the Spider Woman*
(trans. Thomas Colchie)

Jerry Bauer

well as on the cultural foundations of the experimental novel. His second novel, *Heartbreak Tango*, became an instant best-seller when it was published in 1969. Written in the format of popular literature, each chapter was intended to be read as an episode in a serialized story. Yet the novel is a parody of the *feuilleton* (serialized novel) as, for example, written by Alexandre Dumas (1802-1870). Avoiding the sentimentalism characteristic of the *feuilleton*, Puig reveals the lives of the story's protagonists through intimate letters, meditations, dialogues, religious confessions, prayers, and objective descriptions.

Puig's third novel, *The Buenos Aires Affair,* illustrates in its subtitle, *A Detective Novel,* that the author was again using a popular literary form. Aside from the detective elements, the novel is primarily a psychoanalytic study of its two main characters and a parody of their way of life. As in his two previous novels, Puig's major triumph is on the linguistic level. The book was not a popular success. The Argentine military dictatorship refused to recognize itself in the mirror of Puig's novel. In *Kiss of the Spider Woman*, Puig develops subjects which he had touched upon in his earlier novels: politics and sexuality. The drama, polarized between two male protagonists—one a homosexual and the other a political prisoner—focuses on the relationship between the two men in their shared jail cell. Although footnotes pretend to document events, the story appears to be narrated by the two protagonists themselves. Readers are left to their own interpretations of the characters and events portrayed.

Eternal Curse on the Reader of These Pages, originally written in English, is a novel that takes Puig's narrative discourse to even further lengths. The story of two lonely men, one an old Argentine gentleman, the other his American nurse, and their search for friendship and love is rendered entirely through dialogue. As the narrative progresses, however, the dialogues do not appear to move forward in any apparent order; consequently, readers may begin to question whether they are really confronted with two speakers or with only one who is engaged in dialogue with an imaginary other. In *Blood of Requited Love*, Puig introduces his readers to a new fictional locale: a small rural town

W H A T   T O   R E A D

Heartbreak Tango

Heartbreak Tango (1969) was an immediate best-seller when it appeared. It takes the form of an old-fashioned installment novel, and the reader is drawn along by two major lines of development: how a wondrously handsome young man of a fairly good family came to an impoverished, tubercular end, and how the tense relations between a housemaid and her upwardly mobile seducer culminated in the latter's murder. Further interest comes from following the fates of three other young women: the handsome young rake's scheming sister; a local cattle baron's daughter, who rendezvouses with the rake while waiting to marry into the landed aristocracy; and another of the hero's conquests, an ambitious blonde who can never manage to rise above the lower middle class.

While well-educated urban readers might see the book as turning the members of the provincial middle class into figures of fun, such a reading fails to take into account the great amount of material dedicated to the exploration of Puig's twin themes of popular culture and concepts of sexuality. Language is an especially important

in Brazil. A lost or forgotten past (specifically, the lustful youth of the protagonist), gradually emerges into a desolate present. The novel ends with both a celebration of adolescent sexuality and an elegy in acknowledgment of its demise.

Beneath the disguise of popular literature, in his fiction Puig built an elaborate kind of narrative structure in which each element functions in perfect harmony with the totality of which it is a part. While Puig's countrymen relegated him to the category of "second-class sentimentalist," American critics, for the most part, received Puig's works favorably. They assert that Puig is a writer keenly conscious of how both the novel as a literary form and the kinds of people who serve as its subjects have been

tool, and the characters use the media's phrases, though their own existence has little to do with and the rapturous, adventurous, or "macho" expressions they employ. The incongruity is especially acute in the area of courtship mores, and the reader sees a small society in which both marriage and informal liaisons are heavily governed by questions of prestige and economic power, while the characters see love through a haze of dreamily romantic phrases.

On the surface, the unmarried women are expected to remain chaste, while men are given more leeway, although they are required to satisfy conditions of respectability. Overlapping this Victorian standard is the code of *machismo*, which demands of the young men a constant effort to conquer numbers of women and to cultivate a swaggering style.

Of the various liaisons contracted during the novel, all are somehow colored by the dream of acquiring an advantageous match in marriage. Puig is unmistakably critical of this scenario, in which sex and courtship are made part of the politics of class standing. He offers a condemnatory portrait of this system, making his attitude clear by portraying popular culture as stressing the acquisition of an impressive lover or spouse.

— *Naomi Lindstrom*

caught up in the clichés of popular literature. While some critics say that Puig's stylistic methods are, at times, too inventive and even superfluous, others say that Puig's extraordinary inventiveness demonstrates new ways of rendering familiar material, thereby making accessible a reality that might have remained inaccessible through other narrative angles.

— *Genevieve Slomski and Christine R. Catron*

Learn More

Bacarisse, Pamela. *Impossible Choices: The Implications of the Cultural References in the Novels of Manuel Puig.* Calgary, Alberta: University of Calgary Press, 1993. An excellent critical study of Puig's work. Includes bibliographical references and an index.

_____. *The Necessary Dream: A Study of the Novels of Manuel Puig.* Totowa, N.J.: Barnes & Noble Books, 1988. Chapters on the major novels. The introduction provides a useful overview of Puig's career and themes. Includes notes and bibliography.

Colas, Santiago. *Postmodernity in Latin America: The Argentine Paradigm.* Durham, N.C.: Duke University Press, 1994. Puig is discussed in this study of Argentine works, which also examines Julio Cortázar and Ricardo Piglia.

Kerr, Lucille. *Suspended Fictions: Reading Novels by Manuel Puig.* Urbana: University of Illinois Press, 1987. Chapters on each of Puig's major novels, exploring the themes of tradition, romance, popular culture, crime, sex, and the design of Puig's career. Contains detailed notes but no bibliography.

Lavers, Norman. *Pop Culture into Art: The Novels of Manuel Puig.* Columbia: University of Missouri Press, 1988. Lavers finds a close relationship between Puig's life and his literary themes. Biography, in this case, helps to explain the author's methods and themes.

Levine, Suzanne Jill. *Manuel Puig and the Spider Woman: His Life and Fictions.* Madison: University of Wisconsin Press, 2001. A full-length biography by one of Puig's translators, focusing on the intersections between his life and his art.

Tittler, Jonathan. *Manuel Puig.* New York: Twayne, 1993. The best introduction to Puig. Tittler provides a useful survey of Puig's career in his introduction and devotes separate chapters to the novels. Includes detailed notes and an annotated bibliography.

Rachel de Queiroz

Brazilian novelist

Born: Fortaleza, Brazil; November 17, 1910
Died: Rio de Janeiro, Brazil; November 4, 2003

LONG FICTION: *O quinze*, 1930; *João Miguel*, 1932; *Caminho de pedras*, 1937; *As três Marias*, 1939 (*The Three Marias*, 1963); *Dôra, Doralina*, 1975 (English translation, 1984); *O galo de ouro*, 1985; *Memorial de Maria Moura*, 1992.

DRAMA: *Lampião*, pr., pb. 1953; *A beata Maria do Egito*, pr., pb. 1958.

CHILDREN'S LITERATURE: *O menino mágico*, 1969; *Cafute e Pena-de-Prata*, 1986; *Andira*, 1992.

NONFICTION: *A donzela e a moura torta*, 1948; *100 crônicas escolhidas*, 1958; *Histórias e crônicas*, 1963; *O Brasileiro perplexo*, 1964; *O caçador de Tatu*, 1967; *As menininhas, e outras crônicas*, 1976; *Mapinguari: Crônicas*, 1989; *Matriarcas do Ceara: Don Federalina de Lavras*, 1990; *As terras asperas*, 1993; *O nosso Ceará*, 1994 (with Maria Luiza de Queiroz); *Tantos anos*, 1998 (with Maria Luiza de Queiroz); *O Não me Deixes*, 2000 (with Maria Luiza de Queiroz).

MISCELLANEOUS: *Obra reunida*, 1989 (5 volumes).

Rachel de Queiroz (rah-SHEHL thay kay-ee-RAWSH) is regarded as a significant voice of neoregionalism in Brazil and as a protofeminist writer. She was born in the capital city of the state of Ceará in Brazil's northeastern region, the setting of most of her fiction. After the great drought of 1915, her family moved to Rio de Janeiro and then to Belém do Pará. Returning to Fortaleza, she graduated from a Catholic girls' school in 1925 and two years later began work as a journalist. Throughout her career she has written *crônicas*, the Brazilian genre of commentary, social observation, or sketches of life and customs. At the age of twenty, Queiroz published her first novel, which received a national book award. Like many intellectuals of the day concerned with

WHAT TO READ

Dôra, Doralina

The action of *Dôra, Doralina* (1975) is located in the consciousness of the protagonist, Maria das Dores (nicknamed Dôra or Doralina). The novel's first section revolves around Dôra's bitter struggle with her mother, Senhora. A beautiful widow, Senhora tyrannically manages the family ranch, Soledade, while showing no love toward her daughter, and the depth of Dôra's alienation is evidenced in Dôra's desperate need to be loved. This desire seems to be realized when she marries Laurindo Quirino, but soon she realizes that he is a violent, morally hollow opportunist. Dôra discovers that he is having an affair with her mother. Dôra is shattered by this revelation, and her sense of imprisonment deepens, only lessening when her husband is killed in a mysterious hunting accident.

No longer able to tolerate her mother, Dôra leaves the ranch and moves to the city. The second section of the novel describes how she escapes her haunted past. Dôra joins a ragtag theater group as a fledgling actress and be-

social issues, she had a brief association with the Communist Party (1931-1933) and faced imprisonment for expressing her ideas. In the late 1930's Queiroz moved permanently to Rio de Janeiro, but she continued to make annual visits to the family ranch in the interior of Ceará. In recognition of her defense of the disadvantaged she was chosen to represent her country at the 1966 United Nations Commission on Human Rights, after which she joined the Federal Council of Culture. In 1977 she became the first woman to be elected to the Brazilian Academy of Letters.

Queiroz is noted for her profound understanding of the language, landscape, and human drama of northeastern Brazil. The second generation of Brazilian Modernism, which included such authors as Jorge Amado, was characterized by the nationally focused social novel of the 1930's. As a member of this gen-

gins experiencing the larger world. The company gives her the sense of family that she has always desired. Eventually, Dôra meets the man who fulfills her dreams: Asmodeu Lucas, a river captain.

Their relationship is the heart of the novel's final section. When the pressures of World War II force the theater group to disperse, Dôra and the Captain begin to live together in teeming Rio de Janeiro. The two remain in love, and the novel climaxes with the Captain's death from typhoid. Unable to cope with her grief in Rio, Dôra returns to the more familiar solitude of the ranch and becomes the new Senhora.

Queiroz's artistic vision resists morbidity because it vividly depicts the characters' deep-seated need to struggle against time. This struggle enlivens the novel, especially since Queiroz plays the comic second section off the tragic first and third parts. There is a kind of tragic exultation in Dôra's persistent, unsparing, and honest attempt to remember and to confront her ever-fading past. By trying to rescue her memories—an act which brings more pain to her already desolate existence on the ranch—she rejects the temptation to give in to time.

— *James Grove*

eration, Queiroz sought to bring pressing issues to light in honest examinations of conditions in her land of birth. Themes of social conflict, poverty, and forced migration structure Queiroz's fiction. The physical and mental suffering caused by drought is examined in *O quinze* (fifteen, or 1915), which is based on first-hand acquaintance with the people and places of the backlands and cities affected by the drought. In the face of wretched situations Queiroz avoids defeatism, preferring to portray the stoicism of the people. In *João Miguel* (John Michael) she turns to the social psychology of violence in the backlands. The novel is a study of a protagonist who is imprisoned for murder. *Caminho de pedras* (road of stones), more historically oriented, presents the persecution of political dissidents and organizers. Queiroz examines, in a provincial situation, stages of development, class

> *He snooped around and found a postcard and a book, both with a man's name in the same handwriting. He found the insignia of the sergeant's regiment and concluded that the object of his wife's murmurs, sighs, and silences was not only a man but a soldier. Finally he made the supreme discovery. . . . For he discovered the love letters, bearing airmail stamps, a distant postmark, and the sergeant's name.*
>
> —from "Metonymy: Or, The Husband's Revenge"
> (trans. William L. Grossman)

structure, and relations of power. While less distinguished than her fiction, Queiroz's dramatic works also concern the problematic Northeast. Social banditry and heroic folk verse emerge in a play based on the life of a famous renegade, Lampião. *A beata Maria do Egito* (Saint Mary of Egypt) relates hagiological legend to parallel circumstances in Brazil.

Queiroz is also known for her treatment of women's issues, which are in varying degrees important in all of her fictional works. The protagonist of *O quinze* is a young woman who strives for an independent position in the midst of general crisis. The oppression of women is also taken up in the social portrait of *Caminho de pedras*. Such issues are at the fore of Queiroz's two works which have appeared in English. The protagonists of *The Three Marias* confront life in the fictional present through reminiscences about adolescent experiences in a convent school. The novel details their attempts to deal with current frustrations and to come to terms with their sexuality and their roles as citizens, mothers, and spouses. Queiroz addresses the inadequacies of the educational system, especially with regard to women, the inequalities of male-female relations, and the difficulties of emancipation. In *Dôra, Doralina* a retrospective narrative technique is again adopted. The heroines' trajectories are presented in three "books," or stages of life, as the relations of mother, daughter, and a male figure are examined. The women confront traditional values and interpersonal problems from different generational perspectives. Here one senses more positive imaging of self and greater potential for freedom and fulfillment. Queiroz's gallery of strong female characters continues in *Memorial de Maria Moura* (Maria Moura's memorial), a novel about a woman who leads a group of *cangaceiros* (bandits) in the backlands of Ceará.

Rachel de Queiroz occupies a dual position in the Brazilian canon. Besides having a significant role in the regionalist novel of the 1930's, she was one of the very first to integrate gender issues into Brazilian fiction. She is thus a forerunner of contemporary writers who probe the social psychology of women's roles and dramatize their conflicts.

— Charles A. Perrone and Cristina Ferreira-Pinto

Learn More

Courteau, Joanna. "*Dôra, Doralina:* The Sexual Configuration of Discourse." *Chasqui: Revista de Literatura Latinoamericana* 20 (May, 1991): 3-9. A discussion of the narrative style of the novel, Queiroz's treatment of the character, Dôra Maria das Dores, and a psychoanalytic examination of the book.

_____. "The Problematic Heroines in the Novels of Rachel de Queiroz." *Luso Brazilian Review* 22 (Winter, 1985): 123-144. An excellent analysis of the women characters and the female problematic in Queiroz's novels.

Ellison, Fred P. "Rachel de Queiroz." In *Brazil's New Novel: Four Northeastern Masters.* Berkeley: University of California Press, 1954. A good starting point for study of Queiroz's early work, particularly in the context of the 1930's Brazilian social novel.

_____. "Rachel de Queiroz." In *Latin American Writers*, edited by Carlos A. Solé and Maria I. Abreu. Vol 3. New York: Charles Scribner's Sons, 1989. Offers a comprehensive and critical discussion of Queiroz's life and works. Provides a selected bibliography for further reading.

Wasserman, Renata R. "A Woman's Place: Rachel de Queiroz's *Dôra, Doralina.*" *Brasileira: A Journal of Brazilian Literature* 2 (1989): 46-58. A discussion of the role of women in Brazilian society as reflected in *Dôra, Doralina*.

Horacio Quiroga

Uruguayan short-story writer

Born: El Salto, Uruguay; December 31, 1878
Died: Buenos Aires, Argentina; February 19, 1937
Also known as: Horacio Silvestre Quiroga y Forteza

SHORT FICTION: *Los arrecifes de coral,* 1901; *El crimen del otro,* 1904; *Cuentos de amor, de locura y de muerte,* 1917; *Cuentos de la selva para los niños,* 1918 (*South American Jungle Tales,* 1923); *El salvaje,* 1920; *Anaconda,* 1921; *El desierto,* 1924; *La gallina degollada,* 1925 (*The Decapitated Chicken, and Other Stories,* 1976); *Los desterrados,* 1926 (*The Exiles, and Other Stories,* 1987); *Más allá,* 1935.

LONG FICTION: *Historia de un amor turbio,* 1908; *Pasado amor,* 1929.

Horacio Quiroga (hoh-RAH-syoh kee-ROH-gah) holds much the same position in Spanish American literature as does Edgar Allan Poe in North American letters. Like Poe, whom Quiroga admired and who influenced the Uruguayan writer's work significantly, Quiroga dedicated his literary efforts almost entirely to the short-story genre, and in the process he not only penned some of the most famous and most anthologized stories to be found in Spanish American literature but also wrote about the genre, even offering a decalogue of suggestions to other writers on how they should approach writing the short story.

Quiroga published approximately two hundred short stories, many of which are considered classics within the Spanish American literary canon. Most of the author's stories, classics or not, fall within one (or more) of the following three general categories: Poesque stories of horror, often punctuated by madness and/or genetic defect; stories of human beings against a savage and thoroughly unromanticized nature; and Kiplingesque animal stories that frequently contain an underlying moral mes-

539

sage. The vast majority of Quiroga's stories are dramatic, intense, even memorable tales that captivate the reader and in general reveal a true master of the genre at work.

Two elements played significant roles in Horacio Quiroga's life and also frequently find their way into some of the writer's most famous stories. These two elements are tragic violence and the Uruguayan author's fascination with the jungle-filled Mi-

---

WHAT TO READ

"The Decapitated Chicken"

"The Decapitated Chicken" opens with a couple's four "idiot" sons seated on a bench on a patio, their tongues sticking out, their eyes staring off into space. The couple had hoped for a "normal" child and each blamed the other for the defective genes that produced the "idiot" sons. Finally, the couple's fifth child, a daughter, is "normal." She receives all the couple's attention, while the sons are relegated to the care of a servant.

One day, the four sons wander into the kitchen as the servant is cutting the head off of a chicken to prepare it for lunch. Later, by accident, both the sons and the daughter are left unattended. The daughter attempts to climb the garden wall on the patio, where her brothers sit, her neck resting on the top as she works to pull herself up the wall. Captivated, the sons drag her into the kitchen and behead her just as the servant beheaded the chicken.

This story features several classic Quiroga traits, including the early mention of something that will be important later in the story—the decapitation of the chicken. The narrator mentions that, though believed incapable of true learning, the four sons do possess a limited ability to imitate things that they see—again the decapitation of the chicken. This story also demonstrates Quiroga's penchant for surprise and horrifying endings, endings that place Quiroga among the best writers of this type of tale.

— *Keith H. Brower*

---

siones region of northern Argentina. The first of these elements, tragic violence, punctuates Quiroga's life—so much so, in fact, that were his biography offered as fiction, it would almost certainly be roundly criticized for being unbelievable, for no one's life, in the real world, could be so tragically violent, especially when a good portion of said violence comes through accident. The author's fascination with the harsh jungles of Misiones cost him at least one wife and possibly a second in real life, while this unforgiving environment provided him at the same time with the setting and thematic point of departure for many of his most famous stories.

Quiroga was born on December 31, 1878, in El Salto, Uruguay, the youngest of four children born to Prudencio Quiroga and Pastora Forteza. Three months after Horacio's birth, don Prudencio was killed when his hunting rifle went off accidentally as he was stepping from a boat. Quiroga's mother, doña Pastora, ashore with infant son Horacio in her arms, witnessed the tragic event and fainted, dropping her son to the ground. Later the same year, doña Pastora moved the family to the Argentine city of Córdoba. She remarried in 1891, taking Ascencio Barcos as her second husband, and the family moved to Montevideo, Uruguay. On a September afternoon in 1896, don Ascencio, having suffered a cerebral hemorrhage earlier, took his own life with a shotgun. Seventeen-year-old Horacio was the first to arrive on the scene.

Personal tragedy followed Quiroga in 1901 with the death of both his brother Prudencio and his sister Pastora. Then in 1902, the budding writer, who had published his first book, *Los arrecifes de coral* (coral reefs), the previous year, accidentally shot and killed one of his closest friends and literary companions, Federico Ferrando. After teaching off and on for several years in Buenos Aires, in September of 1909 Quiroga married Ana María Cirés and moved with her to San Ignacio, in the Misiones section of Argentina. Quiroga had first visited this jungle hinterland in 1903, with friend and Argentine writer Leopoldo Lugones. Enamored of the region, he bought land there in 1906 and divided his time between Misiones and Buenos Aires for the rest of his life. In 1915, unable to cope with the hardships

> *Once the snakes decided that they would give a costume ball; and to make the affair a truly brilliant one they sent invitations to the frogs, the toads, the alligators and the fish.*
>
> *The fish replied that since they had no legs they would not be able to do much dancing, whereupon, as a special courtesy to them, the ball was held on the shore of the Paraná.*
>
> —from "How the Flamingoes Got Their Stockings"

of living in the jungle, Ana María poisoned herself, leaving Quiroga a widower with the couple's two children. The following year, the writer returned to Buenos Aires, and over the next ten years he saw the publication of his most famous collections of stories, *Cuentos de amor, de locura y de muerte* (stories of love, madness, and death), *South American Jungle Tales, Anaconda,* and *The Exiles, and Other Stories,* all the while moving periodically between the backlands and the Argentine capital. He remarried in 1927, taking a nineteen-year-old friend of his daughter as his second wife (he was forty-nine). Quiroga and his new wife moved to Misiones in 1931, but she returned to Buenos Aires with their infant daughter the following year. Quiroga's health deteriorated significantly in 1934. He returned to Buenos Aires in 1936, where he was diagnosed with cancer in 1937. He took a lethal dose of cyanide to end his life in February of the same year.

Quiroga is without a doubt one of the most highly regarded and most widely read short-story writers in the history of Spanish American literature and is considered by most to be the foremost Spanish American short-story writer prior to the arrival of Jorge Luis Borges, Julio Cortázar, and other writers of the so-called new narrative on the Spanish American literary scene. While critical interest in Quiroga diminished during the Borges and post-Borges eras, the Uruguayan writer's popularity among readers did not—all of which, perhaps, is just as well, for Quiroga's stories, with rare exception the highly polished gems of a consummate short-story writer, lend themselves far more to reader enjoyment than to literary criticism.

— *Keith H. Brower*

Learn More

Berg, Mary G. "Horacio Quiroga." In *Poe Abroad: Influence, Reputation, Affinities*, edited by Lois Davis Vines. Iowa City: University of Iowa Press, 1999. Berg explains how Quiroga was influenced by the work of Edgar Allan Poe.

Brushwood, John S. "The Spanish American Short Story from Quiroga to Borges." *The Latin American Short Story: A Critical History*, edited by Margaret Sayers Peden. Boston: Twayne, 1983. Brushwood dedicates a portion of this chapter to Quiroga. The critic comments on Quiroga's place in the Spanish American short story, discusses the author's decalogue for the perfect short-story writer, and considers various aspects of the stories "The Decapitated Chicken," "Juan Darién," and "The Dead Man."

Englekirk, John. "Horacio Quiroga." In *Edgar Allan Poe in Hispanic Literature*. New York: Instituto de las Españas, 1934. In a lengthy study of Edgar Allan Poe's influence on numerous Spanish and Spanish American writers, Englekirk dedicates his longest chapter to Poe's influence on Quiroga.

Peden, William. "Some Notes on Quiroga's Stories." *Review* 19 (Winter, 1976): 41-43. Peden reviews the chief characteristics of Quiroga's stories and briefly refers to a number of stories that contain these characteristics. Succinct and on target, and especially useful for its English translation of Quiroga's decalogue of the "Perfect Short Story Writer." Published as part of a twenty-page "Focus" section on Quiroga.

Pupo-Walker, Enrique. "The Brief Narrative in Spanish America: 1835-1915." In *The Cambridge History of Latin American Literature*. Vol. 1, edited by Robert González Echevarria and Enrique Pupo-Walker. Cambridge, England: Cambridge University Press, 1996. Provides a valuable historical and cultural context for Quiroga by charting the development of short narrative in Spanish America in the nineteenth century through the early part of the twentieth century.

San Roman, Gustavo. "Amor Turbio, Paranoia, and the Vicissitudes of Manliness in Horacio Quiroga." *The Modern Language Review* 90 (October, 1995): 919-934. Discusses the theme of love in Quiroga's fiction, focusing on the novella *Historia de un amor turbio.* Comments on the links between the story and paranoia, and argues that Quiroga's texts are more like those of a victim than those of a self-controlled author.

Schade, George D. "Horacio Quiroga." In *Latin American Literature in the Twentieth Century: A Guide,* edited by Leonard S. Klein. New York: Ungar, 1986. Largely a three-page version of Schade's introduction to Margaret Sayers Peden's *The Decapitated Chicken and Other Stories,* listed below. Provides concise discussion of the writer's life, career, and chief characteristics and limited consideration of specific stories. Includes a list of "Further Works" (most in Spanish) by Quiroga and a brief bibliography (most in Spanish).

_____. Introduction to *The Decapitated Chicken and Other Stories.* Edited and translated by Margaret Sayers Peden. Austin: University of Texas Press, 1976. In this introduction to Peden's English-language collection of twelve of Quiroga's stories, Schade provides an introduction to Quiroga for the uninitiated reader, discussing the writer's life and career and the chief characteristics of his works. In the process, he comments briefly on the stories included in the collection, among them "The Feather Pillow," "The Decapitated Chicken," "Drifting," "Juan Darién," "The Dead Man," "Anaconda," and "The Son."

John Rechy

Mexican American novelist

Born: El Paso, Texas; March 10, 1934
Also known as: John Francisco Rechy

LONG FICTION: *City of Night*, 1963; *Numbers*, 1967; *This Day's Death*, 1970; *The Vampires*, 1971; *The Fourth Angel*, 1972; *Rushes*, 1979; *Bodies and Souls*, 1983; *Marilyn's Daughter*, 1988; *The Miraculous Day of Amalia Gómez*, 1991; *Our Lady of Babylon*, 1996; *The Coming of the Night*, 1999; *The Life and Adventures of Lyle Clemens*, 2003.

DRAMA: *Momma as She Became—Not as She Was*, pr. 1978; *Tigers Wild*, pr. 1986.

MISCELLANEOUS: *The Sexual Outlaw: A Documentary, a Non-fiction Account, with Commentaries, of Three Days and Nights in the Sexual Underground*, 1977, revised 1985.

John Francisco Rechy (REH-chee), son of Roberto Sixto Rechy and Guadalupe Flores de Rechy, was descended from Mexican and Anglo-Saxon forebears. Born in El Paso, Texas, he spoke Spanish until he began school. Rechy remained in El Paso for his undergraduate education, receiving his bachelor's degree from Texas Western College. He continued his education at the New School for Social Research in New York City. His residence there shaped much of his future career as a novelist.

Despite his Mexican background, Rechy, until the publication of *The Miraculous Day of Amalia Gómez*, drew less on Chicano themes than he did upon the acculturation he received in New York's gay society in the late 1950's and early 1960's. His writing career was bolstered in 1961 when his short story, "The Fabulous Wedding of Miss Destiny," a gay-oriented story, received the Longview Foundation Fiction Prize. This award communicated to Rechy that he was an estimable writer and that a story focusing on gay topics could garner public recognition.

Winning the Longview award led to Rechy's obtaining a publishing contract for *City of Night*. He had begun it in 1959, but it remained unfinished until 1963. Much influenced by Tennessee Williams's plays, particularly *Suddenly Last Summer* (1958), Rechy focuses in *City of Night* on the peregrinations and sexual adventures of a hustler who wanders from New York to the gay enclaves in Chicago, Los Angeles, San Francisco, and New Orleans. The first-person narration closely parallels Rechy's own adventures during the 1950's.

When *City of Night* was published, the homosexual novel was still considered somewhat unusual, despite earlier appearances of works containing gay themes such as Radclyffe Hall's *The Well of Loneliness* (1928), Lillian Hellman's play *The Children's Hour* (1934), Gore Vidal's *The City and the Pillar* (1948), and James

Tony Korody

> *It should begin* now, *in the* present *present, when I am in seclusion in my quarters in the country, within the château of my beloved husband, the handsome Count du Muir, murdered in the Grand Cathedral by his twin brother, Alix, in collusion with their sister, Irena, and perhaps—yes!—the Pope himself.*
>
> —from *Our Lady of Babylon*

Barr's *Quatrefoil* (1950). Major publishers did not encourage such works, fearing the backlash they could unleash against their companies. The public had been somewhat enlightened by Alfred Kinsey's *Sexual Behavior in the Human Male* (1948), but attitudes regarding gay behavior and identity regarded it as abnormal or deviant behavior.

Rechy's first novel, an immediate best-seller in the United States and abroad, is much in the eighteenth century picaresque tradition of Henry Fielding's *Tom Jones* (1749) and Tobias Smollett's *The Adventures of Peregrine Pickle* (1751). Episodic in its development, each portion is virtually a discrete entity welded to the whole by the unifying thread of first-person narration.

Rechy, capitalizing on the book's popularity and a more accepting public climate, in 1967 followed *City of Night* with *Numbers*, a gay novel in which the protagonist, Johnny Río, once a male prostitute in Los Angeles, returns after three years with the goal of making three conquests a day for ten days. Cruising Griffith Park, he easily achieves his aim, indeed exceeding it by seven.

This novel, although it reached the best-seller list, evoked scorn from critics and dismay from many readers. It was widely viewed as borderline pornography rather than as Rechy's existential revelations about a protagonist trying to thwart death by living riotously.

WHAT TO READ

City of Night

John Rechy's first and best-known novel, *City of Night* (1963) explores sexuality and spirituality as they develop during the protagonist's quest for salvation. Combining Chicano heritage, autobiographical material, and a poetic rendering of the restless loneliness of America's sexual underground, *City of Night* investigates difficulties and rewards of an individual's search to claim the many identities that intersect in a single life.

The unnamed protagonist's journey begins with his childhood in El Paso, Texas. Rechy draws on stark, lonely imagery (the fiercely unforgiving wind, the father's inexplicable hatred of his son, the mother's hungry love) to portray a childhood and adolescence denied any sense of connection and certainty. Disconnected and detached from his home, the protagonist stands before the mirror confusing identity with isolation. He asserts a narcissistic removal from the world ("I have only me!") that his quest at first confirms, then refutes.

The first-person narrative chronicles the protagonist's wanderings through New York City, Los Angeles, Hollywood, San Francisco, Chicago, and New Orleans. For Rechy, these various urban settings are "one vast City of Night" fused into the "unmistakable shape of loneliness." Working as a male prostitute, the protagonist navigates this landscape, portraying the types of sexual and spiritual desperation he encounters along the way. His journey is a pilgrimage first away from home and then back to it, as he accepts the possibility that he might come to terms with his family, his childhood, and himself.

City of Night interweaves chapters that describe the geographies of the cities the protagonist passes through with chapters that portray people condemned to these dark cities. Sometimes humorous, sometimes bitter, sometimes indifferent, these portraits of people trapped in the loneliness and cruelty of the cities mirror the protagonist's quest. He is like and unlike the denizens of this world.

— *Daniel M. Scott III*

Perhaps stung by the reception of *Numbers,* Rechy next wrote *This Day's Death,* a well-controlled bifurcated novel about the encroaching death of Jim Girard's mother, a situation that parallels his trial on trumped-up charges of sexual perversion; although innocent, he is convicted. His conviction scuttles his hope of becoming an attorney and raises serious questions about whether the justice system works when homosexuality is part of the equation.

The Vampires introduces gay themes and has a preponderance of gay characters, but it focuses more on evil than on the sexual matters Rechy emphasized in his earlier novels. *The Fourth Angel,* built around a teenage, thrill-seeking trio, the Angels, and its recruitment of a fourth Angel, Jerry, studies the dominant Angel, Shell, who rejects sentimentality in counterdistinction to the fourth Angel, Jerry, who needs love and epitomizes the softness that Shell disparages.

A grant from the National Endowment for the Humanities in 1976 enabled Rechy to research his next book, *The Sexual Outlaw: A Documentary,* which is alternately documentary and fictional. Rechy explores the psychology behind the gay male's frantic search for homosexual encounters, finding it to be, at least in part, a way of rebelling against oppressive authority.

Rushes is set in Rushes, a bar that attracts gays with leather and uniform fetishes, macho men who, although gay, are contemptuous of their orientation and of other gay men less butch than they are. In *Bodies and Souls,* a work strongly influenced by Williams's *Cat on a Hot Tin Roof* (1954), the evangelistic protagonist is left a seven-figure bequest by a wily follower who attaches conditions to it, in much the way conditions were attached to the bequest in Friedrich Dürrenmatt's play *The Visit* (1956). Rechy's first book to reflect the Chicano viewpoint was *The Miraculous Day of Amalia Gómez.* Set in the Los Angeles barrio, it traces the life of a Chicano family in Los Angeles, incorporating not only working-class realism but also the magic realism of religious and Mexican fables.

In 1996, Rechy again mixed realism and myth in *Our Lady of Babylon,* in which a woman accused of murdering her husband dreams of maligned women in history, only to discover that her dreams are memories of past lives. In 1999, *The Coming of the Night*, Rechy returned to his Los Angeles setting and some of his themes in *City of Night* to narrate the events of a windy day in 1981, at the dawn of the AIDS epidemic, and a cast of gay characters who meet a group of gay bashers in a West Hollywood park. *The Life and Adventures of Lyle Clemens*, as its title suggests, traces the picaresque exploits of its protagonist from his conservative, fundamentalist Texas hometown to liberal, liberated Los Angeles.

A winner of PEN West's Lifetime Achievement Award, Rechy maintains an active career as writer, lecturer, and respected teacher of writing—although he remains true to his iconoclastic image. In the October 6, 2002, edition of the *Los Angeles Times*, he debunked the Terrible Three rules of writing: "Show, don't tell"; "Write about what you know"; and "Always have a sympathetic character for the reader to relate to." Rechy's three: "[S]howing may be created through refined telling"; "Write about whatever you want"; and "Write about characters, good or evil, who fascinate."

— *R. Baird Shuman*

Learn More

Bredbeck, Gregory W. "John Rechy." In *Contemporary Gay American Novelists: A Bio-Bibliographical Critical Sourcebook*, edited by Emmanuel S. Nelson. Westport, Conn.: Greenwood Press, 1993. Considers Rechy's life, his works, and the reception of his writings.

Casillo, Charles. *Outlaw: The Lives and Careers of John Rechy*. Los Angeles: Advocate Books, 2002. This full-length biography includes explorations of the street hustling, writing, and academic career of Rechy, and the inspirations and tensions created by living a life of contradictions. Also includes a look at Rechy's unpublished works.

Ortiz, Ricardo. "L.A. Women: Jim Morrison with John Rechy." In *The Queer Sixties*, edited by Patricia Juliana Smith. New York: Routledge, 1999. Discusses the eroticism of life in Los Angeles's 1960's counterculture. Argues that the songs "L.A. Woman" and "Back Door Man" connect the Doors with Rechy's work, queer sexuality, the Beats, and the questioning of dominant ideas on popular culture.

_____. "Sexuality Degree Zero." *Journal of Homosexuality* 26 (August/September, 1993). Discusses pleasure and power in Rechy's novels.

Pérez-Torres, Rafael. "The Ambiguous Outlaw: John Rechy and Complicitious Homotextuality." In *Fictions of Masculinity: Crossing Cultures, Crossing Sexualities,* edited by Peter F. Murphy. New York: New York University Press, 1994. An analysis of the treatment of homosexuality and masculinity in Rechy's work, focusing on *The Sexual Outlaw.*

Rechy, John. Interview by Debra Castillo. *Diacritics* 25 (Spring, 1995). Rechy discusses Latino culture, homosexuality, and critical work on his writings.

_____. "John Rechy." http://www.johnrechy.com/. Accessed March 22, 2005. This Web site includes summaries and reviews of each of his books, photos, and some of his thoughts on writing and on current events.

Steuervogel, T. "Contemporary Homosexual Fiction and the Gay Rights Movement." *Journal of Popular Culture* 20 (Winter, 1986). Relates Rechy's writing to gay politics during the early days of the AIDS epidemic.

Alfonso Reyes

Mexican poet and critic

Born: Monterrey, Mexico; May 17, 1889
Died: Mexico City, Mexico; December 27, 1959

POETRY: *Huellas*, 1923; *Ifigenia cruel*, 1924; *Pausa*, 1926; *Cinco casi sonetos*, 1931; *Romances del Rio de Enero*, 1933; *A la memoria de Ricardo Güiraldes*, 1934; *Golfo de Mexico*, 1934 (*Gulf of Mexico*, 1949); *Yerbas del Tarahumara*, 1934 (*Tarahumara Herbs*, 1949); *Infancia*, 1935; *Minuta*, 1935; *Otra voz*, 1936; *Cantata en la tumba de Federico García Lorca*, 1937; *Poema del Cid*, 1938 (modern version of *Cantar de mío Cid*); *Villa de Unión*, 1940; *Algunos poemas*, 1941; *Romances y afines*, 1945; *La vega y el soto*, 1946; *Cortesía*, 1948; *Homero en Cuernavaca*, 1949; *Obra poética*, 1952.

SHORT FICTION: *El plano oblicuo*, 1920; *Quince presencias*, 1955; *Alfonso Reyes: Prosa y poesía*, 1977 (includes "Major Aranda's Hand," "Silueta del indio Jesús," and "El testimonio de Juan Peña").

TRANSLATIONS: *Viaje sentimental por Francia e Italia*, 1919 (of Laurence Sterne's *A Sentimental Journey*); *El candor de Padre Brown*, 1921 (of G. K. Chesterton's detective stories); *Olalla*, 1922 (of Robert Louis Stevenson's stories); *Historia de la literatura griega*, 1948 (of C. M. Bowra's *Ancient Greek Literature*); *Eurípides y su época*, 1949 (of Gilbert Murray's *Euripides and His Age*); *La Ilíada de Homero*, 1951 (of Homer's *Iliad*).

NONFICTION: *Cuestiones estéticas*, 1911; *Cartones de Madrid*, 1917; *Visión de Anáhuac*, 1917 (*Vision of Anáhuac*, 1950); *Retratos reales e imaginarios*, 1920; *Simpatías y diferencias*, 1921-1926; *Cuestiones gongorinas*, 1927; *Discurso por Virgilio*, 1933; *Capítulos de literatura española*, 1939; *La crítica en la edad ateniense*, 1941; *La experiencia literaria*, 1942; *Ultima Thule*, 1942; *El deslinde: Prolegómenos a la teoría literaria*, 1944; *Grata compañía*, 1948; *The Position of America, and Other Essays*, 1950 (includes *Vision of Anáhuac*); *Árbol de pólvora*, 1953; *Parentalia: Primer libro*

de recuerdos, 1954; *Albores: Segundo libro de recuerdos,* 1960; *Mexico in a Nutshell, and Other Essays,* 1964.
MISCELLANEOUS: *Obras completas,* 1955-1967.

A lfonso Reyes (al-FOHN-soh RAY-yays) wrote "the art of expression did not appear to me as a rhetorical function, independent of conduct, but a means of realizing human feeling." Thus this Mexican writer defined and justified his literary vocation, so faithfully and completely fulfilled during the fifty years of his writing that he has justly been called "the most accomplished example of the man of letters in Mexico."

Born in Monterrey, capital of the state of Nuevo Leon, on May 17, 1889, he was the son of General Bernardo Reyes, at that time governor of the state and a prominent politician in the regime of President Porfirio Díaz. Having begun his schooling in his native city, Reyes moved later to Mexico City, where in 1913

© Alberto Dallal

he received the professional title of lawyer. There he became part of a generation of writers engaged in a vigorous intellectual revolution that had enormous repercussions in Mexican culture. These writers were united in a movement called El Ateneo de la Juventud (The Athenaeum of Youth). Reyes was the youngest member of this group, and he labored side by side with other writers who became primary figures in the intellectual life of modern Mexico, including José Vasconcelos, Antonio Caso, Martín Luis Guzmán, and Enrique González Martínez. The basic aims of this group were the study and understanding of Mexican culture, the assimilation of the emerging post-positivist philosophies, and the development of literary criticism, all grounded in the universal ideas and values of the Enlightenment. The coming revolution, however, produced a rift among those aims: the dream of a harmonious insertion of the Mexican culture into the universal one proved complicated. Each member of the generation pursued his own path out of the impasse.

Immersed in these intellectual currents, Reyes left for Europe in the service of Mexican diplomacy. In Madrid he collaborated with the emerging Center of Historical Studies under the direction of D. Ramón Menéndez Pidal, and he was also invited to contribute to the pages of *El Sol*, headed by José Ortega y Gasset. In 1939, after twenty-five years—except for a few intermissions—of diplomatic service, he returned to Mexico and pursued his literary activities with the greatest enthusiasm. Reyes used the presence in Mexico of exiled Spanish intellectuals to found El Colegio de México, which became the primary Mexican institution of higher learning. The Universities of California, Havana, and Mexico as well as Tulane, Harvard, and Princeton Universities conferred honorary degrees on him. In 1957, in recognition of his faithful and constant dedication to letters, he was named president of the Mexican Academy of Language, of which he had been a corresponding member since 1918.

Reyes's body of work is extensive. During his more than fifty years as a writer—in 1906, at the age of seventeen, he wrote his first sonnet, "Mercenario"—his indefatigable pen produced no fewer than three hundred titles, among them poems, criticism,

WHAT TO READ

Vision of Anáhuac

Written in Madrid in 1915 and published in San José de Costa Rica two years later, *Vision of Anáhuac*, which appeared in English translation in the 1950 collection *The Position of America*, is one of those seminal works in which significance or influence bears no relationship to bulk. It is a prose poem, a landscape painting, a patriotic invocation, a study in history, an archaeological reconstruction, a literary critique, an exercise in style. The famous Chilean poet Gabriela Mistral called it the best single piece of Latin American prose.

Anáhuac was the Nahuatl name for the Valley of Mexico, site of the great city of Tenochtitlán and the center of the Aztec civilization that fell to the conquistadores under Hernán Cortés in 1521. In a style that is subtle, evocative, and varied, Alfonso Reyes re-creates the confrontation between two societies. He laments the loss of the indigenous poetry of the Indians, saying that reconstructions contain only suggestions of what that poetry must have been, for even altered and indirect in the surviving versions it exhibits a degree of sensibility not characteristic of the translating Spanish missionaries. One poem, "Ninoyolonotza," is quoted as an example of man's search through the world of the senses for a concept of the ideal. Another, paraphrased in part from the Quetzalcóatl cycle, contains echoes of an ancient fertility myth and promises a rebirth that, if fulfilled, might have destroyed the blood-drinking gods of the Aztecs and so altered the somber history of Anáhuac.

Discussion can do no more than suggest the magnificence of the writing in *Vision of Anáhuac*. All of pre-conquest Mexico is seen here, evoked out of a vast and prodigal storehouse of history and legend, every detail viewed through the eyes of a poet conferring impressions. The unique style is in keeping with the theme: language rises from the page to the slow swing of its rhythms, setting the standard for a new kind of poetry.

> *Sometimes an effluence rises,*
> *made of nothing, from the ground.*
> *Suddenly, hiddenly,*
> *a cedar sighs its scent.*
> *We who are a secret's*
> *tenuous dissolution,*
> *our soul no sooner yields*
> *than dream wells over.*
>
> —from "Scarcely . . ." (trans. Samuel Beckett)

essays, memoirs, plays, novels, short stories, prefaces, newspaper articles, nonliterary works, and translations. A constant element of his work, as much in his prose as in his verse, is a lyricism that gives to his books a tone that is agreeable and gracious, ingenious and subtle. In his poetry are evident the influences of Luis de Góngora and Stéphane Mallarmé, combined with a personal taste for the picturesque and colloquial. In his preferred medium, the essay, he treats a great variety of subjects. His best literary criticism is to be found in the essays of *La experiencia literaria*, in which he pours forth his own experiences in the profession of a writer, and in "Sobre la estetica de Gongora," with which he opens the doors to the modern study and understanding of that baroque Spanish poet. Important among his strictly literary works is *Vision of Anáhuac*, a poetic evocation of pre-Columbian Mexican history. Among the humanistic studies, *Discurso por Virgilio* (address in behalf of Vergil), contains both profound classical and American flavor; among the works with fantastic and dreamlike themes is *Árbol de pólvora* (tree of powder).

With a profound understanding of the function of a writer, Reyes produced his greatest critical work, *El deslinde* (the boundary line). In it, he analyzes the artistic import of expression, style, aesthetic problems, semantics, philology, and the philosophy of language.

"American, European, universal"—thus Federico de Onís described Reyes. These epithets are well applied if one considers that this Mexican writer, through his native sensibility, his classic form, and the universality of his subjects, is, as the same critic avers, "the most successful example of a citizen of the international world of letters, both ancient and modern."

— *Emil Volek*

Learn More

Aponte, Barbara Bockus. *Alfonso Reyes and Spain: His Dialogue with Unamuno, Valle-Inclán, Ortega y Gasset, Jiménez, and Gómez de la Serna.* Austin: University of Texas Press, 1972. The author explores the dialogues that Reyes maintained with Spanish literary contemporaries. Their correspondence sheds light upon the lives and works of these writers. Reyes relied upon this form of communication to maintain friendships and share ideas. As a member of the Mexican intellectual elite, Reyes recognized that his Spanish contacts were vital to his literary development.

Carter, Sheila. *The Literary Experience.* Mona, Jamaica: Savacou, 1985. A critical analysis of *El deslinde*, with bibliographic references.

Conn, Robert T. *The Politics of Philology: Alfonso Reyes and the Invention of the Latin American Literary Tradition.* Lewisburg, Pa.: Bucknell University Press, 2002. Conn explains how Reyes's work helped establish the role of the writer as public intellectual in Latin America. He also examines how Reyes helped forge a sense of unity among the Latin American writers of his generation.

Robb, James W. "Alfonso Reyes." In *Latin American Writers,* edited by Carlos A. Solé. Vol. 2. New York: Charles Scribner's Sons, 1989. A thorough article from the Scribner writers series.

_____. *Patterns of Image and Structure.* New York: AMS Press, 1969. Critical analysis of the essays of Alfonso Reyes.

Shreve, Jack, and Carole A. Champagne. "Alfonso Reyes." In *Critical Survey of Poetry,* edited by Philip K. Jason. 2d rev. ed. Pasadena, Calif.: Salem Press, 2003. A thorough overview of Reyes's life and career, emphasizing his poetry.

Alberto Ríos

Mexican American
poet and short-story writer

Born: Nogales, Arizona; September 18, 1952

POETRY: *Elk Heads on the Wall*, 1979; *Whispering to Fool the Wind*, 1982; *Five Indiscretions*, 1985; *The Lime Orchard Woman*, 1988; *The Warrington Poems*, 1989; *Teodoro Luna's Two Kisses*, 1990; *The Smallest Muscle in the Human Body*, 2002.
SHORT FICTION: *The Iguana Killer: Twelve Stories of the Heart*, 1984; *Pig Cookies, and Other Stories*, 1995; *The Curtain of Trees: Stories*, 1999.
NONFICTION: *Capirotada: A Nogales Memoir*, 1999.

Both in fact and in spirit, Alberto Ríos (al-BEHR-toh REE-ohs) is a native of the Southwest. He was born to a Mexican father, Alberto Alvaro Ríos, a justice of the peace, and an English mother, Agnes Fogg Ríos, a nurse. Early in his life he was nicknamed Tito, a diminutive of Albertito, that is, "Little Albert." The nickname referred to his small physical frame and differentiated him from his father. In 1975 the future author earned a bachelor of arts degree, with a major in psychology, from the University of Arizona. He then entered the university's law school, only to find that poetry rather than the law was to be his calling. After one year of legal training he switched to the graduate program in creative writing, taking a master of fine arts degree in 1979. He joined the faculty of Arizona State University in 1982 and became Regents' Professor of English there in 1994. He maintains an active schedule of writing, teaching, readings, and lecturing.

Ríos grew up on the Mexican American border, and the work that first brought him widespread attention, *Whispering to Fool the Wind*, addressed most of all the splay of his roots. This volume won for Ríos the prestigious Walt Whitman Award from the National Academy of American Poets in 1981. His first collection of short fiction, *The Iguana Killer,* winner of the Western States Book Award for fiction some two years later, dealt with similar concerns. Taken together, these works identified Ríos as a first-generation American artist chronicling an ethnic experience that had too long gone unexplored in American letters. After their publication, Ríos was warmly praised and widely anthologized, often embraced for this subject matter.

Ríos's work extended beyond the provincial with the publication of the collection of poems *Teodoro Luna's Two Kisses* and his second short-fiction collection, *Pig Cookies, and Other Stories.* These works still spoke of a culture in transition, but they also displayed an evolving artistic vision, one having as much to do with the human condition as it has to do with an ethnic experience per se. Ríos's writing began to manifest something beyond the tangible. A man spits on the pavement in order to rid himself of an intolerable thought. A priest's soul leaves his body, with animal-like instinct. A fat man's body is proof of a weight within him having nothing to do with scales or the flesh. A number of critics noted Ríos's ability to make the commonplace seem strange—as well as his capacity to make the familiar seem magical—and aligned him in this regard with the Latin Magical Realists, such as Gabriel García Márquez.

And everything I expect has been taken away, like that, quick:
The names are not alphabetized.
They are in the order of dying,
An alphabet of—somewhere—screaming.
I start to walk out. I almost leave
But stop to look up names of friends,
My own name. There is somebody
Severiano Ríos.

—from "The Vietnam Wall"

Ríos's vision is important in its own right, however. In an early short story, "The Birthday of Mrs. Pineda," a character brings a cup of coffee to his face only to discover the aroma pulling his head toward the lip of the cup. A short story published a decade later brings this conceit to fruition. "The Great Gardens of Lamberto Diaz" begins with these words:

> A person did not come to these gardens . . . to admire them or simply to breathe them in. No. One was breathed in by them, and something more. In this place a person was drawn up as if to the breast of the gardens, as if one were a child again, and being drawn up was all that mattered and meant everything.
>
> •

Often in his interviews Ríos speaks of "situational physics," of "emotional science." Readers are asked in reading Ríos not simply to revise their suppositions about natural law but to relocate themselves, to reconsider their relationship to all that is tangible. People must reconfirm their presence on the planet, and then reconfirm this presence to one another; the process must begin by listening to language.

Ríos is bilingual, and from the beginning he has called on the idioms and syntax of both English and Spanish in his work. He has also concerned himself with what he calls "a third language," a language that our bodies speak to one another with or without our conscious knowledge—the wink, the nod, the small and still smaller gesture. The reader encounters this type of language even in such early poems as "Nani," in which a small boy speaks English, his grandmother, only Spanish. She serves him lunch each week, and the old woman and the boy discover a shared understanding, bringing them closer than words ever could.

Ríos has placed increasing importance on such means of bridging the gulfs that divide people. In the title poem of *Teodoro Luna's Two Kisses*, aged Teodoro Luna and his equally aged wife know an intimacy that the young are denied—a glance from one to the other, an eyebrow raised that turns a public event into a private experience between them. Kissing is the single act that most occupies Ríos's attention. It illustrates

W H A T   T O   R E A D

"The Purpose of Altar Boys"

In "The Purpose of Altar Boys" the adult Alberto Ríos assumes the voice of a mischievous altar boy who "knew about . . . things." For example, when he assisted the priest at Communion on Sundays, he believed he had his own mission. On some Sundays, he says, his mission was to remind people of the night before. Holding the metal plate beneath a communicant's chin, he would drag his feet on the carpet, stirring up static electricity. He would wait for the right moment, then touch the plate to the person's chin, delivering his "Holy Electric Shock" of retribution.

The sense of ease and speed in the poem's narration is facilitated by the poet's use of a relatively short poetic line, usually containing six or seven syllables. Although the lines are short, the sentences are long. The combination of short lines and long sentences creates a sense not only of speed but also of breathlessness—these features express the altar boy's excitement as he tells his story of good and evil, judgment and temptation. His excitement is also conveyed by repetition. For example, the boy's repeated use of the pronoun "I" reflects his self-assertion and reveals the pride he takes in fulfilling his mission.

The altar boy is a comic character, a prankster whose mischief is essentially harmless. What is harmless in a child, however, may be evil in an adult. A voyeur is not an attractive person. Far worse are people who commit murder and claim that God told them to do it. The altar boy is merely flirting with the sin of pride when he takes upon himself the authority to judge and punish others. Thus, it is important that the poem is written in the past tense. The adult narrator has experience that he lacked as a boy, and his concepts of good and evil are no longer naïve.

— *James Green*

both the enormity of human desire and the inability of people to express themselves in commensurate proportions. It stands for all that divides people and all that might bring them together. Ríos is often at his best when he is exploring how people turn public events into private experience and what they must dare in order to show themselves to the world. Certainly this is the case in several of the stories in *Pig Cookies*. Lazaro, the small boy in the title story, is so consumed with love for a neighbor girl that his very being is shaken, his baker's hands overcome. To put this love of her into words is a much different matter, as the story's ending reminds us: "The most difficult act in the world, he thought with his stomach, was this first saying of *hello*. This first daring to call, without permission, Desire by its first name."

In 1999 Ríos published a memoir, *Capirotada*, named for a Mexican bread pudding made, as Ríos notes, from "a mysterious mixture of prunes, peanuts, white bread, raisins, *quesadilla* cheese, butter, cinnamon and cloves . . . and things people will not tell you," like his life; it won the Latino Literary Hall of Fame Award. In 2002 he published *The Smallest Muscle in the Human Body*, in which poems honed from fable, parable, and family legend use the "intense and supple imagination of childhood to find and preserve history beyond facts"; this collection was a finalist for the National Book Award. In addition to winning these honors, Ríos is the recipient of the Arizona Governor's Arts Award, fellowships from the Guggenheim Foundation and the National Endowment for the Arts, the Walt Whitman Award, the Western States Book Award for Fiction, and six Pushcart Prizes in both poetry and fiction. In 2002, he won the Western Literature Association's Distinguished Achievement Award, the group's highest distinction for authors whose work has defined and influenced the literature and study of the West.

—*Jay Boyer*

Learn More

Logue, Mary. Review of *Whispering to Fool the Wind*, by Alberto Ríos. *Village Voice Literary Supplement*, October, 1982. This extended review was among the first to explore Ríos's talents and is still the best.

Ríos, Alberto. *Capirotada: A Nogales Memoir.* Albuquerque: University of New Mexico Press, 1999. Ríos recalls his experiences growing up in Nogales, an Arizona border town. He has drawn upon these experiences to write some of his short stories.

_____. "Words Like the Wind: An Interview with Alberto Ríos." Interview by William Barillas. *Américas Review* 24 (Fall/Winter, 1996). An insightful interview with Ríos.

Ullman, L. "Solitaries and Storytellers, Magicians, and Pagans: Five Poets in the World." *Kenyon Review* 13 (Spring, 1991). Reviews Ríos's *Teodoro Luna's Two Kisses.*

Wild, Peter. *Alberto Ríos.* Boise, Idaho: Boise State University Press, 1998. Part of the Western Writers series. A brief introduction to the author's work.

Tomás Rivera

Mexican American novelist

Born: Crystal City, Texas; December 22, 1935
Died: Fontana, California; May 16, 1984

LONG FICTION: . . . *y no se lo tragó la tierra*/. . . *and the earth did not part*, 1971 (also as *This Migrant Earth*, 1985; . . . *and the earth did not devour him*, 1987).

SHORT FICTION: *The Harvest: Short Stories*, 1989 (bilingual).

POETRY: *Always, and Other Poems*, 1973; *The Searchers: Collected Poetry*, 1990.

MISCELLANEOUS: *Tomás Rivera: The Complete Works*, 1991.

Rarely has a literary reputation been so securely based on one slim novel as that of Tomás Rivera (toh-MAHS rih-VAYR-ah). Though he was also highly regarded as a college administrator and educator—becoming, in 1979, the first Chicano to be named a chancellor in the University of California system—and though he published a small collection of poems (*Always, and Other Poems*) in 1973 and scattered poems, essays, and short stories afterward, it is on his striking episodic novel, . . . *and the earth did not part*, that his literary reputation rests.

Born on December 22, 1935, the son of migrant workers Florencio and Josefa Hernández Rivera, Tomás Rivera himself did migrant work until 1957. He received a bachelor's degree in education in 1958 and a master's degree in educational administration in 1964 from Southwest Texas State University; he subsequently studied at the University of Oklahoma, from which he earned a doctorate in Romance languages and literature in 1969. His novel . . . *and the earth did not part* was first published in 1971, in an edition that printed both the original Spanish and its translation into English; it won the Quinto Sol National Chicano Literary Award. In 1978 he married Concepción Garza, and in 1979 he became chancellor of the University of California at Riverside.

> *There's nothing I can do now. But I can't tell the others 'cause they'll sin like me. I better not go to communion. Better that I don't go to confession. I can't, now that I know, I can't. But what will Mom and Dad say if I don't go to communion? And my godfather, I can't leave him there waiting. I have to confess what I saw.*
>
> —from "First Communion"
> (trans. Evangelina Vigil-Piñón)

Not a conventional novel, . . . *and the earth did not part* may appear to some at first reading to be a collection of loosely connected short stories and sketches. While the separate chapters are written and can be read as individual stories, critics agree that the deeper structure of the work as a whole demands that it be read as a novel.

The book begins with a chapter entitled "The Lost Year," which introduces the theme of lost time that will continue through the novel. When the narrator describes a recurring dream in which the unnamed protagonist "would suddenly awaken and then realize that he was really asleep," the reader may be put in mind of the beginning of Marcel Proust's *À la recherche du temps perdu* (1913-1927; *Remembrance of Things Past*, 1922-1931, 1981), in which the narrator wakes with the candle extinguished and cannot remember whether he has slept. As Rivera's book continues, the reader understands that the period the narrator is describing as a year is actually several years, which have blended together into a single year. The fragmentation of the chapters that follow highlights less the memory loss of the protagonist than the slow regaining of memory he is experiencing.

The novel follows the effects of migrant living and working not only on the main character but also on the community of workers. Typically, the chapters alternate sections of tersely de-

W H A T   T O   R E A D

. . . and the earth did not part

Rivera's . . . *and the earth did not part* (1971) has exerted a great influence on Chicano literature. The book explores the psychological and external circumstances of a boy who is coming of age in a Mexican American migrant family. The novel is a collection of disjointed narratives, including twelve stories and thirteen vignettes, told with various voices. This unusual structure evokes impressions of a lifestyle in which the continuity of existence is repeatedly broken by forced migration and in which poverty creates a deadening sameness that erases time.

The story begins with "The Lost Year," which indicates the boy has lost touch with his identity and with the reality of events. Several sections portray the dismal, oppressed condition of migrant farmworkers. In "A Silvery Night," the boy first calls the Devil, then decides that the Devil does not exist. Religious awakening continues in the title chapter, in which the boy curses God and is not punished—the earth remains solid.

The nature of sin, the mystery of sex, and the injustices and tragedies visited upon his people are all confusing to the boy. Brief moments of beauty are eclipsed by injuries and horrible deaths. A mother struggles to buy a few Christmas presents for her children. In a swindle, a family loses their only photograph of a son killed in the Korean War. The boy becomes a man, hiding under his house. The final scene offers a glimmer of hope, as he climbs a tree and imagines that someone in another tree can see him.

The simple language and humble settings make the book accessible, but the novel's unique structure and symbolism present challenges to the reader. The book has been reprinted several times, and a retelling in English (*This Migrant Earth*, 1985) was published by Rolando Hinojosa. A film version, *And the Earth Did Not Swallow Him*, was released in 1994.

— *Laura L. Klure*

scribed action with equally terse dialogue between unnamed speakers—sometimes between the characters of the story being told and sometimes between two people who are discussing this story, which might be well known to both of them. At the end of "The Children Couldn't Wait," a story about a child being shot for taking a drink of water, two people talk about how the boss who shot him went crazy and lost all of his money. Similarly, both "The Little Burn Victims" and "The Night the Lights Went Out"—the first a story of children burned to death and the second a story of a jealous lover who electrocutes himself—end with the voices of people casually discussing these tragedies. Not only do the tragedies belong to the entire community, but they are accepted almost as everyday, if fascinating, occurrences.

Side by side with these apocalyptic stories are the stories that seem to center on the main protagonist himself; though it is not certain that the young boy who appears in many of these stories is the same one, it is certain that the stories are presented as if they might be about the same person. Just as the tragedies belong not only to the people to whom they happen but also to the entire community, each story about the growth and disappointments of a young boy belongs not only to the boy himself but also to people like him. In "It's That It Hurts" the boy, having been expelled from school for fighting back when attacked by a couple of what the principal calls "our kids," and unable to imagine breaking the news to his parents, tries to convince himself that maybe he was not expelled. The irony is that his expulsion from school marks the beginning of his real education. Three stories, "A Silvery Night," "... and the earth did not part," and "First Communion," trace his growing mistrust of religion as he calls on the Devil to appear, curses God for letting his father and little brother both get sunstroke, and lies to a priest at confession. In each case he expects some sort of retribution to occur, but instead he comes to the sudden recognition that the Devil will not appear and that the earth will not open up and swallow him.

His astonishment at learning that apocalypses need not occur leads up to the "The Portrait," in which a man who has been

567

swindled by a person who promised to make a portrait of his dead son searches out the swindler and forces him to make the portrait from memory. For the first time in the book, forceful action taken by a Chicano against an exploiter produces a desirable result. In the penultimate chapter, "When We Arrive," migrant workers on a truck that has broken down discuss what they will do when they arrive, even after one of them says, "We never arrive." They never arrive at anything except waiting for the next job, the next arrival; still, in this constant waiting, a community is forged.

Before his death, Rivera was working on a second novel, *La casa grande*, sections of which had appeared in various journals, but no final product was released. Regardless, on the basis of his one short novel . . . *and the earth did not part*, which has become a standard text in North American Hispanic and Chicano literature classes, his literary reputation is secure. Partly because his novel was written in Spanish and was translated into English, many critics of Chicano literature view it as a text that liberated other Chicano writers to find their authentic voices. When the journal *Revista Chicano-Riqueña*, which Rivera helped to found, published a special double issue, *International Studies in Honor of Tomás Rivera*, after his death, many of the contributors recalled not only his presence as a writer but also his generosity as an educator and friend.

— Thomas J. Cassidy

Learn More

Castañeda-Shular, Antonia, Tomás Ybarra-Frautos, and Joseph Sommers, eds. *Chicano Literature: Text and Context.* Englewood Cliffs, N.J.: Prentice-Hall, 1972. A rich source of information on Mexican American life, history, criticism, and literature, with Rivera's place in the Chicano literary canon clearly delineated.

Kanellos, Nicolás, ed. *Short Fiction by Hispanic Writers of the United States.* Houston, Tex.: Arte Público Press, 1993. Calling Rivera "one of the most beloved figures in Chicano literature," Kanellos offers an overview of Rivera's academic career, and an introduction to . . . *and the earth did not part.*

_____. "Tomás Rivera." *The Hispanic Literary Companion.* Detroit: Visible Ink, 1996. Includes quotes from other criticism of Rivera's work and a list of his writings. Kanellos further discusses Rivera's deep devotion to Chicano education and belief in the ability of literature to enlighten and inform.

Lattin, Vernon E., Rolando Hinojosa, and Gary D. Keller, eds. *Tomás Rivera, 1935-1984: The Man and His Work.* Tempe, Ariz.: Bilingual Review/Press, 1988. A collection of overview articles.

Martinez, Manuel Luis. *Countering the Counterculture: Rereading Postwar American Dissent from Jack Kerouac to Tomás Rivera.* Madison: University of Wisconsin Press, 2003. Compares the works of Kerouac and other Beat writers with works by Chicano authors. Martinez concludes that the migrant writers, Rivera and Ernesto Galarza, expressed a distinctly radical and inclusive vision of democracy in their work.

Olivares, Julían, ed. *International Studies in Honor of Tomás Rivera.* Houston, Tex.: Arte Público Press, 1986. A reprint of the double issue of *Revista Chicano-Riqueña* devoted to Rivera. An excellent source of information on Rivera and his work; it contains reminiscences of the man, a poem by Evangelina Vigil-Piñon written in his memory, close examinations of his work, and essays on Chicano and Hispanic literature.

Saldívar, Ramón. "Tomás Rivera." In *Heath Anthology of American Literature.* Vol. 1. Lexington, Mass.: D. C. Heath, 1994. A compact biography covering Rivera's life and work, and his literary influences. There is a useful long essay, balancing between historical and literary details, which provides a broad background from 1945 through the 1980's.

Augusto Roa Bastos

Paraguayan
novelist and short-story writer

Born: Asunción, Paraguay; June 13, 1917
Died: Asunción, Paraguay; April 26, 2005
Also known as: Augusto Antonio Roa Bastos

LONG FICTION: *Hijo de hombre*, 1960 (*Son of Man*, 1965); *Yo, el Supremo*, 1974 (*I the Supreme*, 1986); *Vigilia del almirante*, 1992; *El fiscal*, 1993; *Contravida*, 1994; *Madama Sui*, 1995.

SHORT FICTION: *El trueno entre las hojas*, 1953; *El baldío*, 1966; *Madera quemada*, 1967; *Los pies sobre el agua*, 1967; *Moriencia*, 1969; *Cuerpo presente, y otros textos*, 1972; *Antología personal*, 1980; *Contar un cuento, y otros relatos*, 1984; *Cuentos completos*, 2000.

SCREENPLAYS: *Hijo de hombre*, 1960 (adaptation of his novel); *Shunko*, 1961; *Alias Gardelito*, 1962; *Castigo al traidor*, 1966; *Don Segundo Sombra*, 1969 (adaptation of Ricardo Guiraldes' novel).

POETRY: *El ruiseñor de la aurora, y otros poemas*, 1942; *El naranjal ardiente: Nocturno paraguayo, 1947-1949*, 1960; *Poesías reunidas*, 1995.

NONFICTION: *El tiranosaurio del Paraguay da sus últimas boqueadas*, 1986; *Carta abierta a mi pueblo*, 1986.

CHILDREN'S LITERATURE: *El pollito de fuego*, 1974; *Carolina y Gaspar*, 1979.

MISCELLANEOUS: *Metáforismos*, 1996.

Augusto Roa Bastos (ow-GOOS-toh ROH-ah BAHS-tohs) is undoubtedly the most prominent figure in modern Paraguayan literature and one of the leading novelists of Latin America. He spent his childhood in Iturbe, a small village in the Guaitá region, where he learned both Spanish and Guaraní, which is the dominant language of the country. Thus, he was exposed to a particular form of rural bilingualism as a child, which provided one of his most distinguishing traits as a writer.

During his formative years Roa Bastos was sent to the capital city of Asunción to receive formal education at the Colegio de los Padres de San José. While living there and under the tutelage of his maternal uncle Hermenegildo Roa, who later became bishop of Asunción, Roa Bastos read the universal classics—Homer, Dante Alighieri, William Shakespeare, Miguel de Cervantes—and the principal French thinkers of the Enlightenment—Denis Diderot, Jean-Jacques Rousseu, and Voltaire.

When he was fifteen years old, he joined the national army and participated in the Chaco War between Paraguay and Bolivia (1932-1935), a conflict which became a major subject of his novel *Son of Man*. When the war was finally won by Paraguay, Roa Bastos returned to civilian life to work as a bank employee. He began his literary career with a never-published novel, *Fulgencio Miranda*, which received the Ateneo Paraguayo Prize in 1937. In the next decade he wrote *El niño del rocío* and *Mientras llega el día*, two unpublished plays that were presented by the Elenco del Ateneo Paraguayo in Asunción.

For years he was a contributor and a staff member of the Paraguayan newspaper *El País*. Thanks to a British Council Fellowship, Roa Bastos spent time in England studying journalism. This trip gave him the opportunity to witness the devastation suffered by Europe during World War II. He also visited the North of Africa, Germany, Sweden, and while in France he interviewed General Charles De Gaulle.

> *Striped, swallowed up by darkness; they had no face.*
> *Nothing more than their vaguely human silhouettes,*
> *both bodies reabsorbed in their own shadows. Alike*
> *and so different nonetheless. One inert, traveling the*
> *earth's surface with the passivity of innocence or the*
> *most absolute indifference. The other bent over,*
> *panting from the effort of dragging him through the*
> *brush and refuse.*
>
> —from "The Vacant Lot"

W H A T   T O   R E A D

Son of Man

Son of Man (1960) is a novel of "man crucified by his fellow man." The plot includes nine stories not in chronological order; each appears at first to be independent of the others. The novel jumps from one time to another to introduce an important event or to present a character, acquiring its unity from the repetition of certain symbols and events, and from the voice of Miguel Vera, who is the protagonist-narrator in five of the stories and the omniscient spectator-narrator in the other four.

Central to *Son of Man* is the juxtaposition of two main characters, Vera and Cristóbal Jara, or Kiritó. Vera represents the intellectual who cannot completely become one with the oppressed. Vera is aware of the need for social revolution in Paraguay, yet is too introverted and sentimental to contribute to that revolution. He simply observes the tragedy from the sidelines, unwittingly becoming a Judas figure. He denounces his comrades, he shoots Kiritó, and, by becoming mayor, he even becomes an official member of the oppressors.

Kiritó is a silent, uneducated man, the antithesis of Vera. He leads his people by the force of his character, symbolizing the potential for the salvation of mankind by man himself. Kiritó sacrifices himself for his fellow men, and he is fully conscious that this is his mission: "For now the only thing that mattered was to go on, always at all costs. . . . That was his destiny."

The main theme in the novel is the desire for the social redemption of a country. Like many writers, Roa Bastos sees the Christ figure as a powerful symbol of man's redemption by man himself. Hence, the figure of the "son of man" appears throughout the book as an outstanding individual who reveals himself in death. His death may not reduce the people's oppression, but it supports them by reinforcing their belief in brotherhood.

— *Mercedes Jimenez Gonzalez*

Back in his own country, he was appointed Paraguayan cultural attaché in Buenos Aires, but the civil war, which resulted in the long-lasting dictatorship of General Alfredo Stroessner (1954-1989), forced him to remain in exile beginning in 1947. His literary activity before this moment, which includes most of his poetic attempts and several lost pieces of writing, corresponds unquestionably to a period of apprenticeship. As Roa Bastos himself has recognized, the exile experience was very significant in helping him to develop a committed stance against political violence and Paraguay's appalling historical record with regard to human rights. Roa Bastos attempted several times to visit his home country, and in 1982 he was accused of trying to promote civil disobedience among youths. As a result, authorities revoked his passport; only after the overthrow of General Stroessner did he recover his citizenship.

In 1959 his novel *Son of Man* won first prize in an international literary contest organized by Editorial Losada of Buenos Aires. Soon after, he was asked to prepare a screenplay from the novel, and the resulting film won its own prize from the Argentine Institute of Cinematography, thus allowing for a widespread recognition of this Paraguayan writer. In 1961 he was invited by the German Federation of Writers and the Ibero-American Institute of Berlin to participate in a seminar along with writers such as the Argentine Jorge Luis Borges, the Colombian Germán Arciniegas, and the Guatemalan Miguel Ángel Asturias.

During the 1960's Roa Bastos wrote scripts for the Argentine film industry and published several collections of his short stories, some of them including already published pieces and adding a few new ones.

After holding a John Simon Guggenheim Foundation Fellowship for creative writers in 1971, Roa Bastos reached the peak of fame with his 1974 novel *I the Supreme*. The novel, based on the life of José Gaspar Rodríguez de Francia, dictator of Paraguay between 1814 and 1840, explores the complex relationships between fiction and history. Although Roa Bastos has been considered a Modernist writer of the Boom generation, this novel has many characteristics attributed to postmodern narrative such as the use of parody, the carnivalization of historical discourse, and the questioning of the concept of narrative authority. These post-Boom concerns influenced the writing of the younger generation of Latin American novelists which includes Mempo Giardinelli, Isabel Allende, and Luisa Valenzuela.

After ten years of working as a professor of Guaraní and Latin American literature at the University of Toulouse in France, Roa Bastos retired in 1985. In 1989 he was awarded the Miguel de Cervantes Prize, the highest recognition that a Spanish-speaking writer can receive.

— *Daniel Altamiranda*

Learn More

Balderston, Daniel. "The Making of a Precursor: Carlyle in *Yo, el Supremo.*" *Symposium* 44 (Fall, 1990): 155-164. Discusses the influence of Thomas Carlyle's 1843 essay on Doctor Francia on Roa Bastos's novel.

Cuadernos hispanoamericanos 493/494 (July/August, 1991). Special issue devoted to Roa Bastos's work. Contains a very detailed biobibliography by José L. Roca Martinez and Virgilia Gil Amante. In Spanish.

Escritura 15, no. 30 (1990). Special issue devoted to Roa Bastos's work. In Spanish.

Foster, David William. *Augusto Roa Bastos.* Boston: Twayne, 1978. Offers a structuralist overview of Roa Bastos's literary production, interpretive readings of his major writings, and a useful chronology.

_____. *The Myth of Paraguay in the Fiction of Augusto Roa Bastos.* Chapel Hill: University of North Carolina Press, 1969. Considers *El trueno entre las hojas* as a tentative program of artistic experimentation, in the way the author sought to create a prophetic vision of humankind which becomes the basis of his *Son of Man.*

Weldt-Basson, Helene Carol. *Augusto Roa Bastos's "I, the Supreme": A Dialogic Perspective.* Columbia: University of Missouri Press, 1993. Studies the use of narrative voice, symbolism, history, and intertextuality in the novel and makes a strong case for considering this a key text in Latin American postmodern writing.

Abraham Rodriguez, Jr.

Puerto Rican
novelist and short-story writer

Born: Bronx, New York; 1961

LONG FICTION: *Spidertown*, 1993; *The Buddha Book*, 2001.
SHORT FICTION: *The Boy Without a Flag: Tales of the South Bronx*,
1992.

Abraham Rodriguez (AY-brah-ham roh-DREE-gehs), Jr., is a contemporary Puerto Rican writer. Having been raised in the Bronx, he writes stories that depict the experiences of "Nuyoricans." The concept of Nuyorican varies from generation to generation; Puerto Ricans living in New York during the 1950's experienced life in that city differently than do members of today's Nuyorican population. However, the struggle of Puerto Ricans, whether on the island of Puerto Rico or on the American mainland, continues to involve issues of culture and identity not easily revealed in the literature of social sciences,

---

Her mother was always asking her if she'd had any Lotto dreams, especially this week, with the fifty-million dollar pot in the balance. Dalia would run through her dream bit by bit while her mother whipped some eggs into froth. "You said there were how many men with beards?" she'd ask, deriving a number from inane symbols. Her mother believed in the power of dreams. She believed God was going to disclose to her winning numbers.

—from "The Lotto"

fiction, or elsewhere. The issues are generally complex, and work that tells the stories of the Puerto Ricans living in New York is of value both to the community in New York and to the communities of Puerto Rican people on Puerto Rico and throughout the mainland.

Colonization of Borinquén (Puerto Rico's indigenous name) resulted in cultural conflicts for those whose parents migrated to New York in several waves. Puerto Ricans, although citizens of the United States, find their identities in terms of culture, race, and class re-categorized by the establishment in the United States. These categories often conflict with their family and traditional beliefs—hence the conflicts and problems with their sense of self-identification and how to express their identification to two countries. Rodriguez gives voice to that experience.

In *The Boy Without a Flag*, Rodriguez retells the stories he has heard from his father about American imperialism, specifically the conquest of Puerto Rico in 1898. Conscious of this history, the narrator refuses to salute the American flag. In other stories, Rodriguez depicts violence and poverty in barrio life. He uses the language of the streets and the rhythms of the island from which his family comes. Drugs, promiscuity, and other social issues are addressed in his other works. They reveal the intimate knowledge of a man born and raised in New York's South Bronx. This area is home to people from various ethnic groups, where they live often in poverty but never in a culturally poor environment. Salsa, guns, and early death are all part of Rodriguez's milieu, and his writing evokes passion underlying the story lines.

In the novel *Spidertown*, Rodriguez portrays the life of a young man, Miguel, who works as a drug runner for his friend and "mentor," Spider. He seems satisfied with the world he lives in until he becomes involved with a beautiful, practical-minded young woman. He then sees the lack of substance to his life and realizes he must make some choices. Comments about this work praise Rodriguez's use of language, the pacing of the story, and the realism of the lives portrayed. It is a portrait of poor, urban Puerto Rican lives.

W H A T   T O   R E A D

The Boy Without a Flag

The Boy Without a Flag: Tales of the South Bronx (1992) is the first book of fiction from Abraham Rodriguez, Jr., a young Puerto Rican American whose greatest strength is his ability to capture the salsa-driven rhythms and late-night bodega rap sessions of a streetcorner posse in a raw prose style. These stories, Rodriguez declared, are "about the rancid underbelly of the American Dream. These are the kids no one likes to talk about. I want to show them as they are, not as society wishes them to be."

The narrator of "The Boy Without a Flag" is a precocious eleven-year-old schoolboy who refuses to stand up to salute the American flag during a school assembly, an act of defiance that, he hopes, will impress his father, a frustrated poet and Puerto Rican nationalist.

As it turns out, though, the plan backfires, and the boy's father, when summoned to the school, is nothing but meekly apologetic and self-critical for his son's "crazy" behavior. The boy must come to terms with his father's betrayal, which triggers a preadolescent passage into disillusion. Later, though, he realizes that his father has, in fact, provided him with a valuable lesson. He has learned that he must break away from his father's sphere of influence and must find his own means of independence. The narrator works his way up from this epiphany, and it is clear that he has pledged allegiance to no one but himself, "away from the bondage of obedience."

The successes of this book—Rodriguez's portrayal of the South Bronx, a place that inhabits his characters, brought to life with an affection, a sympathy that is in no way sentimental—cancel out its scattering of stylistic shortcomings. Rodriguez's depictions of lost childhoods are true and brutal, and he is a writer driven by the impulse to tell the stories belonging to those who are voiceless. Their stories deserve to be heard.

— *Peter Markus*

In 1993 Rodriguez earned *The New York Times* Notable Book of the Year award for *The Boy Without a Flag*. He also won the 1995 American Book Award for *Spidertown*, which was also published in British, Dutch, German, and Spanish editions. In conjunction with Scan/LaGuardia and the National Book Foundation's donation of copies of *The Boy Without a Flag*, Rodriguez conducted a workshop for youths and others at Scan/LaGuardia Memorial House in East Harlem, New York, in the spring of 2001. His works have appeared in anthologies and literary magazines including *Boricuas, Growing up Puerto Rican, Story, Best Stories from New Writers, The Chattahoochee Review*, and *Alternative Fiction and Poetry*.

Rodriguez received a grant from the New York Foundation for the Arts in 2000, and he served as a literary panel member on the New York State Council of the Arts. His involvement with both the literary foundation and the Scan/LaGuardia Memorial House demonstrates his commitment to his community and to his art. In 2001, he wrote the narration for a film called *Chenrezi Vision* and started an East Coast small press named Art Bridge.

— *Louise Rodríguez Connal*

Learn More

Flores, Juan. *From Bomba to Hip-Hop: Puerto Rican Culture and the Latino Identity*. New York: Columbia University Press, 2000. Flores investigates the historical experience of Puerto Ricans in New York. Includes a discussion of Nuyorican literature.

Hernandez, Carmen Dolores. *Puerto Rican Voices in English: Interviews with Writers*. Westport, Conn.: Praeger, 1997. This book of fourteen interviews includes a lengthy one with Rodriguez.

Richard Rodriguez

Mexican American essayist

Born: San Francisco, California; July 31, 1944

NONFICTION: *Hunger of Memory: The Education of Richard Rodriguez*, 1982; *Days of Obligation: An Argument with My Mexican Father*, 1992; *Brown: The Last Discovery of America*, 2002.

With the publication of his autobiography, *Hunger of Memory*, in 1982, Richard Rodriguez (rawd-REE-gehz) rose to immediate national attention as a fine, if controversial, essayist. Born Ricardo Rodriguez in San Francisco, California, in 1944, the son of Mexican immigrants, he moved with his family to Sacramento, where they had purchased a small home. Ricardo spoke only Spanish at home with his parents and siblings. In *Hunger of Memory* he describes his first experience of English-language society, encountered in the Catholic elementary classroom which transformed him from Ricardo to Richard. When his parents began to speak only the "public" language of English at home, at the recommendation of his Irish nun teachers, Richard suffered a loss of intimacy with his family. He later decided that the educational process itself accounted for his separation from his parents, rather than simply "public" (English) versus "private" (Spanish) language.

Rodriguez was raised Catholic and attended Catholic primary and secondary schools. He earned a B.A. from Stanford University in 1967 and an M.S. from Columbia University in 1969. He did graduate work at the University of California, Berkeley, and at the Warburg Institute in London. He received a Fulbright Fellowship (1972-1973) and a National Endowment for the Humanities Fellowship (1976-1977). Though he was offered several university teaching positions, he declined the offers because he suspected that he was benefitting from a misplaced affirmative action. That is, he was offered such positions because as a Mexican American he was a member of an under-represented ethnic group, while he believed that his entire education and preparation had resulted in his complete assimilation into the majority. Rodriguez became an editor at Pacific News Service, where he served for more than two decades, and a contributing editor for *Harper's, U.S. News & World Report,* and the Sunday "Opinion" section of the *Los Angeles Times.* He has written for the *New York Times, Wall Street Journal, American Scholar, Time, Mother Jones, New Republic,* and other publications.

Rodriguez spent six years writing *Hunger of Memory,* sections of which first appeared in magazines. *Hunger of Memory* is autobiographical, but rather than presenting a chronological view of Rodriguez's growth and development, it presents his life in essays focused on his development as related to broader issues. Having learned the public language of English and entered successfully into the linguistic and cultural discourse of the dominant culture, Rodriguez reflects on the relationship between language, family, and intimacy. Having been raised Mexican American and Catholic, he examines his Catholic faith and comments on liturgical changes to Catholic rites. Though Rodriguez was awarded funding for college and postgraduate study based on merit, assistance was also based partly on his minority status.

> *Like those whose lives are bound by a barrio, I was reminded by Spanish of my separateness from* los otros, los gringos *in power. But more intensely than for most barrio children—because I did not live in a barrio—Spanish seemed to me the language of home. (Most days it was only at home that I'd hear it.) It became the language of joyful return.*
>
> —from *Hunger of Memory: The Education of Richard Rodriguez*

Having thus benefitted from affirmative action, he critiques it as a misguided approach that—because it helps people based on ethnicity or race—often helps those who are no longer disadvantaged. Affirmative action, argues Rodriguez, should focus on class rather than race. Rodriguez also criticizes bilingual education as a program that prevents more rapid assimilation of non-English speakers, consequently maintaining or even aggravating their disadvantaged status in relation to the majority culture. Furthermore, Rodriguez sees education as a transformative process that gives the individual an identity as a member of a group, an identity denied the student of a bilingual program. *Hunger of Memory* exploded on the literary scene when first published: The book received more attention from mainstream critics than any other single work by a Chicano author.

W H A T   T O   R E A D

Brown

Hunger of Memory (1982) and *Days of Obligation* (1992) were the first two installments of "a trilogy on American public life and my private life" that *Brown* (2002) completes. Though it is doubtful that Rodriguez has identified "the last discovery of America," as his book's subtitle claims, in *Brown* he musters considerable evidence to support his thesis that brown—not the red, white, and blue of the "Stars and Stripes"—is the quintessential American color.

Rodriguez believes that "America is browning" and that this process is unavoidable; increasingly, Americans are unable to clearly define where they come from, no matter how detailed their family trees may be. This process continues even—often especially—when Americans oppose it, and they may fail to see the passion of "browning" because of their individualism. Overlooking how profoundly "the 'we' is a precondition for saying 'I,'" Americans underplay the very impurity that enriches

---

Mexican American critics and Latin Americanists immediately responded to the polemical nature of the text. Advocates of affirmative action and bilingual education registered the betrayal that only one of their own could elicit.

Like *Hunger of Memory*, much of *Days of Obligation* appeared as separate essays prior to being collected. Though many of the essays take Rodriguez's life as a point of departure, *Days of Obligation* is a more distanced, less polemical narrative than his first book. Rodriguez recalls, in "Asians," the Sacramento neighborhood of his childhood and his Chinese dentist. He examines the apparent decline of Catholicism and the rise of Protestantism among Hispanics in the United States and Latin America, referencing his own Catholicism. He details the consequences of the acquired immunodeficiency syndrome (AIDS) epidemic on the

both the American "I" and "we," a theme that Rodriguez calls his most important. Thus, making the identification his "mestizo boast," Rodriguez gladly describes himself as "a queer Catholic Indian Spaniard at home in a temperate Chinese city in a fading blond state in a post-Protestant nation." Rodriguez makes no mistake in linking the personal to the public and political. The roots of individual American identities, often oppressed and oppressing, are increasingly entangled, so much so that "righteousness should not come easily to any of us."

Rodriguez's parents emigrated from their native Mexico to California, where Richard, the third of their four children, was born. Although American census classifications have dubbed him "Hispanic," a category he attacks, Rodriguez sometimes underscores the complexity of American identity by contending that he is "Irish," because of the formative influence of Irish nuns who taught him English. In its "brown" form, English becomes a language best called "American," and it is to the multiple expressions of that tongue that Rodriguez owes much of his hard-earned optimism.

— *John K. Roth*

gay population of San Francisco, making no effort to avoid revealing his own homosexuality. As in *Hunger of Memory*, he focuses predominantly on Mexican and Mexican American culture and history, particularly in relation or contrast to the United States. In "Nothing Lasts a Hundred Years," the closing essay, he recalls the argument he had with his father when he was fourteen and his father was fifty. His father told him that life is harder than he thinks. Nearly his father's age, he now agrees with him, and honors him, fulfilling the obligation of the book's title. Broader in its investigation, less personal and less specifically autobiographical than *Hunger of Memory, Days of Obligation* nonetheless continues the discourse Rodriguez initiated in his first book and proves him to be an outstanding essayist and a major figure in Chicano literature.

Brown, published in 2002, is a collection of essays on a broad variety of topics, from the cleaning of the Sistine Chapel to Broadway musicals, in which the author works to subvert the notion of race in America as a distinction between black and white and suggests the color brown as a means of understanding both America's future and its past. The book was nominated for the 2002 National Book Critics Circle Award for general nonfiction.

During the 1990's and early 2000's, Rodriguez was often seen on the Public Broadcasting System's *NewsHour with Jim Lehrer* in his capacity as an essayist. His abiding theme was the reexamination of race, and identity in general, in American society. His awards include the Frankel Medal from the National Endowment for the Humanities (now known as the National Humanities Medal) and the International Journalism Award from the World Affairs Council of California. In 1997 he received the coveted George Foster Peabody Award, recognizing his "outstanding achievement in broadcasting and cable." He lives in San Francisco.

— *Linda Ledford-Miller*

Learn More

Challener, Daniel D. *Stories of Resilience in Childhood: The Narratives of Maya Angelou, Maxine Hong Kingston, Richard Rodriguez,*

John Edgar Wideman, and Tobias Wolff. New York: Garland, 1997. Challener examines *Hunger of Memory* and autobiographical works by four other authors to determine how bilingual education, family, community, ethnic discrimination, and other factors contributed to the authors' resilience.

Christopher, Renny. "Rags to Riches to Suicide: Unhappy Narratives of Upward Mobility—*Martin Eden, Bread Givers, Delia's Song,* and *Hunger of Memory.*" *College Literature* 29 (Fall, 2002). Discusses upward social and class mobility and the accompanying sense of loss, and includes an excerpt from *Hunger of Memory.*

Danahay, Martin A. "Richard Rodriguez's Poetics of Manhood." In *Fictions of Masculinity: Crossing Cultures, Crossing Sexualities,* edited by Peter F. Murphy. New York: New York University Press, 1994. The chapter on Rodriguez is part of a collection that looks at the "gendered" work of male authors and how they address masculinity and sexuality.

Foster, David William. "Other and Difference in Richard Rodriquez's *Hunger of Memory.*" In *Postcolonial and Queer Theories: Intersections and Essays,* edited by John C. Hawley. Westport, Conn.: Greenwood Press, 2001. Analysis of Mexican American identity, male homosexuality, and ethnic communities in Rodriguez's book is included in this collection of essays about gay cultures that do not fit the Western paradigm.

Guajardo, Paul. *Chicano Controversy: Oscar Acosta and Richard Rodriguez.* New York: Peter Lang, 2002. Argues for looking anew at Rodriguez's work and including him in the canon of Chicano literature.

Rodriguez, Richard. "A View from the Melting Pot: An Interview with Richard Rodriguez." Interview by Scott London. In *The Writer's Presence,* edited by Donald McQuade and Robert Atwan. New York: Bedford/St. Martin's Press, 2000. Interview with Rodriguez on race, ethnic and cultural identity, academia, affirmative action, bilingual education, class, and other subjects.

Saldaña-Portillo, Josefina. "Who's the Indian in Aztlán? Rewriting Mestizaje, Indianism, and Chicanismo from the Lacandón." In *The Latin American Subaltern Studies Reader,* edited by Ileana

Rodriguez. Durham, N.C.: Duke University Press, 2001. This collection of essays about the treatment of poor people in Latin American literature includes analyses of the treatment of Mexican American identity and indigenous cultures in *Hunger of Memory, Days of Obligation,* and *An Argument with My Mexican Father.*

Sedore, Timothy. "Violating the Boundaries: An Interview with Richard Rodriguez." *Michigan Quarterly Review* 38 (Summer, 1999). Rodriguez discusses his sense of community and Chicano literature.

José Rubén Romero
Mexican novelist and poet

Born: Cotija de la Paz, Michoacán, Mexico;
September 25, 1890
Died: Mexico City, Mexico; July 4, 1952

LONG FICTION: *Apuntes de un lugareño,* 1932 (*Notes of a Villager,*
1988); *Desbandada,* 1934; *El pueblo inocente,* 1934; *Mi caballo, mi
perro y mi rifle,* 1936; *La vida inútil de Pito Pérez,* 1938 (*The Futile
Life of Pito Pérez,* 1966); *Una vez fui rico,* 1939; *Rosenda,* 1946.
SHORT FICTION: *Cuentos rurales,* 1915.
POETRY: *Fantasías,* 1908; *La musa heroica,* 1912; *Sentimental,* 1919;
Tacámbaro, 1922.
MISCELLANEOUS: *Breve historia de mis libros,* 1942.

During his sixty-two years José Rubén Romero (hoh-SAY
rew-BAYN raw-MAY-roh) was, among other things, a poet,
short-story writer, grocer, haberdasher, civil servant, revolutionary, diplomat, novelist, and essayist—more or less in that order.
His lifetime (1890-1952) was for the most part a period of violent and sweeping change unparalleled in Mexican history; not

> *We sat down on the outside edge of the tower with
> our legs dangling down. My new shoes, next to
> Pito's, were well polished and they shone with that
> foolish pride of the rich. . . . Our feet epitomized our
> entire social world filled with its injustices and
> inequalities.*
>
> —from *The Futile Life of Pito Pérez*
> (trans. William O. Cord)

W H A T   T O   R E A D

The Futile Life of Pito Pérez

The Futile Life of Pito Pérez (1938) takes a critical look at
Mexican society of the 1920's and 1930's through the
eyes of Pito Peréz, who tells the unnamed narrator of the
various escapades he unwittingly suffers from childhood
until the day of his death.

As the town drunk, Pito sees himself as life's loser, a
pattern established early in his life when his mother
adopted a child and ensured that he had more food,
comfort, and love than her own son. By Pito's own account, his life has been "downhill" ever since. His gentle
and optimistic demeanor blinds him to the devastation
which greets his every turn. That he should happen to select unworthy friends is a paltry second to his uncanny instinct for becoming love's foil and fool. Repeatedly, he
risks all to better his lovers' lives. Without fail, his prize is
to watch them marry someone deemed more socially ac-
ceptable, and with each devastation, Pito increases both
his hopes for a better future and his expectation of even
more cruel results. He finally strikes upon his solution to

even the war of independence from Spain (1821) was as pro-
tracted or witnessed such carnage.

Although Romero did not participate in the military phase of
the revolution, through the influence of his father he was
named private secretary to the revolutionary governor of the
state of Michoacán. Accused of political agitation, Romero fled
the state capital, Morelia, for Mexico City, later settling in
Tacámbaro, where he engaged in the politically safe professions
of grocer and haberdasher. At the age of twenty-eight, however,
literary fame and political connections brought him back to
Morelia to serve the new governor, Pascual Ortíz Rubio. Once
again on the move, he returned to Mexico City in 1920 as the
emissary of the governor and to take a position in the diplo-

life's inconstancy: to betroth himself to Caneca, a female skeleton for whom he works as a street peddler.

The novel ends with Pito's death. His body, significantly, is found on a rubbish heap. In his pocket, Pito has placed his last will and testament, a bitter document which he asks his readers to accept as accurate, since he was mad and therefore able to perceive the truth. In it, he denounces most of the highly held human sentiments of liberty, equality, fraternity, humanity, friendship, and love. Instead, he extols thievery, dishonesty, greed, and ambition.

Romero's resolutely cynical view of Mexico's infrastructure precludes any characterization based on values of trust or love. The inference that madness and death are the principled individual's response to the hypocritical, deceitful world is borne out in Pito's last will and testament, which is a resounding denouncement of all institutions. The pervasive irony of the work makes its social critique successful. Such a serious tone would seem to preclude a wide readership for the novel, yet since its publication Romero's novel has maintained a vast audience as it has been "discovered" by successive generations.

— *John Knowles*

matic service, an appointment he held until his retirement eight years before his death.

The first diplomatic posting for Romero outside Mexico occurred in 1930 during the presidency of his mentor, Ortíz Rubio. While he was in Barcelona, Spain, nostalgia for his homeland inspired an autobiographical novel, *Notes of a Villager,* published in 1932. The title of this novel seems a foreshadowing of two characteristics that reappeared in his later fiction: a preference for anecdote at the expense of plot and the use of rural settings. By the end of the 1930's Romero was the author of seven novels and the subject of two critical studies.

Before the age of forty-two Romero wrote only rather uninspired poetry and unread short stories. The publication of *Notes*

of a Villager signaled a change in his literary fortunes. In novel writing he at last achieved the leisurely pace and the discursive nature that best suited the shrewdly crafted, yet seemingly disorderly memories which were to become the basic ingredients of his fiction. The broad sweep of the novel also provided him with a vehicle for the portrayal of the social, political, and economic ills that preceded, survived, and transformed the revolution.

The sentiments of the rural and village poor to which his novels gave voice were also present in his poetry, but not even in his best book of poems, *Tacámbaro*, are they expressed as clearly and as effectively as in the fiction. Like many uninspired young poets, Romero chose as his principal subject the passions of youth, a theme which he could not separate from the worn-out rhetoric of popular Romanticism. Aside from the sentimentality and general poverty of expression, the weakness of his poetry is in its predilection for the consciously literary, resonant phrase to the exclusion of the simple articulation of felt experience. A success among readers of poetry in his home state, Romero owed his popularity more to the revolutionary fervor of the times than to the quality of his verse.

In his novels, however, Romero was more concerned with the forceful rendering of character and incident than with sonority. Furthermore, by the time he began to write his novels, youthful optimism and revolutionary fervor no longer seemed appropriate; it had become clear that the revolution had betrayed the ideals of his youth and of "the innocent people" who provide the title for his third novel, *El pueblo inocente.*

Essentially a moralist in the tradition of the Spanish and Mexican picaresque, Romero was skilled at detecting hypocrisy and exposing hypocrites. In his best-known and still widely read novel *The Futile Life of Pito Pérez,* the protagonist is granted representative status. Endowed with the capacity of simple people to see the truth about life, Pito comes to embody the nub of Mexican experience. An expert liar and swindler, he knows the truth about the lives of his dishonest, self-deceiving victims better than they do. The sins of Pito against his victims' property and his own purity are depicted, therefore, as a form of moral resistance or revenge against duplicity, mere innocent pleasures at the expense of those who have no use for innocence. In his final novel, *Rosenda,* Romero returns to the theme of innocence betrayed. This time, however, the subject of the introspection is an archetypal, self-sacrificing Mexican woman, and the meditations about Mexican life are from a female perspective.

The warmth and color of *The Futile Life of Pito Pérez* contrast with the allegorical dryness of Romero's earlier fiction. Pito's joyful misanthropy and verbal play are an antidote to the cynicism that darkens the final pages in this and other works. Paradoxically, this novel proves that as long as there are false pieties and official lies, there is reason for cheer; there is reason to celebrate life as a comedy of deceit. Without liars and cheats to defraud, Romero implies, life would offer little fun.

— Charles A. Piano

Learn More

Brushwood, John S. *Mexico in Its Novel: A Nation's Search for Identity.* Austin: University of Texas Press, 1966. An analysis of the novel in Mexican literature, including a profile and overview of the work of José Rubén Romero.

Chandler, Richard E., and Kessel Schwartz. *A New History of Spanish American Fiction.* Rev. ed. Baton Rouge: Louisiana State University Press, 1991. This survey of Spanish American fiction contains a discussion of Romero's novels.

Langford, Walter M. *The Mexican Novel Comes of Age.* South Bend, Ind.: University of Notre Dame Press, 1971. Romero's importance in the development of the Mexican novel is discussed.

Mackegney, James Cuthbert. "Some Non-fictional Aspects of *La vida inútil de Pito Pérez.*" *Romance Notes* 6 (1964). Draws connections between the novel and history.

Juan Ruiz de Alarcón

Mexican playwright

Born: Mexico City, Mexico; 1581
Died: Madrid, Spain; August 4, 1639
Also known as: Don Juan Ruiz de Alarcón
y Mendoza

DRAMA: *Los favores del mundo*, pr. c. 1616-1618; *Las paredes oyen*, pr. 1617 (*The Walls Have Ears*, 1942); *Algunas hazañas de las muchachas de don García Hurtado de Mendoza, marqués de Cañete*, pb. 1622 (with Luis de Belmonte y Bermúdez, Guillén de Castro y Bellvís, Antonio Mira de Amescua, Luis Vélez de Guevara, and others); *El anticristo*, pr. 1623, pb. 1634; *Siempre ayuda la verdad*, pr. 1623, pb. 1635; *La industria y la suerte*, pb. 1628; *El semejante a sí mismo*, pb. 1628; *La cueva de Salamanca*, pb. 1628; *Mudarse por mejorarse*, pb. 1628; *Todo es ventura*, pb. 1628; *El desdichado en fingir*, pb. 1628; *Parte primera de las comedias*, pb. 1628; *La verdad sospechosa*, pb. 1630 (as *El mentiroso* in Lope de Vega Carpio's *Parte veynte y dos de las comedias del fénix de España Lope de Vega Carpio; The Truth Suspected*, 1927); *Ganar amigos*, pb. 1633; *El examen de maridos*, pb. 1633; *Los empeños de un engaño*, pb. 1634; *El dueño de las estrellas*, pb. 1634; *La amistad castigada*, pb. 1634; *La manganilla de Melilla*, pb. 1634; *El tejedor de Segovia, I*, pb. 1634; *El tejedor de Segovia, II*, pb. 1634; *La prueba de las promesas*, pb. 1634; *Los pechos privilegiados*, pb. 1634; *La crueldad por el honor*, pb. 1634; *Parte segunda de las comedias*, pb. 1634; *La culpa busca la pena, y el agravio la venganza*, pb. 1646; *Quien mal anda en mal acaba*, pb. c. 1652; *No hay mal que por bien no venga: O, Don Domingo de don Blas*, pb. 1653 (*Look for the Silver Lining*, 1941); *Comedias escogidas*, pb. 1867 (3 volumes); *Obras completas de Juan Ruiz de Alarcón*, pb. 1957-1968 (3 volumes); *Teatro*, pb. 1992 (2 volumes).

on Juan Ruiz de Alarcón (hwahn rew-EES thay ahl-ahr-KOHN) was born in Mexico City or nearby, possibly in Taxco. His parents had emigrated from Spain, but very little is known about them beyond the fact that both bore illustrious family names. The father had some connection to the silver mines of Taxco, perhaps as an overseer, and the mother was known as Doña Leonor. The playwright's ostentatious addition of the title "Don" later in life derives from a claim to hereditary nobility through the maternal line of Mendoza.

Ruiz de Alarcón completed several courses in canon law at the Royal and Pontifical University of Mexico by 1600, but apparently he did not graduate. By October of that year, he was in Spain, enrolled at the University of Salamanca. In very short order—a matter of two weeks—he received a bachelor's degree in canon law and immediately registered to pursue the equivalent degree in civil law.

Records at the University of Salamanca suggest that he initially matriculated as simply Juan Ruiz. In time, he added "de Alarcón," and as he became more acclimatized to a new and often hostile environment, the mother's family name was appended, which served to justify the addition of Don at the beginning. By the time his name assumed its full form, he was established in Madrid as a dramatist. At least one wit of the day

> *If he were reckless, restless, and inclined*
> *To pick a fight at the least provocation,*
> *Or married far below his station,*
> *If he were to die, I still would find*
> *The strength to bear these things and control*
> *My grief. But to know he's a liar! Oh,*
> *What a horrible fault! It's so*
> *Repugnant to my very soul.*
>
> —from *The Truth Can't Be Trusted*
> (trans. Dakin Matthews)

made the comment that Ruiz de Alarcón's name had by then come to exceed the bearer's height by its inordinate length. Another commented that the somewhat questionable use of D. (the abbreviation of Don) could serve as the writer's half portrait in profile, as he was both humpbacked and pigeon-breasted. Another observed that it was impossible to tell, seen from a distance, whether he was coming or going. It was also held against him that he had reddish hair, as, according to popular superstition, hair of that shade indicated complicity with the powers of the netherworld. Nor was it in his favor that he was a Creole, by virtue of his birth in the New World, who had come to Spain against the tide of emigration.

The future playwright received a degree in civil law in 1602 and then spent three more years studying toward the equivalent of a master's, which he did not receive, likely owing to the great expense it would have entailed. He finally did receive a licentiate degree from the University of Mexico in 1609, and during the next four years he aspired to a university chair but was unsuccessful. Meanwhile, he practiced law in various capacities. By April 24, 1614, however, he had settled again in Spain, this time in Madrid, where he would spend the remainder of his life.

The legal background he possessed made Ruiz de Alarcón unique among the coterie of playwrights then active in Madrid, most of whom were or would become churchmen. His considerable training and experience in the law served to foster a predominantly secular outlook and helps to explain the proposed legal and social reforms expressed in two plays in particular, *El dueño de las estrellas* and *La crueldad por el honor.* It also helps one understand the advocacy of reason, his characteristically concise and precise style, and the pains taken everywhere in his work to offer logical explanations for behavior and to analyze actions and motivations. This intellectual formation and predisposition serve to explain many aspects that strike the casual reader as being different in his theater.

The difference, one notes, has been attributed to other factors, among them the resentment he must have felt at being treated so ill by his fellow men of letters, by fortune, and by nature; his having been born and reared in Mexico; and his supposed classical bent. The supposed "Mexicanness" of his production has been held for naught by at least one distinguished modern Mexican critic, Antonio Alatorre, and the other two factors fare little better when submitted to scrutiny.

Finally, he was unique in that he wrote primarily to keep body and soul together while aspiring to other things, specifically to a

---

W H A T   T O   R E A D

The Truth Suspected

The Truth Suspected (1630) presents the misadventures of a young man who elevates falsehood to a fine art. Don García's creative imagination and verbal dexterity deceive and amaze all with whom he comes in contact. His objective, he discloses, is to become famous by whatever means necessary, and because his forte is fabrication, that will serve his purpose. It is left for the audience to decide whether Don García is a compulsive liar who thus rationalizes his defect or is in fact consciously pursuing a perverted notion of fame by attempting to excel at what he does best. It is clear, in any event, that his actions are counterproductive, as his father and his manservant frequently remind him.

In the end, he is obliged to marry Lucrecia when he is in fact in love with Jacinta, partly as a result of mistaken identity earlier in the play, but mainly because he has persisted in spinning a tissue of lies. Although Don García might be said to be punished in this manner, by frustration, the resolution is patently unfair to Lucrecia. Pierre Corneille, Ruiz de Alarcón's better-known French contemporary, realized this, and changed the ending to make it more palatable to the audience of his adaptation, *Le Menteur* (1644; *The Liar*, 1671). The ending Ruiz de Alarcón provides need not be taken to illustrate poetic justice but may be seen merely as the continuation of a venerable tradition of comedy, that of the arbitrary pairing off at the end.

— *James Allan Parr*

civil service post for which his legal training had equipped him. Because playwriting was only an avocation, beyond his regular work on the Council of the Indies, the professional dramatists reviled Ruiz de Alarcón, and performances of his plays were frequently interrupted by unexplained accidents on the stage. Discouraged, he did little writing during the last ten years of his life. Once he secured the civil service post, in 1626, he continued to avoid the theater, and he turned his back on it definitively when he received a promotion in 1633 that allowed for a modicum of affluence. Ignoring the good advice of an Italian acquaintance, Ruiz de Alarcón willingly exchanged "ambrosia for chocolate." He died on August 4, 1639.

— James Allan Parr

Learn More

Claydon, Ellen. *Juan Ruiz de Alarcón: Baroque Dramatist.* Chapel Hill: University of North Carolina Press, 1970. Claydon presents a study of the life and works of Ruiz de Alarcón. Includes bibliography.

Halpern, Cynthia Leone. *The Political Theater of Early Seventeenth Century Spain: With Special Reference to Juan Ruiz de Alarcón.* New York: Peter Lang, 1993. Halpern examines the political theater that existed during the seventeenth century in Spain, focusing on Ruiz de Alarcón and his works. Includes bibliography.

Parr, James A., ed. *Critical Essays on the Life and Work of Juan Ruiz de Alarcón.* Madrid: Editorial Dos Continentes, 1972. A collection of essays discussing the life and plays of Ruiz de Alarcón. Includes bibliography.

Poesse, Walter. *Juan Ruiz de Alarcón.* New York: Twayne, 1972. A basic study of the life and works of the early Spanish dramatist. Includes bibliography.

Whicker, Jules. *The Plays of Juan Ruiz de Alarcón.* Rochester, N.Y.: Tamesis, 2003. Discusses the preoccupation with deception in the plays of Ruiz de Alarcón. Whicker maintains the playwright's concern with truth-telling in literature, and his seriousness and moral orthodoxy, can be viewed both positively and negatively.

Juan Rulfo

Mexican novelist and short-story writer

Born: Barranca de Apulco, Jalisco, Mexico;
May 16, 1918
Died: Mexico City, Mexico; January 7, 1986

LONG FICTION: *Pedro Páramo*, 1955, revised 1959, 1964, 1980 (English translation, 1959, 1994).

SHORT FICTION: *El llano en llamas*, 1953, revised 1970, 1980 (*The Burning Plain, and Other Stories*, 1967).

SCREENPLAYS: *El gallo de oro y otros textos para cine*, 1980 (partial translation, "The Golden Cock," 1992).

NONFICTION: *Juan Rulfo: Autobiografía armada*, 1973 (Reina Roffé, compiler); *Inframundo: El México de Juan Rulfo*, 1980 (*Inframundo: The Mexico of Juan Rulfo*, 1983).

MISCELLANEOUS: *Toda la obra*, 1992 (critical edition); *Los cuadernos de Juan Rulfo*, 1994.

Juan Rulfo (hwahn REWL-foh) has been recognized as one of the greatest modern Mexican novelists, one of the forerunners of the "boom" in Latin American fiction of the 1960's, and one of the initiators of Magical Realism. He was born to a landowner family impoverished by the Mexican Revolution. Both his parents died in his early childhood; his father and various other relatives were assassinated. The brutality of the countryside Cristeros uprising of 1926 to 1929 persisted in his memory. Rulfo was raised both in an orphanage and by relatives. He studied law in Guadalajara, but he soon moved to Mexico City to pursue his literary ambitions. He scraped a bare living working as an immigration officer, a salesman for a tire company, a movie scriptwriter and television producer, and, after 1962, as the director of the editorial department of the National Institute of Indian Affairs. As adviser to the Mexican Center of Writers, he helped to educate generations of Mexican literati. In

1970 Rulfo received the National Prize for Literature; in 1980 he became a member of the Mexican Academy of Language; and in 1985 he was awarded the prestigious Cervantes Prize in Spain.

Rulfo's fame rests on two slim volumes, the collection of short stories *The Burning Plain, and Other Stories* and, especially, the novel *Pedro Páramo*, in which he distilled his stark vision of the Mexican countryside ravaged by the revolution, poverty, and violence. *Páramo* can be translated as "wasteland." His photographs in *Inframundo* are a powerful companion to his vision of Mexican barren landscapes. Although he began to write earlier, Rulfo found his characteristic voice in the mid-1940's when he began to craft, one by one, his masterpiece stories. Behind the deceptively simple facade of his rustic characters and their discourse stripped to "bare bones" hides a stunning virtuosity of narrative technique. Each story is narrated in a different way, yet the experiment is not showcased for the sake of experiment itself but blends with the other elements to convey the author's bleak view of modern, revolutionary, and postrevolutionary Mexico. "Luvina," one of his best stories, adds a magic—almost fantastic—dimension, and through myth, modern and provincial Mexico stands for the universal condition of modern humankind.

Pedro Páramo appeared at a time when Mexico was consolidating its postrevolution and wartime gains and dreamed of participating, although belatedly, at the banquet of modernity. In his

> *Because what happened is that Natalia and I killed Tanilo Santos between the two of us. We got him to go with us to Talpa so he'd die. And he died. We knew he couldn't stand all that traveling; but just the same, we pushed him along between us, thinking we'd finished him off forever. That's what we did.*
>
> —from *Talpa* (trans. George D. Schade)

Bunny Adler

novel, Rulfo magnificently tied together the different threads from his stories and mixed them together in an anguished parable of the modern and yet ageless Mexico, violently torn between history and myth.

What makes *Pedro Páramo* a unique achievement is its masterful blend of the stark realities evoked, in which murder, death, rape, and incest destroy life; of modern experimental techniques, which turn the apparent chaos of fleeting narrative fragments into an artistic structure executed with a clockwork precision; and of Mexican folklore and traditional culture, which put familiar faces on any absurdity. As if in homage to the Day of the Dead (celebrated in Mexico on November 2), all the characters of the novel are long dead; their "souls in pain" cannot rest in peace; the monsoon rains resuscitate them, and the skeletons begin to remember and to replay their squalid lives. Black hu-

W H A T   T O   R E A D

Pedro Páramo

Pedro Páramo (1955) is one of the most important Mexican novels of the second half of the twentieth century. In episodes that recall a number of universal myths, and with Mexican characters who recall Greek heroes such as Odysseus, Telemachus, Oedipus, and Electra, Rulfo tells about people searching for identity in love, family origins, and interpersonal relationships. The novel is presented in two sections. In the first, which has no chronology, the point of view is Juan Preciado's, who is dead when the novel begins. The second section has an omniscient narrator who gives the history of Comala from Páramo's childhood to the moment of his death. Thus, the time of the second section is prior to that of the first one.

In the first part, Juan Preciado is sent by his mother Dolores to find Pedro Páramo, the father who abandoned Juan and Dolores before Juan was born. Juan's half-brother Abundio guides him to Comala, located "at the mouth of Hell," where ghosts speak from the grave to describe the sinister influence of Pedro Páramo on

mor, absurdity of situations and dialogue, and an overall dream-like character all bring the novel close to surrealism, a connection borne out in Rulfo's later film scripts.

Rulfo continued to work on the text of his novel for the next quarter of a century, sometimes augmenting, sometimes deleting. Thus in each edition, the textual sequence is broken up into different narrative fragments. In the 1980 edition, he strengthened the graphic markers and established seventy segments. With hindsight, it is relatively easy to identify the nuclear narratives; the hard part comes when the reader attempts to relate them to the historical chronology. Yet the degree to which the historical background can be reconstructed is surpris-

the town and its inhabitants. Juan dies without discovering his identity, since he never meets his father. Páramo died years before Juan's arrival, murdered by his son Abundio.

Among the ghostly voices of Comala (in the second section) is that of Susana San Juan, Páramo's childhood sweetheart and his life's obsession. When young Susana left Comala in the company of her father, Bartolomé, Páramo waited thirty years for her return. When she reappeared, she was psychologically disturbed by an incestuous relationship forced upon her by Bartolomé. In her delirium, Susana confuses Bartolomé and Páramo with a third man: Florencio. Florencio is Susana's husband, or perhaps he is a sublimation of the father figure in Susana's mind. Susana finds happiness and fulfillment in fantasies about her relationship with Florencio, but her madness makes her inaccessible to Páramo. Like Juan, Páramo dies without finding the identity sought, in Páramo's case, in the love of Susana San Juan.

The fragments of *Pedro Páramo* are like the shards of a broken mirror. They reflect the characters, their relationships, and their identities. It is up to the reader to reconstruct the mirror in order to discover the truth reflected in it.

— *Warren L. Meinhardt*

ing. What is even more interesting is that Rulfo, who had up to a point striven to establish the historical, chronological, and geographical points of reference for the story, started to demolish them with vengeance. In *Pedro Páramo*, realism and its conventions become but a pretext for their own subversion and parody.

Readers have recognized from early on that behind the father-son relation in the novel hides the Oedipus myth. Allegorical readings have sprung up based on everything from classical and Aztec myths to psychoanalysis. Yet the mythical layer of the novel relies more on the haunting Mexican realities than on the Greek, modern West European, or pre-Columbian myths. *Pedro*

Páramo closes the cycle of Mexican postrevolutionary rural novel and has become a part of the Mexican national myth, one of Mexico's founding fictions.

— *Emil Volek*

Learn More

Detjens, Wilma Else. *Home as Creation: The Influence of Early Childhood Experience in the Literary Creation of Gabriel García Márquez, Agustín Yáñez, and Juan Rulfo.* New York: Peter Lang, 1993. Detjens analyzes the relationship of childhood to the creative process in *Pedro Páramo* and novels by Latin American authors.

Dove, Patrick. *The Catastrophe of Modernity: Tragedy and the Nation in Latin American Literature.* Lewisburg, Pa.: Bucknell University Press, 2004. Dove analyzes *Pedro Páramo* and works by other authors to determine how literature reflects and comes to terms with societal catastrophe in Latin America.

Jordan, Michael S. "Noise and Communication in Juan Rulfo." *Latin American Literary Review* 24, no. 27 (January-June, 1996): 115-130. Excellent analysis of several short stories and *Pedro Páramo*, investigating the presence of noise and abundance of "speech acts" in a narrative universe in which real communication is ultimately impossible.

Leal, Luis. *Juan Rulfo.* Boston: Twayne, 1983. The first full-length study in English of Rulfo's work. Relates Rulfo's first unpublished novel, "The Son of Affliction," to his difficult childhood. Divides his writing into the first prose work, the early stories, and the later stories, then focuses on the novel *Pedro Páramo.* Also includes a brief chapter on Rulfo's screenplays and the films made from them as well as his public lectures. Includes an excellent bibliography.

Mendez Rodenas, Adriana. "Narcissus in Bloom: The Desiring Subject in Modern Latin American Narrative: María Luisa Bombal and Juan Rulfo." In *Latin American Women's Writing: Feminist Readings in Theory and Crisis,* edited by Anny Brooksbank Jones and Catherine Davies. New York: Oxford University Press, 1996. Mendez Rodenas applies psychoanalytic theory and a feminist approach to compare Rulfo's use of the Narcissus myth in *Pedro Páramo* with María Louisa Bombal's use of the myth in *The Shrouded Woman.*

Reinhardt-Childers, Ilva. "Sensuality, Brutality, and Violence in Two of Rulfo's Stories: An Analytical Study." *Hispanic Journal* 12, no. 1 (Spring, 1991): 69-73. Discusses "At Daybreak" and "The Burning Plain" from the perspective of the extreme and unpredictable violence they contain.

Rulfo, Juan. *Juan Rulfo's Mexico: Essays.* Translated by Margaret Sayers Peden. Washington, D.C.: Smithsonian Institution Press, 2002. A collection of 175 of Rulfo's photographs of Mexico. Also contains six essays analyzing Rulfo's images, including "Forms That Defy Oblivion" by Carlos Fuentes.

Ernesto Sábato

Argentine novelist and essayist

Born: Rojas, Argentina; June 24, 1911

LONG FICTION: *El túnel,* 1948 (*The Outsider,* 1950; also known as *The Tunnel*); *Sobre héroes y tumbas,* 1961 (*On Heroes and Tombs,* 1981); *Abaddón, el exterminador,* 1974, revised 1978 (*The Angel of Darkness,* 1991).

NONFICTION: *Uno y el universo,* 1945; *Hombres y engranajes: Reflecciones sobre el dinero, la razón y el derrumbe de nuestro tiempo,* 1951; *Heterodoxia,* 1953; *El caso Sábato,* 1956; *El otro rostro del peronismo,* 1956; *El escritor y sus fantasmas,* 1963; *Tango: Discusión y clave,* 1963; *Tres aproximaciones a la literatura de nuestro tiempo: Robbe-Grillet, Borges, Sartre,* 1968; *Itinerario,* 1969; *La convulsión política y social de nuestro tiempo,* 1969; *Mitomagia: Los temos del misterio,* 1969; *Ernesto Sábato: Claves políticas,* 1971; *La cultura en la encrucijada nacional,* 1973; *El escritor y la crisis contemporánea,* 1976 (*The Writer in the Catastrophe of Our Time,* 1990); *Diálogos,* 1976; *La robotización del hombre y otras páginas de ficción y reflexion,* 1981; *Entre la letra y la sangre: Conversaciones con Carlos Catania,* 1989; *Lo mejor de Ernesto Sábato,* 1989; *Antes del fin,* 1998; *Medio siglo con Sábato: Entrevistas,* 2000 (interviews); *La resistencia,* 2000.

EDITED TEXT: *Cuentos que me apasionaron,* 1999-2000 (2 volumes).

MISCELLANEOUS: *Obra completa,* 1997 (2 volumes).

Ernesto Sábato (ehr-NAYS-toh SAH-bah-toh) emerged from the Argentine pampas to examine his nation's character and to explore the existential crisis of modern humanity. He was born on June 24, 1911, in Rojas, Argentina, where his Italian immigrant parents owned the local flour mill. One of the searing events in Sábato's life came in 1924, when his parents sent him to La Plata to attend secondary school. Torn from his community and large family, Sábato suffered a nervous collapse. He regained stability by immersing himself in the orderly world of mathematics and science. In 1929 he entered the Institute of Physics at the National University of La Plata, where he became involved with anarchist and communist student groups. In 1934 he attended a student communist congress in Brussels, Belgium, and once more fell into mental despondency. He fled to Paris, again finding peace by immersing himself in science. He returned to La Plata, completed his doctorate in 1937, and received a fellowship to study with French physicist Irène Joliot-Curie. After his time in France, he spent a year at the Massachusetts Institute of Technology. In 1940 he accepted professorships in theoretical physics at schools in La Plata and Buenos Aires.

Although science had provided him with needed mental stability, Sábato came to believe that humanity's desire to rest its physical, mental, and spiritual well-being on science and reason had led to disaster. Thus, he left science by using his teaching positions to finance his literary apprenticeship, served by writing regularly for *Sur* and *La Nación*. In 1945 the dictator Juan Perón, offended by Sábato's writing, forced him to resign his professorships, which had the effect of freeing him to devote himself fully to literature. It was the first of several times that Sábato's staunch support of freedom of speech got him in trouble with Argentine caudillos. In 1945 Sábato published a book

A terrible anxiety began to weigh on his spirit, as though in the middle of some unknown territory night had fallen and he found he had to orient himself by tiny lights in far-off huts inhabited by people who were utter strangers to him, or by the glow of a great fire off at some unreachable distance.

—from *The Angel of Darkness*
(trans. Andrew Hurley)

of essays, *Uno y el universo* (one and the universe), which earned for him national recognition. In 1948, with Albert Camus's help, he found a publisher for his first novel, *The Outsider*, which gained for Sábato international recognition. Two further volumes of essays followed, and in 1955 he became editor of *Mundo Argentino* until his support of freedom of speech and press brought him into conflict with the military government of Pedro Aramburu. Sábato was forced to resign his position, a decision he made again in 1958, when, as director of cultural relations in the Arturo Frondizi government, he became dissatisfied with government policy.

He had published further volumes of essays in the 1950's, but it was his second novel, *On Heroes and Tombs*, appearing in 1961, that assured his stature in Latin American letters. *On Heroes and Tombs* encompassed themes that concerned Sábato throughout his literary career. The novel begins in May, 1953, when seventeen-year-old Martín meets and falls in love with the myste-

W H A T   T O   R E A D

The Outsider

The Outsider (1948) has become a classic of Argentine literature and has brought international fame to Sábato's work. In the book, Sábato develops two themes present in many of his other works: the isolation of the individual and love's inability to provide total happiness. The main character, Juan Pablo Castel, is a painter who has been jailed for murder. He narrates the circumstances of his crime from prison, guiding the reader through the murky maze of his thoughts, and, importantly, through a series of three dreams that reveal a great deal about his character and state of mind. The novel never delves into description of the novel's setting (Buenos Aires) or of other characters. Instead, Castel probes his memories with an artist's eye for detail, painting a bleak portrait of the world and his place in it.

Castel is utterly alienated and detached from society. He is without friends or family and, at the point at which his story begins, without a lover. When he meets María Ibarne Hunter, a woman who seems to understand his paintings, he becomes obsessed with her, and the two develop a deep, dark, and complicated relationship. Their affair, like every other aspect of Castel's life, is scarred by the narrator's inflexibility, his inability to communicate, and his morbid existentialism. Unsurprisingly, the relationship ends unhappily, and Castel is imprisoned for María's murder. However, he has long since been trapped in a mental prison of his own making, and this does not change in jail: His world view continues to be colored by his unhappy solitude and his distorted, disordered, and detached vision of reality. Indeed, the Spanish title, *El túnel,* has also been translated as *The Tunnel* (1988) as well as *The Outsider* (1950), a clear reference to the main character's isolation.

— *Anna A. Moore*

rious Alejandra. In June, 1955, she kills her father, Fernando, and then commits suicide. To explain the events of those two years, Martín and other central characters journey through 150 years of Argentine history, come into contact with the major social classes and ethnic groups of Argentina, and confront the painful events of their own lives as they try to comprehend the tragedy of Fernando and Alejandra. Few writers have described the existential crisis of modern times more powerfully and clearly than does Sábato in *On Heroes and Tombs.*

More volumes of essays followed *On Heroes and Tombs,* and in 1974, Sábato published his third novel. A nervous condition restricted further literary output, but he has retained his preeminent position in the Argentine literary world. His support of freedom continued to win for him respect. After the brutal military dictatorship that lasted from 1976 to 1983, President Raúl Alfonsín appointed Sábato to head the National Commission for the Disappearance of Persons. Sábato is in the forefront of post-World War II Latin American writers. Recognition of his importance continues to grow in the United States and elsewhere.

— *William E. Pemberton*

Learn More

Bachman, Caleb. "Ernesto Sábato: A Conscious Choice of Words." *Americas* 43 (January/February, 1991): 14-20. A look at Sábato's life and work. Addresses the dark tone of his novels, as well as comments by critics "who feel that his 'black hope' is several shades too dark."

Busette, Cedric. *"La familia de Pascual Duarte" and "El túnel": Correspondences and Divergences in the Exercise of Craft.* Lanham, Md.: University Press of America, 1994. Little in English is available on Sábato; this study reveals some of his overall concerns, expressed also in *The Outsider.* Includes bibliographical references.

Cheadle, Norman. "Mise en abyme and the Abyss: Two Paintings in Ernesto Sábato's Trilogy of Novels." *Hispanic Review* 63 (Autumn, 1995): 543-553. Discusses Sábato's use of iconic metaphors in his novels.

Flores, Angel. *Spanish American Authors: The Twentieth Century.* New York: H. W. Wilson, 1992. A good overall view of Sábato's work. Offers a brief critical analysis of selected novels and common themes that thread through Sábato's fiction.

Oberhelman, Harley Dean. *Ernesto Sábato.* New York: Twayne, 1970. An excellent biography of Sábato. Oberhelman brings together the man and his works in one of the best biographies in the Twayne series.

Gustavo Sainz

Mexican novelist

Born: Mexico City, Mexico; July 13, 1940

LONG FICTION: *Gazapo*, 1965 (English translation, 1968); *Obsesivos días circulares*, 1969; *La princesa del palacio de hierro*, 1974 (*The Princess of the Iron Palace*, 1987); *Compadre lobo*, 1977; *Fantasmas aztecas*, 1982; *Paseo en trapecio*, 1985; *Muchacho en llamas*, 1987; *A la salud de la serpiente*, 1991; *Retablo de inmodernaciones y heresiarcas*, 1992; *La muchacha que tenía la culpa de todo*, 1995; *Salto de tigre blanco*, 1996; *Quiero escribir pero me sale espuma*, 1997; *La novela virtual: Atrás, arriba, adelante, debajo y entre*, 1998; *Con tinta sangre del corazón*, 2000; *A troche y moche*, 2002.

NONFICTION: *Gustavo Sainz*, 1966 (autobiography).

Gustavo Sainz (gews-TAH-voh saynz), Mexican novelist, critic, and journalist, is best known as a founder of the literature of *la onda*, a mid-1960's countercultural movement in Mexico representative of the growing restlessness of youth and defined particularly by a lack of concern toward Mexican national identity.

Sainz's early life was marked by the absence of the mother he did not know until adulthood and the influence of the father who raised him. Engaging his son in adventures such as mountain climbing, Sainz's father shared his love of literature that eventually spawned an interest in language and writing. Nonetheless, poverty and a broken home were hardships, and the difficulties of his adolescence would later be reflected in his early work.

Between 1959 and 1962, Sainz published a number of short stories. He attended the National Autonomous University of Mexico, where a grant from the Centro Mexicana de Escritores allowed him to complete and preview the novel *Gazapo*. Initial reaction to the work was negative; however, when it was published several years later, the program's director and others praised the book and welcomed Sainz's entry into Mexican letters.

Published in 1965, *Gazapo* portrays a week in the lives of a group of middle-class teenagers in the Mexican capital. Seeking refuge in his mother's vacant apartment, Menelao and his friends play out their fantasies through a series of conversations. Sainz employs several techniques to develop the narrative of the novel, most notably the fragments of tape recordings from which the protagonist splices together his own novel. The collage of real and imagined scenes defines the character's emotional and sexual self-obsession. *Gazapo* captures the language and nuances of adolescence in rebellion against meaninglessness and sheer boredom.

Gazapo was an immediate best-seller in Mexico and was translated into English, French, German, Italian, and Portuguese. Although its fragmentary narrative, thematic concerns,

and youthful appeal were criticized by some as overly trendy, others praised the work as marking an important chapter in Mexican literary history. Sainz, along with fellow Mexican author José Agustín, was dubbed a leader of *la onda* (the happening). This new literature was a colloquial expression of disillusionment, self-indicting and without solutions. Criticized by some as "adolescent," the literature of *la onda* lacked the socially comprehensive and epic qualities of Latin American *Modernismo*, characterized by writers like Mario Vargas Llosa and Carlos Fuentes, and the unambiguous language of *Gazapo* heralded the emergence of postmodernism in Mexican literature.

In 1968 Sainz received a Rockefeller grant to attend the International Writing Program of the University of Iowa, where he wrote his second novel. *Obsesivos días circulares*, complete with a qualifying self-disparaging epigraph, was considered by most to be a disappointing second effort. The language, tone, and complexity were criticized as pretentious, and the work attained little recognition aside from serving as evidence that the author had broken with the genre of *la onda*.

More favorable attention fell on his third novel, *The Princess of the Iron Palace*, which presents the recollections, dreams, and frustrations of a former department store salesgirl in Mexico City. The novel received critical acclaim and was awarded the prestigious Xavier Villaurrutia Prize for Literature. Sainz's continued success led to a Guggenheim grant to fund his next novel. Published in 1977, *Compadre lobo* tells the story of a writer and an artist in love with the same woman. Although the work garnered Sainz another grant, this time from the Tinker Foundation, the author himself described *Compadre lobo* as a "botched . . . narrative essay," and most critics agreed.

A string of novels followed, including *Fantasmas aztecas* in 1982, his most experimental work. Set during the excavation of an Aztec temple, the narrative moves through numerous unsuccessful attempts to differentiate past from present. Though not widely read, *Fantasmas aztecas* was praised for its wit and depth. His next novel, *Paseo en trapecio*, was a commentary on Mexico narrated by a ghost.

W H A T   T O   R E A D

Gazapo

Most of the action of *Gazapo* (1965) takes place as the characters drive around Mexico City, searching for something meaningful to do. The action centers on the young and misunderstood Menelao, who has been abandoned in a seedy apartment by his divorced mother. Menelao's independence is accidental. His mother, divorced from his father, who has married the domineering Matriarca, has gone away, leaving Menelao with no means of support. His father, overcome by his second wife, has sacrificed his son to his indecision. Left to his own devices, Menelao divides his time between Gisela and his friends, with no direction or aim. With precision, Menelao traces his routes through the city, giving the person familiar with Mexico City a very accurate picture of his whereabouts.

Two matters preoccupy Menelao and serve as catalysts for the action: his relationship with Gisela, whom he wants to seduce, and the disintegration of his family. He convinces Gisela to go to his apartment, where he makes his advances. Although Menelao is thoroughly infatuated with Gisela, he mistrusts her. He also blames her for the break with his father, who dislikes her because she is of a lower social status. The relationship is further complicated by Menelao's lies to his friends about having "scored" with Gisela. When they repeat the story in a taxi, the driver, Gisela's father, overhears and forbids her to see Menelao again. Throughout the novel, nevertheless, the two lovers defy the adults by seeing each other when they should be in school.

In *Gazapo*, the things one generally regards as important are trivialized, while banal things are stressed. This is a reminder of the fact that Menelao, his peers, and the society in which they live are disoriented and confused. In the end, nothing happens. Sainz suggests that reality does not have a structure as a conventional novel does, with a beginning, a middle, and an end.

— *Stella T. Clark*

615

> *By the time we girls would get out of classes, get out*
> *of school, right?, we were ready to go crazy. I mean*
> *really, those afternoons, oh, we thought we were sooo*
> *worldly, and so wild, too, because we'd leave school*
> *and go over to the Zero Zone, which was very in*
> *then, or someplace like that. . . . That's how we let*
> *our hair down, right?*
>
> —from *The Princess of the Iron Palace*
> (trans. Andrew Hurley)

Sainz has continued to receive the critical praise of his admirers. Rejecting his association with *la onda* of the 1960's, Sainz matured as a writer in the 1980's and 1990's, and he continues to contribute to the Mexican literary landscape. The process of writing, the function of language within a text, and the role of the writer are recurring concerns in his novels.

— *Steven Clotzman*

Learn More

D'Lugo, Carol Clark. *The Fragmented Novel in Mexico: The Politics of Form.* Austin: University of Texas Press, 1997. Sainz is one of several writers discussed in this study that links the fragmentation of narrative to an underlying fragmentation in political and social life that belies the myth of Mexican national unity.

Fernandez, Salvador. *Gustavo Sainz: Postmodernism and the Mexican Novel.* New York: P. Lang, 1999. Provides a comprehensive analysis, attempting to draw some general conclusions about the body of Sainz's work.

Gyruko, Lanin A. "Twentieth Century Fiction." In *Mexican Literature: A History,* edited by David William Foster. Austin: University of Texas Press, 1994. In English, an excellent overview of twentieth century Mexican fiction with some reference to the place of Sainz.

Shaw, Donald L. *The Post-Boom in Spanish American Fiction.* Albany: State University of New York Press, 1998. Shaw includes a chapter about Sainz in his examination of Latin American fiction that first appeared in the mid-1970's. This literature differed from the works published in the preceding "Boom" period: It was more reader-friendly, situated in the here and now, and not readily assimilated into the postmodern movement.

Williams, Raymond L. *The Postmodern Novel in Latin America: Politics, Culture, and the Crisis of Truth.* New York: St. Martin's Press, 1995. In his chapter on Mexican writers, Williams places Sainz in the "first wave" of the Mexican postmodernist movement.

Florencio Sánchez

Uruguayan playwright

Born: Montevideo, Uruguay; January 17, 1875
Died: Milan, Italy; November 7, 1910

DRAMA: *Canillita*, pr. 1902; *M'hijo el dotor,* pr. 1903 (*My Son, the Lawyer,* 1961); *La gringa,* pr. 1904 (*The Foreign Girl,* 1942); *Barranca abajo,* pr. 1905 (*Retrogression,* 1961; also known as *Down the Ravine*); *Los muertos,* pr. 1905 (*The Dead,* 1979).
MISCELLANEOUS: *Obras completas,* 1968 (3 volumes).

Florencio Sánchez (floh-REHN-syoh SAHN-chays) was born in 1875, the first of eleven children of a middle-class family. His father's political activities kept the family on the move and prevented the children from receiving much of a formal education. As a young man Sánchez worked as a secretary and in various jobs on newspapers. His first play was written for the entertainment of a club of political protesters to which he belonged. His second attempt was censored by city officials of Rosario, where he was a newspaper reporter, but when its performance was prevented, he worked all night setting it in type and had it ready for the public to read the next morning. He rewrote his first play as a musical comedy, *Canillita,* which

> *Bet your dowry on me, and you'll see how common sense wins. People think because they've been down to the university, they know more than an old man that's passed his whole life in the country behind the plow.*
>
> —from *The Foreign Girl* (trans. Alfred Coester)

takes its title from its newsboy hero. The success of the play put that word into the Argentine language as a nickname for all newsboys.

In 1903 Sánchez wrote his first important play, *My Son, the Lawyer.* During the six years following the success of this tragedy he produced a total of twenty plays, eight long dramas and twelve one-act sketches. He wrote rapidly, often on telegraph blanks, and did his best work in noisy bars and in crowds. He reportedly declared that he needed only one day to complete the four-act *The Foreign Girl,* called by one critic "the tragedy of the Argentine race." Critics have pointed out certain technical flaws, but the emotions of the play and the realistic pictures of people and life on the pampas made it Sánchez's most popular

W H A T   T O   R E A D

The Foreign Girl

The Foreign Girl (1942) raises an important issue: What traditions should be preserved in the face of technological advances? Sánchez answers this question in the various types of characters he uses to define the social groups involved in the controversy.

Don Nicola is an immigrant landowner who works hard on his farm and expects his laborers to do the same. Privately, his workmen and less ambitious neighbors criticize him because he makes his wife and children get up at two o'clock in the morning to begin their daily chores. One of his neighbors is Don Cantalicio, an easygoing creole farmer deeply in Don Nicola's debt. Próspero, his son, works for Don Nicola and is in love with Victoria, his employer's pretty daughter. Cantalicio is unable to pay the debt, but he refuses to give up the property, and he loses the lawsuit that might have let him keep his property. Próspero is fired after María, Don Nicola's wife, discovers Próspero with her daughter.

Two years later, Don Nicola has made many changes to the farm. To make room for a new building, he now

play. Technically better is *Retrogression* (sometimes called *Down the Ravine*), the tragedy of a good gaucho driven to despair and suicide by the unworthy and nagging women about him. Sánchez usually shows neither interest in nor sympathy with the women of his plays, who serve merely to develop his ideas and story.

From 1905 on, Sánchez turned his attention to the city and wrote nine plays about the lower classes and five tragedies about the middle and upper classes. These works are characterized by realistic treatment that tends toward naturalism. Sánchez was no follower of Émile Zola, however; he saw a tragic fatality of character and circumstance, but he also had sympathy for his creations as the victims of the society in which they live. In his wish-

---

plans to have the workmen chop down the ancient ombu tree, symbol of the old-time Argentine gaucho. Old Cantalicio turns up unexpectedly and protests the tree's removal, saying that it belongs to the land. After angrily mounting his horse, Cantalicio is thrown and badly injured. Victoria nurses him back to health, insisting that he stay with her family, because she is carrying Próspero's child. Próspero returns, having proved himself a prodigious worker in the outside world, and he is permitted to marry Victoria.

The play achieves dramatic tension by contrasting Don Nicola's desire for quick wealth with the local people's more relaxed work ethic. Sánchez's stand is clear: The conflict between Don Nicola and Don Cantalicio is not due to one man working harder than the other, but to Don Nicola's exploitation of the land and his lack of attachment to the country. *The Foreign Girl*'s happy ending reflects Latin American society's positive attitude at the turn of the twentieth century. Sánchez recognizes, however, that native values are in jeopardy, and he urges that modern Latin American society observe a balance between the ancient, local South American customs and the ideas of European industrialism.

— *Rafael Ocasio*

ing to make them over, he showed similarity with Henrik Ibsen, thereby gaining his nickname, "El Ibsen criollo."

Once he dominated the Argentine and Uruguayan theater, Sánchez longed for a hearing in Europe. Several of his plays had already been translated and played in Italian. In 1909 he persuaded his government to send him to Italy, but soon after arriving there he contracted tuberculosis. On November 7, 1910, the dramatist who had helped introduce realism into the theater of the River Plate died and was buried in Milan. In 1921 the Uruguayan government brought home the ashes of its most distinguished playwright.

Sánchez's writing is uneven, and some of his situations trite and weak. His lasting contribution, however, is that he inspired writers in his own land, and his many good qualities have made his theater a cultural heritage of the region.

— *Emil Volek*

Learn More

Costa, René de. "The Dramaturgy of Florencio Sánchez: An Analysis of *Barranca abajo*." *Latin American Theater Review* 7, no. 2 (1974). Costa examines the theatrical techniques and composition of the play.

Foster, David W. "Ideological Shift in the Rural Images in Florencio Sánchez's Theater." *Hispanic Journal* 11, no. 1 (1990). Studies how the themes of the countryside and immigration are treated in *La gringa* and *Barranca abajo*.

Jones, Willis K. "Florencio Sánchez." In *Behind Spanish American Footlights*. Austin: University of Texas Press, 1966. Sánchez's work is included in this examination of Spanish American playwrights.

_____. "The *Gringa* Theme in River Plate Drama." *Hispania* 25 (1942). A study of plays by Sánchez and other Argentine and Uruguayan playwrights.

Richardson, Ruth. *Florencio Sánchez and the Argentine Theatre*. 1933. Reprint. New York: Gordon Press, 1975. A rare English-language book about Sánchez.

Luis Rafael Sánchez

Puerto Rican novelist and playwright

Born: Humacao, Puerto Rico; November 17, 1936

LONG FICTION: *La guaracha del Macho Camacho,* 1976 (*Macho Camacho's Beat,* 1980); *La importancia de llamarse Daniel Santos,* 1988.

SHORT FICTION: *En cuerpo de camisa,* 1965, revised 1971.

DRAMA: *La espera,* pr. 1959; "Cuento de cucarachita viudita," wr. 1959; *Farsa del amor compradito,* pb. 1960; *Los ángeles se han fatigado,* pb. 1960 (*The Angels Are Exhausted,* 1964); *La hiel nuestra de cada día,* pr. 1962, pb. 1976 (*Our Daily Bitterness,* 1964); *Casi el alma: Auto da fe en tres actos,* pr. 1964, pb. 1966 (*A Miracle for Maggie,* 1974); *La pasión según Antígona Pérez,* pr., pb. 1968 (*The Passion According to Antígona Pérez,* 1968; also known as *The Passion of Antígona Pérez,* 1971); *Teatro de Luis Rafael Sánchez,* pb. 1976 (includes *Los ángeles se han fatigado, Farsa del amor compradito,* and *La hiel nuestra de cada día*); *Quíntuples,* pr. 1984, pb. 1985 (*Quintuplets,* 1984).

NONFICTION: *Fabulación e ideología en la cuentística de Emilio S. Belaval,* 1979; *No llores por nosotros, Puerto Rico,* 1997.

The success of his novel *Macho Camacho's Beat* catapulted the Puerto Rican playwright, short-story writer, and essayist Luis Rafael Sánchez (lwees rah-FYEHL SAHN-chehz) to international fame. Sánchez was born to a working-class family in a small coastal town in Puerto Rico. He went to San Juan to study theater at the University of Puerto Rico. For a time he moved back and forth between his native land and New York City. Sánchez spent a year at Columbia University, where he studied theater and creative writing. Later he returned to New York to pursue a master's degree in Spanish literature at New York University. He began but did not complete his doctoral studies at Columbia University; he would receive his Ph.D. in 1973 from the University of Madrid. He then taught Latin American and

WHAT TO READ

Quintuplets

Quintuplets (1985) is written for two performers, each playing several roles. Critics have said that it is necessary to consult one's playbill to make sure that only two performers are involved because each one acts so convincingly in the variety of roles undertaken. Sánchez has called the play a parody of suspense comedy. It is played as a family vaudeville act that, in the course of its unfolding, comments sociopolitically and philosophically on what it means to act and what it means to produce drama.

The play is acted out before the delegates at a Conference on Family Affairs. The participants, the Morrison Quintuplets and their father, each occupy one of the play's six acts, presenting a monologue that details his or her perceptions of what it is to be a member of the Morrison family. Among the Morrisons, Dafne is cast as a bombshell, radiant in a provocative red dress. She rejects traditional femininity but adopts the mask of femininity. In contrast is Bianca, whose sexual identity is not clearly revealed, although it is

Spanish literature at the University of Puerto Rico, occasionally traveling and living abroad.

Sánchez began his writing career as a playwright. While there is some low-key experimentalism in his drama, typical of the Latin American scene of the 1960's, the thrust of his works lies in social criticism, with heavy moralizing, rhetoric, and transparent allegories. His political stance is that of an *independentista* (represented by the left-wing intellectual elite proposing independence for his native island), which in the Puerto Rico of the late twentieth century had become inextricably entangled with upholding Fidel Castro's Cuban Revolution of 1959 as the model for such independence.

The mastery of language and the hyperbolism employed in *Farsa del amor compradito* recall Ramón María del Valle-Inclán's

suggested that she has lesbian tendencies. All three Morrison boys are named Ifigenio, so they adopt names that distinguish them from each other: Baby and Mandrake are particularly telling among these assumed names.

The father, Papá Morrison, referred to as El Gran Semental (the great stud), is viewed quite differently by each of the quintuplets. For Dafne, he represents perfection and is to be emulated. For Mandrake, he is the competition as a performer but also in an Oedipal sense. Bianca considers him a controlling, domineering patriarchal archetype. Baby, the least secure of the quintuplets, sees his father as someone whose example he can never live up to no matter how hard he tries.

According to Sánchez's directions, each member of the family improvises his or her part in a vaudevillian style. The play comments stingingly on patriarchy and, indirectly, on the paternalism of the United States toward Puerto Rico, a topic that Sánchez injects into most of his writing. The play's lengthy stage directions also comment on the meaning of acting and drama; hence, on different levels, *Quintuplets* is rewarding both to see in performance and to read.

— *R. Baird Shuman*

farcical *esperpentos* from the early twentieth century. This quality continues through the short stories *En cuerpo de camisa* and reaches a high point in *Macho Camacho's Beat*. Sánchez turns his back on the romantic icon of Puerto Rican cultural identity, the mainly white, peasant *jíbaro*. Instead, he focuses on the new Puerto Rico that emerged, after postwar industrialization and Americanization, in the cities. In these early works Sánchez starts learning to "write in this new Puerto Rican," developing a neobaroque language that celebrates popular urban culture, discourse, music, and humor.

The Passion According to Antígona Pérez is generally considered one of the highlights of the first period of Sánchez's work. However, the tragic moral dilemma of the Sophoclean Antigone is considerably weakened in this version, and the story is transformed into a predictable political allegory that criticizes stale stereotypes and situations in Latin America (such as the mutual support of church and state). Read decades later, the drama does not seem to have withstood the ravages of time, history, and failed master ideologies. Indeed, the dictatorship in Sánchez's apocryphal Latin American "banana republic" bears a striking, if unintentional and ironic, resemblance to Castro's regime in Cuba.

Macho Camacho's Beat, published originally in Argentina, was an instant success. In this novel Sánchez blends the language of an apocryphal popular hit song, real-life commercial hype, and contemporary urban mass-media culture into a masterful stream of radio advertisement babble that unmasks commercialism, superficial journalism, and popular hyperreal lifestyles propagated by commercial radio, all while criticizing some more serious aspects of Puerto Rican political life, such as all-pervasive corruption. While the novel is also based on some worn-out stereotypes (such as the corrupt senator and his mulatto mistress), it entertains. The reader might even overlook the underlying ideological framework. The protagonist of the novel seems to be the playful use of language, based on colloquial urban popular usage.

In 1984 Sánchez's play *Quintuplets* was staged, to critical acclaim, in San Juan, New York, Buenos Aires, Santo Domingo,

---

And it is not a question, ladies and gentlemen, friends, of a foolish little number that fills the repertory of a musical group like I mean the Afro Babies, the Latin Provocatives, the Top of the Top, the Monster Feeling, the Creole Feeling. I mean that it's not a question of a ditty or some sugary rubbish to sweeten the cheap taste of long-haired types.

—from *Macho Camacho's Beat*
(trans. Gregory Rabassa)

and Oporto. The play consists of monologues by the five children of the actor The Great Mandrake; criticizing patriarchy, it also deals with the nature of acting and writing. In 1985 Sánchez received a grant from the German academic exchange board and spent that year in Berlin. In 1988 he published *La importancia de llamarse Daniel Santos,* a fictionalized biography of Daniel Santos, a real-life Puerto Rican singer of boleros from the 1940's and 1950's who was both a pop-culture idol and a fervent believer in the island's independence. The text is a hybrid work, a mosaic of essay, fiction, and (pseudo)documentary narrative spiced with fragments of Santos's best-known romantic and sentimental bolero songs.

— Emil Volek

Learn More

Birmingham-Pokorny, Elba D., ed. *The Demythologization of Language, Gender, and Culture and the Re-mapping of Latin American Identity in Luis Rafael Sánchez's Works.* Miami, Fla.: Ediciones Universal, 1999. A collection of essays, some in English and others in Spanish, analyzing the representation of Latin American identity, consumerism, the role of women, patriarchy, Christianity, and other topics in Sánchez's work. Includes an English-language bibliography.

Guinness, Gerald. "Is *Macho Camacho's Beat* a Good Translation of *La guaracha del Macho Camacho?*" In *Images and Identities: The Puerto Rican in Two World Contexts,* edited by Asela Rodriguez de Laguna. New Brunswick, N.J.: Transaction Books, 1987. Explores the techniques of Gregory Rabassa's translation of the novel, with some alternative renderings.

Luis, William. *Dance Between Two Cultures: Latino Caribbean Literature Written in the United States.* Nashville, Tenn.: Vanderbilt University Press, 1997. Contains a section on Puerto Rican literature written in the United States and compares Sánchez's work with that of Cuban novelists Oscar Hijuelos and Guillermo Cabrera Infante.

Navarro, Consuelo. "Loner and Outsider: The Restless 'Anacobero' Revisted in Luis Rafael Sanchez's *La importancia de llamarse Daniel Santos.*" In *The Image of the Outsider in Literature,*

Media, and Society, edited by Will Wright and Steven Kaplan. Pueblo, Colo.: Society for the Interdisciplinary Study of Social Imagery, University of Southern Colorado, 2002. Daniel Santos, the Puerto Rican singer who is the subject of Sánchez's fictional biography, was nicknamed *anacobero,* a Spanish word meaning imp or bohemian. This essay examines Sánchez's treatment of the bohemian outsider in the book.

Perivolaris, John. *Puerto Rican Cultural Identity and the Work of Luis Rafael Sánchez.* Chapel Hill: University of North Carolina Press, 2000. One of the first book-length treatments in English.

Quintana, Hilda E. "Myth and Reality in Luis Rafael Sánchez's *La pasión según Antígona Pérez.*" *Revista/Review interamericana* 19, nos. 3/4 (1989). Focuses on the use of myth in the novel.

Zamora, Lois Parkinson. "Clichés and Defamiliarization in the Fiction of Manuel Puig and Luis Rafael Sánchez." *Journal of Aesthetics & Art Criticism* 41, no. 4 (June, 1983): 421. Examines the use of cliché and defamiliarization in the works of the two writers.

Thomas Sanchez

Spanish and Portuguese American novelist

Born: Oakland, California; February 26, 1944

LONG FICTION: *Rabbit Boss*, 1973; *Zoot Suit Murders*, 1978; *Mile Zero*, 1989; *Day of the Bees*, 2000; *King Bongo: A Novel of Havana*, 2003.

NONFICTION: *Four Visions of America: Henry Miller, Thomas Sanchez, Erica Jong, Kay Boyle*, 1977 (with others); *Native Notes from the Land of Earthquake and Fire*, 1979 (also known as *Angels Burning: Native Notes from the Land of Earthquake and Fire*, 1987).

Thomas Sanchez (SAHN-chays) interweaves historical and current events with fictional narratives of people who live on the margins of society to create powerful social and political commentaries on contemporary American culture. Like many of the characters in his books, Sanchez knows what it means to be an outsider. He was born to a Portuguese mother and a Spanish father who was killed in the Pacific during World War II. His mother and grandmother worked in canning factories to support the family. Sanchez credits his grandmother, an illiterate woman who was a skilled storyteller, with helping him to develop an appreciation of language and literature.

When Sanchez was five, his mother married a man who had originally hailed from the Midwest. Although he kept his Spanish surname, Sanchez grew up in "an Anglo-Saxon world" but had little in common with the Anglo-American society. It was then that he began to perceive himself as the "other."

Sanchez's mother became seriously ill when he was a teenager, and he was sent to the St. Francis School for Boys in northern California. Most of the students were orphans or poor and were from Hispanic, Native American, and African American

> *Tomorrow morning would be good for Bongo's
> business, because tonight people having a good time
> would do bad things—crash cars, walk through
> plate-glass windows, fall into swimming pools and
> go to sleep underwater. . . . All the things Bongo
> needed to make his up-and-coming one-man
> insurance office succeed.*
>
> —from *King Bongo*

backgrounds. He then attended a community college in Sacramento Valley; at the same time he worked as a ranch hand in the High Sierra with Washo Indians and members of other tribes. His experiences at St. Francis and on the ranch enhanced his knowledge of American Indian culture and provided the material for *Rabbit Boss*.

Sanchez first began to work on *Rabbit Boss* when he was twenty-one, while attending San Francisco State University in the 1960's. He was deeply involved in the antiwar movement, Congress for Racial Equality, and the Student Nonviolent Coordinating Committee. After earning a B.A. in 1966 and an M.A. in 1967, he taught at the university and continued to work on the novel. After witnessing a violent protest where students were beaten, he left the country for Spain and there finished *Rabbit Boss*.

Rabbit Boss was published in 1973 after Sanchez returned from Spain. The novel chronicles the lives of four generations of Washo Indians, whose society is slowly decimated by the encroachment of whites on their ancestral lands. Although it begins in 1846, with a chilling description of a young Washo's close encounter with the ill-fated Donner party, and ends with the death of his great-great grandson in the 1950's, *Rabbit Boss* is Sanchez's attempt to come to terms with the war in Vietnam. He saw the American presence in that nation as an "extension of our westward thrust as a country" and used the white culture's subjugation of the Washo tribe as a metaphor for American imperialism. *Rabbit Boss* was a stunning achievement for a young author.

Zoot Suit Murders, Sanchez's second novel, was published in 1978 and is less complex than *Rabbit Boss*. Set in Los Angeles during World War II, it is a murder mystery that takes place at the time of the "zoot-suit riots" in 1943. Mexican American gangs clothed in zoot suits clash with sailors and are beaten, stripped, and shaved by the navy men. Oscar Fuss, an undercover agent posing as a social worker, investigates the murder of two Federal Bureau of Investigation (FBI) agents that has occurred during the riots as well as the fascist and communist

W H A T   T O   R E A D

Mile Zero

Mile Zero (1989), Thomas Sanchez's sweeping vision of Key West, Florida, brilliantly evokes the rich history and lyrical passion of the island. Key West is the southernmost point of the continental United States, where "Mile Zero," the last highway sign before the Atlantic Ocean, symbolizes the end of the American road. While Key West represents the end for the downtrodden Americans who gravitate there, the island promises hope for refugees fleeing Haiti's poverty. Sanchez traces the island's shifting economy from a hub of the cigar industry to "a marijuana republic," then to "a mere cocaine principality," lamenting how the drug trade has corrupted the American Dream.

Mile Zero's main character, St. Cloud, is a former antiwar activist who ponders his inability to sacrifice himself for his beliefs. He feels a strange kinship with MK, once a soldier in Vietnam and now a dangerous smuggler who has fled to South America. MK's mysterious presence and the shadow of Vietnam permeate the book. St. Cloud imagines that his pacifism and MK's violence are two

groups who are trying to gain control of the barrio. Again Sanchez takes up the cause of the downtrodden in his portrayal of the people who live in the barrio and are caught in a power struggle between the American government, the communists, and the fascists. Although the book is well written, Sanchez's treatment of the social and political issues lacks the depth displayed in *Rabbit Boss*.

Sanchez did not publish another novel until 1989, when *Mile Zero* appeared to critical acclaim. *Mile Zero* is a richly textured novel dealing with the complex contemporary issues of drug smuggling, money laundering, acquired immunodeficiency syndrome (AIDS), and the influx of Haitian refugees to the

---

sides of the same coin; after Vietnam, returning soldiers and protesters both found themselves cast out of society.

Justo Tamarindo, a Cuban American police officer, drafts St. Cloud to help him prevent the deportation of a Haitian refugee named Voltaire. Voltaire's sad story reveals how America thrives at the expense of the Third World. Late in the novel, Voltaire escapes from the detention center where he is waiting to be deported. The young, malnourished boy dreams he has reached a heavenly land of plenty at a garish shopping mall before he dies.

Meanwhile, Justo pursues Zobop, an enigmatic killer who is roaming the island and leaving voodoo-inspired clues everywhere. After Zobop is killed, Justo learns that the murderer sought purification by destruction, believing that everything must be wiped out before it can be renewed.

In *Mile Zero*, Sanchez signals the necessity of cultural change. Vietnam is over, Justo thinks, but the bodies of the dead refugees augur the arrival of a new devil. America is doomed if it does not change. The novel's ambiguous ending, in which Justo, who may have contracted AIDS, pulls St. Cloud out of the ocean, brings its readers to mile zero, a place that can be either an ending or a beginning.

— *Trey Strecker*

United States. Set in Key West, Florida, the novel opens with a powerful juxtaposition of images: The space shuttle has just been launched and flies over waters where Haitian refugees huddle on their overcrowded boats, waiting to enter the United States. St. Cloud, an alcoholic and former Vietnam War activist, is recruited by Cuban-born policeman Justo Tamarindo to act as a translator for a Haitian refugee who has AIDS. Meanwhile, St. Cloud also becomes involved in an investigation to discover the whereabouts of MK, a veteran of the Vietnam War and a highly successful drug smuggler. Interwoven with the stories of MK and the Haitian refugees are strange, disjointed letters from Zobop, a mysterious killer and self-styled prophet, who foretells humankind's destruction through environmental disaster. *Mile Zero* is a compelling portrait of the social and political issues that drive modern society as well as an ironic, suspense-filled thriller.

More than a decade after *Mile Zero*, Sanchez produced *Day of the Bees*, in which Francisco Zermano, a famous Spanish painter, and his beautiful French lover Louise Collard endure the German invasion of France during World War II, fleeing Vichy-controlled Provence. Zermano later returns to occupied Paris, but Collard disappears. Fifty years later, their correspondence is discovered by an American historian who then travels to France to seek out Zermano. The novel received mixed reviews, negative for the melodramatic and predictable rhetoric of the lovers' correspondence but positive for its inventive manipulation of point of view. It was followed in 2003 (quickly for Sanchez) by a reprise of *noir* fiction in *King Bongo*, whose protagonist negotiates political intrigues while hunting down a terrorist who exploded a bomb in a Havana nightclub in pre-war Cuba.

— Pegge A. Bochynski

Learn More

Kirkus Reviews. Review of *King Bongo*, by Thomas Sanchez. 71, no. 1 (March 15, 2003): 425. Finds the novel to be a straightforward *noir*, "florid, not quite Chandler."

Marovitz, Sanford E. "The Entropic World of the Washo: Fatality and Self-Deception in *Rabbit Boss*." *Western American Literature*

19 (Fall, 1984). Gives a detailed analysis of the structure, themes, and characters of the novel, focusing on the clash between the Washo culture and the dominant white society.

Rieff, D. "The Affirmative Action Novel." *The New Republic* 202, no. 14 (April 2, 1990). Review of *Mile Zero*.

Sanchez, Thomas. "An Interview with Thomas Sanchez." Interview by Kay Bonetti. *The Missouri Review* 14, no. 2 (1991). Explores how Sanchez's family background, education, and experience as a social activist have influenced the plots and characterizations of his novels.

_____. "The Visionary Imagination." *MELUS* 3, no. 2 (1976). Sanchez discusses how his social and political commitments influence his writing, particularly in *Rabbit Boss*.

Skenazy, Paul. "History as Mystery: Or, Who Killed L.A.?" In *Los Angeles in Fiction: A Collection of Essays*, edited by David Fine. Rev. ed. Albuquerque: University of New Mexico Press, 1995. Compares the treatment of Los Angeles in two mystery novels set in that city: Sanchez's *Zoot Suit Murders* and John Gregory Dunne's *True Confessions*.

Severo Sarduy

Cuban novelist and poet

Born: Camagüey, Cuba; February 25, 1937
Died: Paris, France; June 8, 1993

LONG FICTION: *Gestos*, 1963; *De donde son los cantantes*, 1967 (*From Cuba with a Song*, 1972); *Cobra*, 1972 (English translation, 1975); *Maitreya*, 1978 (English translation, 1987); *Colibrí*, 1984; *Cocuyo*, 1990.

SHORT FICTION: *Pájaros de la playa*, 1993.

RADIO PLAYS: *Para la voz*, 1978 (*For Voice: Four Plays*, 1985).

POETRY: *Big Bang*, 1974; *Un testigo fugaz y disfrazado: sonetos, décimas*, 1985.

NONFICTION: *Escrito sobre un cuerpo: Ensayos de crítica*, 1969 (*Written on a Body*, 1989); *Barroco*, 1974; *La simulación*, 1982; *Nueva inestabilidad*, 1987; *Ensayos generales sobre el barroco*, 1987; *Cartas*, 1996 (correspondence).

MISCELLANEOUS: *El Cristo de la rue Jacob*, 1987 (*Christ on the Rue Jacob*, 1995); *Epitafios, imitación, aforismos*, 1994; *Obra completa*, 1999 (2 volumes).

Severo Sarduy (seh-VAY-roh SAHR-dwee) was the most prominent link between twentieth century Latin American culture and the Parisian poststructuralist intellectual gay circles (the *Tel Quel* group). He was also a promoter of the "boom" of Latin American narrative in France in the 1960's and after. He was born into a working-class family in a provincial Cuban town; at his birth, it was prophesied that he would become a writer. In 1956 he left for Havana to study medicine. There he joined the splinter group of gay writers who had recently abandoned José Lezama Lima's journal *Orígenes* and had begun publishing *Ciclón* (1955-1957). Yet Sarduy remained dazzled by Lezama, whose work continued to be a major influence on his writing and on his concept of Latin American culture. Following Lezama's lead, he developed an interest in art criticism, and visual arts would become an important influence on his novels.

Sarduy welcomed the Cuban Revolution of 1959, working on the "cultural front" until his departure for France at the end of that year to study art criticism at the Louvre. The intellectual ferment in France in the 1960's proved too irresistible for him to return to Cuba after his government scholarship expired; he chose to stay in France and became a French citizen in 1967. An emigrant, and therefore a traitor, in the eyes of the Cuban government, Sarduy was ostracized there almost up to his death from acquired immunodeficiency syndrome (AIDS) in 1993. Sarduy, however, dutifully maintained his faith in the revolution for many years, in spite of the ongoing savage persecution in Fidel Castro's Cuba of gays in general and of his literary mentors, Lezama and Virgilio Piñera, in particular. Only much later would he exchange his faith in modern utopia for Buddhism and Afro-Cuban *santería*; strangely enough, after 1989, the revolution itself took similar steps, selling out its deteriorating rites of "*machismo*-Leninism" for the local syncretistic Afro-Cuban powers.

Yet the revolution to which Sarduy was committed in his heart was found in literature and criticism. Various elements—the Lezamian concept of the baroque (hyperbolic, imagistic,

> *"Chinese atmosphere, girls, come on!"—the Director steps out of a saffron cloud smelling of burnt grass (yes, the same grass you're thinking). He steps out of his pagoda of smoke, pensive, hair greased with sweat, eyes of a jade bulldog—two red balls—hands crossed over his chest (is he reciting the Book?); he walks along a dotted line. He shivers, turns green; the opalescent cloud crumbles in the scenery.*
>
> —from *From Cuba with a Song*
> (trans. Suzanne Jill Levine)

W H A T   T O   R E A D

From Cuba with a Song

From Cuba with a Song (1967) is not a novel in the traditional sense; rather, Sarduy's second work of fiction breaks down the founding conventions of the genre: character, plot, and theme. Instead of telling a story in linear fashion, it reads like a verbal jigsaw puzzle composed of three pieces or narrative sequences attached to a "head"—the introductory "Curriculum Cubense."

This first section traces a drawing that helps the reader assemble Sarduy's experiment in the novel form. An Asian and a black woman flank a blond, white male at the center of the picture. He stands next to Help, one-half of the pair of twins who reappear throughout the work, and close to them the "Waxen Woman," the face of Death, absorbs the entire scene. The drawing displayed in "Curriculum Cubense," "a giant four-leaf clover, or a four-headed animal facing the four cardinal points, or a Yoruba sign of the four roads," fills in the outline of an empty plot. Each figure in the picture corresponds to one of the

and carnivalesque); the French *nouveau roman*; structuralist semiology; the erotic and hedonistic concept of writing "with/on/into the body" developed by the poststructuralistic Roland Barthes; Western pop culture; gay and symbolic transvestism; and the new cosmology of the big bang—all gave rise to a joyous syncretistic Caribbean literary concoction that Sarduy called neobaroque. He was an extremely self-conscious writer, and his theories crisscross both his essays (such as those in *Written on a Body*) and narratives.

Sarduy wrote his first novel, *Gestos*, while still in Cuba in 1959, dealing with a terrorist act in Havana under the waning dictatorship of Fulgencio Batista. *Gestos* is an experimental exercise inspired both by the early *nouveau roman* and by action painting. In France he worked for the radio, covering scientific topics.

three fictions that make up the novel. The Chinese and the black woman become protagonists of their own tales in her piece. The white man, Mortal Pérez, fills the center of the drawing since he is in a relation of desire to the two women. Yet he is also the center of his own supreme fiction, "The Entry of Christ in Havana," first as Everyman and then as a baroque Christ figure. The three tales are designed to depict the linguistic and erotic sensibility proper to the racial layers superimposed on the mosaic of Cuban culture: the Chinese, African, and Spanish elements.

The novel's linguistic texture constructs a verbal archetype or reproduction of Cuba. It appears that the pieces of the puzzle fit together in the totality of a culture: a whole Cuba integrated by its racial-ethnic components, as reflected in the drawing. Metaphor and poetic description qualify the Chinese tale; dialogue, colloquial speech, and a mock tragic tone exhibit the African flair for drama in the second tale. The last section testifies to the origins of Cuban lexicon and intonation in Castilian Spanish; it also bears witness to the Hispanic legacy of mysticism.

— *Adriana Méndez Rodenas*

The intimate knowledge of the medium would reflect in his experimental radio plays. In his own narrative work science seeps through in many ways, but it takes up a carnivalized form, degraded as it is to yet another manifestation of contemporary pop culture. In 1966 Sarduy became editor of the Latin American collection for Editions du Seuil.

From Cuba with a Song puts to the test the later, more experimental *nouveau roman* and his own neobaroque approach in the search for Cuban cultural identity. Sarduy, himself of Cuban Chinese origin, sees Cuban cultural idiosyncrasy as a result of an interaction of three cultural components: Spanish, coming with discovery and conquest; African, introduced through black slaves after the indigenous population disappeared; and Chinese, brought to Cuba in the last century with the agricultural workers, after slavery was abolished. The text exploits, plays on, and parodies cultural stereotypes and, at the same time, explodes traditional narrative forms. The literary result is exhilarating and perplexing. Language is the true protagonist of this antinovel.

The next work, *Cobra*, is a perplexing exercise in narrative experiment. Completely cosmopolitan in its themes, it nonetheless remains profoundly Caribbean in its popular and carnivalesque undertones. The antinarrative constructs and dismantles the story of a beautiful transvestite unhappy about his ugly feet, a motorcycle gang and Tibetan rituals, and the sadistic castration performed by Dr. Ktazob (a multilingual pun meaning "penis cutter") in pursuit of the phantom of feminine perfection. This search for unattainable perfection is paralleled by the topsy-turvy writing understood as verbal transvestism. *Cobra* received the coveted Medicis Prize in 1972.

In the 1970's Sarduy made several trips to India. *Maitreya* uses the myth of the last Buddha and plays on the theme of exile and flight all around the planet, from Java to Cuba, Miami, New York, and the Islamic world. *Colibrí* returns to a Latin American setting and cultural intertexts; its scene is a homosexual brothel at the edge of the Amazonian jungle. *Cocuyo*'s main theme is voyeurism.

— *Emil Volek*

Learn More

Blanchard, Marc. "Site Unseen: Cuba on the Rue Jacob." *Sites* 5 (Spring, 2001): 79-88. Profile of Sarduy focusing on his retention of "cultural difference" after settling in France.

Bush, Andrew. "On Exemplary and Postmodern Simulation: Robert Coover and Severo Sarduy." *Comparative Literature* 44 (Spring, 1992): 174-193. Uses Sarduy and Robert Coover's works as case studies in discussing the relationship between theory and fiction.

Cooppan, Vilashini. "Mourning Becomes Kitsch: The Aesthetics of Loss in Severo Sarduy's *Cobra*." In *Loss: The Politics of Mourning*, edited by David L. Eng and David Kazanjian. Berkeley: University of California Press, 2003. Examines the treatment of mourning and its relation to cultural identity and postcolonialism in Sarduy's novel.

Gosser, Mary Ann. "Cobra." In *Critical Essays on the Literatures of Spain and Spanish America,* edited by Luis T. González-del-Valle and Julio Baena. Boulder, Colo.: Society of Spanish and Spanish American Studies, 1991. Useful for a general reader in English.

Kushigian, Julia. *Orientalism in the Hispanic Literary Tradition: In Dialogue with Borges, Paz, and Sarduy.* Albuquerque: University of New Mexico Press, 1991. Studies Sarduy's Asian connection, the theme of oriental exoticism, and Asian influence on Latin American literature.

Montero, Oscar. *The Name Game: Writing/Fading Writer in "De donde son los cantantes."* Chapel Hill: University of North Carolina Press, 1988. Focuses on the narrative experiment.

Rivero-Potter, Alicia, ed. *Between the Self and the Void: Essays in Honor of Severo Sarduy.* Boulder, Colo.: Society of Spanish and Spanish American Studies, 1998. A collection of essays from a variety of perspectives summing up Sarduy's career.

Salgado, Cesar Augusto. "Hybridity in New World Baroque Theory." *Journal of American Folklore* 112 (Summer, 1999): 316-331. Discusses Sarduy's "neobaroque" theory.

Gary Soto

Mexican American poet and memoirist

Born: Fresno, California; April 12, 1952

POETRY: *The Elements of San Joaquin,* 1977; *The Tale of Sunlight,* 1978; *Where Sparrows Work Hard,* 1981; *Black Hair,* 1985; *Who Will Know Us?,* 1990; *A Fire in My Hands,* 1990; *Home Course in Religion,* 1991; *New and Selected Poems,* 1995; *A Natural Man,* 1999; *One Kind of Faith,* 2003.

LONG FICTION: *Nickel and Dime,* 2000; *Poetry Lover,* 2001; *Amnesia in a Republican County,* 2003.

CHILDREN'S LITERATURE: *Baseball in April, and Other Stories,* 1990; *Taking Sides,* 1991; *Neighborhood Odes,* 1992 (poetry); *Pacific Crossing,* 1992; *The Skirt,* 1992; *Too Many Tamales,* 1993; *Local News,* 1993; *Crazy Weekend,* 1994; *Jesse,* 1994; *Boys at Work,* 1995; *Canto Familiar,* 1995 (poetry); *The Cat's Meow,* 1995; *Chato's Kitchen,* 1995; *Off and Running,* 1996; *Buried Onions,* 1997; *Novio Boy,* 1997 (play); *Petty Crimes,* 1998; *Big Bushy Mustache,* 1998; *Chato Throws a Pachanga,* 1999; *Chato and the Party Animals,* 1999; *Nerdlania,* 1999 (play); *Jesse De La Cruz: A Profile of a United Farm Worker,* 2000; *My Little Car,* 2000; *Body Parts in Rebellion: Hanging Out with Fernie and Me,* 2002 (poetry); *If the Shoe Fits,* 2002; *The Afterlife,* 2003; *Chato Goes Cruisin',* 2004.

NONFICTION: *Living up the Street: Narrative Recollections,* 1985; *Small Faces,* 1986; *Lesser Evils: Ten Quartets,* 1988; *A Summer Life,* 1990 (39 short vignettes based on his life); *The Effect of Knut Hamsun on a Fresno Boy,* 2000.

EDITED TEXTS: *California Childhood: Recollections and Stories of the Golden State,* 1988; *Pieces of the Heart: New Chicano Fiction,* 1993.

G ary Soto (GA-ree SOH-toh), who has been called one of the finest natural talents among Mexican American writers, was born on April 12, 1952, to Manuel and Angie (Trevino)

Soto. Although his parents were born in the United States, Soto's grandfather, Frank Soto, immigrated there to escape economic and political instability in Mexico. He met his future wife, Paola, in Fresno. Soto's parents and grandparents were members of the working class. Every day, the Soto family would join other Mexican American families from their barrio in Fresno and travel to the lush San Joaquin Valley to pick grapes and oranges. At a young age, Gary experienced the grimness of working in mind-deadening, physically exhausting labor, picking cotton in the fields, collecting aluminum cans, all to help his family survive. The lushness of the valley juxtaposed with the backbreaking labor his family had to endure because of their poverty would figure prominently in Soto's poetry and fiction.

M. L. Martinelle

When Soto was five years old, tragedy struck his family; Manuel Soto died as a result of a factory accident at the age of twenty-seven. The father's death left Soto's mother to raise him, his older brother, Rick, and his younger sister Debra. Manuel's death created financial and emotional hardships for the family. They never discussed his death, never dealt with their individual or communal grief. The silence created an emotional chasm for Gary. The effects of Soto's father's death have become a key issue in Soto's writings as he attempts to reconcile his love for his father and his feelings of abandonment with the numbing effects of silence.

Soto grew up in a Catholic family and attended Catholic and private schools. However, his family never stressed the importance of obtaining an education or had books in the house or encouraged him to read. His mother and father left high school to get married when they were eighteen. Even though Soto received no encouragement at home to work hard in school, he did graduate from high school in 1970 and enrolled in Fresno City College to avoid the draft.

A key event occurred in Soto's life after enrolling in college. While browsing through the college library, he discovered a collection of poems titled *The New American Poetry*. After reading several of the poems, he immediately began writing poetry and discovered his poetic voice. He had found his niche.

Seeking the companionship and intellectualism of other writers, Soto transferred to California State University, Fresno, and enrolled in Philip Levine's creative writing class. This decision was life-altering. From 1972 to 1973, Levine nurtured and encouraged Soto's talent as a poet. As he created more poetry under the tutelage of Levine, Soto began to discover his own sense of aloneness, a feeling of being alienated from two cultures, his own because of his education and the Anglo world, which both encouraged and rejected him. Through his writings, he delves into the theme of alienation and learns that it is a human, universal emotion that is not particular to him.

In 1974, Soto graduated magna cum laude from California State University, Fresno. In 1975 he married Carolyn Oda, a native of Fresno and the daughter of Japanese-American farmers

W H A T   T O   R E A D

A Summer Life

A Summer Life (1990) is a collection of thirty-nine vignettes based on Gary Soto's life in California. The book is arranged in three sections covering his early childhood, preadolescence, and the time prior to adulthood. Soto's Latino heritage forms a background, and he identifies himself with this community in his descriptions of everyday realities: his grandfather's wallet is "machine tooled with MEXICO and a *campesino* and donkey climbing a hill"; his mother pounds "a round steak into *carne asada*" and crushes "a heap of beans into *refritos.*" Soto's experiences include the sounds of Spanish and the objects of the barrio, but they seem universal. At heart, the book is a child's movement toward self-awareness.

In the first section, his world is bounded by his neighborhood and his eyes see this world in the sharp, concrete images of childhood. "I was four and already at night thinking of the past," he writes, "The cat with a sliver in his eye came and went. . . . the three sick pups shivered and blinked twilight in their eyes . . . the next day they rolled over into their leaf-padded graves."

In the last story in *A Summer Life*, "The River," Soto is seventeen, and it is the 1960's, the hippie era. He and his friend Scott have traveled to Los Angeles to find themselves amid the "mobs of young people in leather vests, bell-bottoms, beads, Jesus thongs, tied-dyed shirts, and crowns of flowers." As the two of them bed down that night in an uncle's house, Soto seems to find that instant between childhood and adulthood, between the past and the present: "I thought of Braley Street and family, some of whom were now dead, and how when Uncle returned from the Korean War, he slept on a cot on the sunporch. . . . We had yet to go and come back from our war and find ourselves a life other than the one we were losing." In this moment, Soto speaks for all readers who recall that thin edge between yesterday and today.

— *Diane Andrews Henningfeld*

> *When the police left, we came back and some of the*
> *nationals made up stories of how they were almost*
> *caught—how they outraced the police. Some of the*
> *stories were so convoluted and unconvincing that*
> *everyone laughed* mentiras, *especially when one*
> *described how he overpowered a policeman, took his*
> *gun away, and sold the patrol car. We laughed and*
> *laughed, happy to be there to make up a story.*
>
> —from "Black Hair"

who had been imprisoned in internment camps during World War II. At first, his family opposed their marriage, hoping he would marry a good Mexican American girl. Soto discusses their initial reaction and eventual consent in one of his prose memoirs, *Small Faces.* Five years after they were married, Carolyn gave birth to their daughter, Mariko.

Soto earned a master's degree in creative writing from the University of California, Irvine in 1976. He then became writer-in-residence at San Diego State University but left to become a lecturer in the Chicano studies department at the University of California at Berkeley. There, in 1977 he received an associate professorship in both Chicano studies and English. In 1992 he became a senior lecturer in the English department.

While fulfilling his teaching responsibilities, Soto continued to write poetry. In 1977 his first volume of poetry, *The Elements of San Joaquin,* a book he dedicated in part to his grandmother, was published and earned several literary awards. In this volume, Soto gives voice to the grim, impoverished, violent, and soul-deadening world of his childhood: a world that was often filled with human suffering caused by his family's poverty and their inability to become upwardly mobile. He conveys his feelings by using a street as a major motif. Although the street implies movement and a journey, Soto uses the street to imply a dead-end existence on the mean streets of his neighborhood.

In his next two volumes of poetry, *The Tale of Sunlight* and *Where Sparrows Work Hard*, Soto seems to have exorcised his demons because he tempers his social commentary on the poverty his family endured and instead focuses on the human suffering poverty causes. The street motif still exists in these works, but it is used to show that mobility is possible. Creatively, 1985 proved to be a very important year for Soto: He published his fourth volume of poetry, *Black Hair*, in which he fondly remembers his family and friends. He also attempted a new genre, autobiographical prose, when his *Living up the Street: Narrative Recollections* was published and earned for him an American Book Award. In this memoir and the one that immediately followed it, *Small Faces*, Soto vividly re-creates the racially mixed, laboring-class neighborhood in which he was raised, the struggles his family endured to provide the children with a safe environment, and the central dilemma of a life continually lived on the margins as a product of two cultures.

After writing poems and autobiographical memoirs, Soto ventured into children's literature with the publication of *Baseball in April, and Other Stories*. It immediately earned critical recognition, including the Best Book For Young Adults award from the American Library Association. The eleven short stories focus on Mexican American boys and girls and their fears, aspirations, angst, and desires as they enter adolescence. In this collection and his other fiction for children, *Jesse*, *Taking Sides*, and *Pacific Crossing*, Soto depicts real-life situations. Even though his writings are set in ethnic neighborhoods, the conflicts and situations in which he places his characters are universal. To depict these situations, he uses a quiet, often humorous and empathetic tone.

Soto's consistent attention to his craft has earned him the respect of critics and readers. His numerous awards and fellowships, among which include the Guggenheim Fellowship and being nominated for a Pulitzer Prize, attest to his literary genius and his versatility. Gary Soto is a gifted writer who transcends the particular he knew and re-creates a universalized world that touches all of his readers.

— *Sharon K. Wilson*

Learn More

Erben, Rudolf, and Ute Erben. "Popular Culture, Mass Media, and Chicano Identity in Gary Soto's *Living up the Street* and *Small Faces.*" *MELUS* 17, no. 3 (Fall, 1991/1992): 43-52. The authors explore the conflict of dual consciousness and social problems that Soto examines.

Ganz, Robin. "Gary Soto." In *Updating the Literary West,* sponsored by the Western Literature Association. Ft. Worth: Texas Christian University Press, 1997. This collection of essays about writers with a connection to the Western United States includes a discussion of Soto's treatment of the Mexican American experience in his poetry and prose.

Manson, Michael Tomasek. "Poetry and Masculinity on the Anglo/Chicano Border: Gary Soto, Robert Frost, and Robert Haas." In *The Calvinist Roots of the Modern Era,* edited by Aliki Barnstone, Michael Tomasek Manson, and Carol J. Singley. Hanover, N.H.: University Press of New England, 1997. Examines Soto's treatment of cross-cultural values and masculinity and their relationship to Puritanism and Calvinism in *Home Course in Religion.* Compares the treatment of these subjects in Soto's poetry with the handling of these subjects in the poems of Frost and Haas.

Olivares, Julian. "The Streets of Gary Soto." *Latin America Literary Review* 18, no. 35 (January-June, 1990): 32-49. Olivares explores Soto's ability to universalize the situations his characters face.

Soto, Gary. "Gary Soto." http://www.garysoto.com/. Accessed March 22, 2005. The author's Web site has a list of his books, information on his recent accomplishments, and answers to frequently asked questions.

Virgil Suárez

Cuban American novelist and poet

Born: Havana, Cuba; 1962

LONG FICTION: *Latin Jazz,* 1989; *The Cutter,* 1991; *Havana Thurs-days,* 1995; *Going Under,* 1996.

SHORT FICTION: *Welcome to the Oasis, and Other Stories,* 1992.

POETRY: *You Come Singing,* 1998; *Garabato Poems,* 1999; *In the Re-public of Longing,* 1999; *Palm Crows,* 2001; *Banyan,* 2001; *Guide to the Blue Tongue,* 2002.

EDITED TEXTS: *Iguana Dreams: New Latino Fiction,* 1992 (with Delia Poey); *Paper Dance: Fifty-five Latino Poets,* 1995 (with Victor Hernández and Leroy V. Quintana); *Little Havana Blues: A Cuban-American Literature Anthology,* 1996 (with Poey); *American Diaspora: Poetry of Displacement,* 2001 (with Ryan G. Van Cleave); *Like Thunder: Poets Respond to Violence in America,* 2002 (with Van Cleave).

MISCELLANEOUS: *Spared Angola: Memories from a Cuban-American Childhood,* 1997 (short stories, poetry, and essays); *Infinite Ref-uge,* 2002 (sketches, poetry, memories, and fragments of short stories).

Virgil Suárez (VER-hihl SWAH-rays), the son of a pattern cutter and a piecemeal seamstress who worked in the sweatshops of Havana, left Cuba in 1970 with his family. After four years in Madrid, Spain, they went to Los Angeles. A man of many interests and prolific literary output, Suárez raised three daughters with his wife in Florida. His multitude of works in numerous genres deal with immigration, exile, and acclimatization to life and culture in the United States as well as the hopes and struggles of Cubans and Cuban Americans who had to abandon their island home under political duress.

A self-confessed obsessive, whether about his family, his hobbies, or his writing, Suárez is preoccupied by voice. He cites physical place as paramount in the process of finding and producing his voice, whether in prose or poetry. Initially recognized for his fiction, Suárez has written poetry since 1978, though he only began to publish it in the mid-1990's. He believes that voice is most important in poetry because of poetry's space limitations. He feels so strongly about maintaining the authenticity of his personal voice that he discards any poem he believes does not respect and represent his voice.

That voice is of an immigrant who, although he has spent the majority of his life in his adopted land and does not expect to return to Cuba, still does not feel completely acclimated. Suárez writes about what he knows: the nature and travails of exile. Appropriately, given his mixed feelings, Suárez writes in English and includes a sprinkling of Spanish, reiterated in English. Nonetheless, critics characterize Suárez's style as unwavering, definitive, and direct.

Suárez finished his secondary schooling in Los Angeles and received a B.A. in creative writing from California State University, Long Beach, in 1984. He studied at the University of Arizona and received an M.F.A. in creative writing from Louisiana State University in 1987. In addition to having been a visiting professor at the University of Texas in Austin in 1997, Suárez has taught at the University of Miami, Florida International Univer-

> *Xavier, the young-urban Cuban-American. The YUCA, the equivalent of yuppie. Business at hand at all times. In haste, no time to waste. Twenty-four hours a day not being enough time. Seven days a week. No time to rest, for in this magic city of Miami, the Sun Capital, there were many deals to be made, and whoever struck first struck big by making the money.*
>
> —from "Sonny Manteca's Blues"

sity, Miami-Dade Community College, and Florida State University in Tallahassee.

Suárez's poems alone have appeared in more than 250 magazines and journals. He has also been a book reviewer for the *Los Angeles Times, Miami Herald, Philadelphia Inquirer,* and *Tallahassee Democrat.* He is a member of PEN, the Academy of American Poets, the Associated Writing Programs, and the Modern Language Association.

W H A T   T O   R E A D

The Cutter

The Cutter (1991) is the story of a young man's desperate attempt to leave Cuba and its Communist regime. The novel is divided into five sections that mark the stages of his journey away from the island.

The protagonist, Julian Campos, is twenty years old and a university student who has recently returned to Havana after having completed his years of military service. He has been waiting to leave Cuba ever since his parents left five years earlier, and he thinks that the time has finally come—until the government tells him he must do additional "voluntary work" if he wants to leave Cuba.

The work is slave labor, and Julian and his coworkers are mistreated. Suárez depicts Cuba at its worst, leading the reader to understand why Julian is compelled to leave the country. Julian grows increasingly despondent about his prospects for leaving Cuba, particularly when he receives the belated news of his grandmother's death.

When Julian is finally released from the fields and permitted to go home, he realizes that he will never receive an exit notice. His neighbors plan to escape, and Julian joins them. Their group is infiltrated by a government spy, however, and his neighbors are killed. In the novel's final section, Julian reaches the United States. In contrast to most of the Cuban characters, those in the United States are kind to him and are eager to help him adjust to his new country. Julian clearly enjoys his newfound freedom, and, though he appears reluctant to search for his parents, the novel ends with a suggestion that ultimately he will find refuge with them.

Suárez's own family left Cuba in 1970, about the time at which this novel is set. *The Cutter* is his attempt to come to grips with his native Cuba. The novel focuses mainly on the desire for independeonce, but it is also about the loss of innocence and of the belief that if one does the right thing, good will be the end result.

— *Margaret Kent Bass*

Nominated for five Pushcart Prizes, Suárez was a featured lecturer at the Smithsonian Institution in 1997. He received a Florida State Individual Artist grant in 1998 and a National Endowment for the Arts Fellowship in 2001-2002 to write a poetry work. His volume *Garabato Poems* was named *Generation Ñ* magazine's Best Book of 1999. He served as a National Endowment for the Arts Fellowship panel judge in 1999 and a Mid-Atlantic Arts Foundation panelist in 2000.

— *Debra D. Andrist*

Learn More

Alvarez-Borland, Isabel. *Cuban-American Literature of Exile: From Person to Persona.* Charlottesville: University of Virginia Press, 1998. Suárez's work is included in this examination of literature written by Cuban natives living in the United States.

_____. "Displacements and Autobiography in Cuban American Fiction." *World Literature Today* 68, no. 1 (1994): 43-49. Analyzes the theme of exile and displacement in the work of Suárez and other Cuban American writers.

Hospital, Carolina, and Jorge Cantera, eds. *A Century of Cuban Writers in Florida: Selected Prose and Poetry.* Sarasota, Fla.: Pineapple Press, 1996. Suárez is one of the thirty-three writers whose work is included in this anthology of Cubans who have lived, or who are living today, in Florida. The introduction by the editors describes the historical importance of the Cuban connection to Florida's heritage.

Suárez, Virgil. "A Perfect Hotspot." In *Hispanic American Literature,* edited by Rodolfo Cortina. Lincolnwood, Ill.: NTC, 1998. Suárez's short story is included in this anthology.

_____. "Song for the Royal Palms of Miami." In *ReMembering Cuba: Legacy of a Diaspora,* edited by Andrea O'Reilly Herrera. Austin: University of Texas Press, 2001. Suárez's work is included in this collection of writing by Cubans living in other countries.

Sheila Ortiz Taylor

Mexican American novelist

Born: Los Angeles, California; September 25, 1939

LONG FICTION: *Faultline*, 1982; *Spring Forward/Fall Back*, 1985;
Southbound, 1990; *Coachella*, 1998.
POETRY: *Slow Dancing at Miss Polly's*, 1989.
NONFICTION: *Emily Dickinson: A Bibliography, 1850-1966*, 1968;
Imaginary Parents, 1996.

Sheila Ortiz Taylor (SHEE-lah ohr-TEES TAY-lohr) is often considered the first Chicana lesbian novelist. Her first and most acclaimed novel, *Faultline*, was republished in 1995 because of increased awareness of its importance not only in lesbian and Chicano literature but as a significant work of fiction. The novel has been published in British, German, Greek, Italian, and Spanish translations, and in 1995 film rights were bought by Joseph May Productions. The novel also won several awards, although it was often neglected by critics and mainstream reviewers.

Ortiz Taylor grew up in a Mexican American family in Southern California, an experience she records in *Imaginary Parents*. The book, a mixture of fact and fiction, is true to the spirit of her childhood in the 1940's and 1950's. Her older sister's color prints accompany the text and represent a different version of the shared past. In her preface Ortiz Taylor writes that the book could be called autobiography, memoir, poetry, nonfiction, creative nonfiction, fiction, or codex (a manuscript book); she herself calls it an *ofrenda*, an offering of small objects with big meanings set out in order. The book reimagines the past and recreates the parents and extended family who have since died; it also provides an insightful Chicana perspective into what she calls the strange Southern California culture of the war years.

> *I gaze into the cake, a sheet cake decorated to look
> like the swimming pool the Halversons will build
> next summer. Pink children swim in blue-green
> frosting. We lift our voices in song. Mrs. Halverson
> fires off little bulbs from her camera. I am happy, at
> my first real birthday party. I have come here
> without my big sister.*
>
> —from *Imaginary Parents*

It was during the post-World War II years of the early 1950's that Taylor, then twelve or thirteen years old, realized that she wanted to write. She attended California State University at Northridge and graduated magna cum laude. She earned her M.A. from the University of California, Los Angeles, in 1964, and her Ph.D. in English from the same university in 1973 with a dissertation on "Form and Function in the Picaresque Novel."

Taylor's own novels often follow the episodic traditions of the picaresque, although they transform the rogue hero into an adventurous lesbian protagonist who challenges boundaries and resists stereotyped categorization. In *Faultline* the main character, Arden Benbow, who was an English major in college, is the mother of six when she falls in love with another woman. Together they create a loving home life, which includes an African American gay male drag queen as a baby-sitter, an assortment of pets (as many as three hundred rabbits), and various friends and neighbors who are attracted by Arden's energy and enthusiasm. Although he himself is involved with another woman and does not want to be bothered with the children, Arden's former husband files a custody suit on the grounds that Arden's lesbianism makes her an unfit mother. Arden refuses to pretend to be someone she is not, and her life-affirming spirit triumphs. The book ends with a legally nonbinding double wedding between Arden and her lover Alice and between two of their gay male friends.

W H A T   T O   R E A D

Faultline

Faultline (1982) is a comic novel with a serious message. Sheila Ortiz Taylor creates a shining cast of characters who speak about their relationships to the protagonist, Arden Benbow, as Arden battles her ex-husband Malthus for custody of their six children. Malthus has never considered women equal to men, and his ego is hurt when Arden prefers living with a woman to staying with him in their dull marriage.

The theme of acceptance of individual differences runs throughout the novel. It is not until Arden and Alice Wicks fall in love that Arden can see what it means to free oneself to live fully and to develop the creative spirit. Alice too has married because that is what society expected of her, but she learns that she must be herself and follow her own spirit.

The faultline of the title refers to the geography of the setting in Southern California, but it is also a metaphor for unpredictability and the need for adaptability and acceptance of reality. One chapter is in the words of a professor of geophysics who specializes in plate tectonics, which includes the study of the faultlines where earthquakes occur. Earthquakes, he says, are dynamic reactions to changes in the earth's crust that remind people of their mortality and the need to live with enthusiasm. People should not waste their time being prejudiced against others. Although he is a scientist, the professor knows—as Malthus does not—that there is more to life than "facts." In *Faultine*, characters who are rigid and domineering prove to be unhappy, whatever material wealth they may have.

Faultline emphasizes the need for people to celebrate life rather than to oppress others. Arden is, after all, not only a fit mother but an outstanding one who brings to her children and to all around her a sense of fairness and decency and a joy in living and loving.

— *Lois A. Marchino*

A similar sense of hopefulness and triumph in the face of opposition, which some reviewers have referred to as utopian, pervades *Spring Forward/Fall Back*, and the same spirit informs Taylor's poetry and other writings. Taylor has a keen eye for detail and is clear about oppression and stagnated prejudicial attitudes. Her writings also show survival techniques in a hostile culture, among them the invocation of humor, love, and goodwill toward others. Her protagonists refuse to be beaten down, and they enjoy and respect life.

Taylor's professional career has been in teaching English at several universities, most notably at Florida State University, where she began teaching literature in the early 1970's. Her courses include many on women writers, and she has served as Director of Women's Studies. She has given many public readings nationally and internationally, and in 1991 she was awarded a Fulbright Fellowship to teach at the University of Erlangen-Nürnberg.

Taylor's work shows a continuing fascination with the novel form and its many variations. She sees herself as an author who creates convincing forgeries that are intended to illuminate life. Her works show her challenging herself by shifting subject matter, style, and approach. She never repeats simple patterns or formulas from previous works. This approach to writing is also reflected in her central characters, who meet challenges with creativity and vitality and accept risk as a part of the lived life.

Many readers have found Taylor's texts to be engaging. Her work is therefore not restricted to special audiences. Like the literal lesson of the geological faultlines where earthquakes appear, Taylor's works illustrate that chance and change are inevitable, that for individuals and societies it is important to avoid rigidity, and that challenges must be met actively with love, humor, and imagination.

— *Lois A. Marchino*

Learn More

Bruce-Novoa, Juan. *RetroSpace: Collected Essays on Chicano Literature*. Houston, Tex.: Arte Público Press, 1990. Asserts that Taylor's writings show that there is no monolithic Chicano

culture or literature and cites *Faultline* as the best novel written by a Chicana.

_____. "Sheila Ortiz Taylor's *Faultline:* A Third Woman Uto-
pia." *Confluencia: Revista Hispánica de Cultura y Literatura* 6
(Spring, 1991). A lengthy discussion about the novel.

Castillo, Debra A., and María Socorro Tabuenca Córdoba. *Border Women: Writing from La Frontera.* Minneapolis: University
of Minnesota Press, 2002. This examination of writing by
women who live along the United States-Mexican border includes an analysis of Taylor's work. The book describes how
these women writers are rethinking traditional ideas about
the border.

Christian, Karen. "Will the 'Real Chicano' Please Stand Up? The
Challenge of John Rechy and Sheila Ortiz Taylor to Chicano
Essentialism." *Americas Review* 20 (Summer, 1992). An excellent extended treatment of the importance of gay and lesbian writing in Chicano literature, with special attention to
the style and content of *Faultline.*

Harris, Jeane. "Sheila Ortiz Taylor (1939-   )." In *Contemporary Lesbian Writers of the United States: A Bio-bibliographical Critical Sourcebook,* edited by Sandra Pollack and Denise D. Knight.
Westport, Conn.: Greenwood Press, 1993. Contains an essay
about Taylor, featuring biographical information, an analysis
of her writing, and a discussion of the critical reception her
work has received. Also includes a bibliography.

Zimmerman, Bonnie. *Safe Sea of Women.* Boston: Beacon Press,
1990. Taylor is one of several writers discussed in this study of
lesbian fiction in the late twentieth century.